FROM
BEN BRADLEE
TO LENA HORNE
TO CARL REINER,
**OUR MOST FAMOUS
EIGHTY YEAR OLDS**
REVEAL WHY
THEY NEVER
FELT SO YOUNG

80

FROM
BEN BRADLEE
TO LENA HORNE
TO CARL REINER,
**OUR MOST FAMOUS
EIGHTY YEAR OLDS**
REVEAL WHY
THEY NEVER
FELT SO YOUNG

Gerald Gardner & Jim Bellows

SOURCEBOOKS, INC.
NAPERVILLE, ILLINOIS

Published by Sourcebooks, Inc.
P.O. Box 4410, Naperville, Illinois 60567-4410
(630) 961-3900
Fax: (630) 961-2168
www.sourcebooks.com

Library of Congress Cataloging-in-Publication Data

Gardner, Gerald C.
  80 : eighty famous people in their eighties talk about how they got there and live there/by Gerald Gardner and Jim Bellows.
    p. cm.
Includes bibliographical references and index.
1. Older people—United States—Biography. 2. United States—Biography. 3. Biography—20th century. 4. Celebrities—United States—Biography. 5. Entertainers—United States—Biography. I. Bellows, Jim, 1917 - II. Title. III. Title: Eighty.

CT220.G37 2007
920.073—dc22

2007020377

Printed and bound in the United States of America.
RRD 10 9 8 7 6 5 4 3 2

OTHER BOOKS BY GERALD GARDNER

Who's in Charge Here?
Robert Kennedy in New York
All the Presidents' Wits
The Mocking of the President
The Watergate Follies
The Censorship Papers
The Quotable Mr. Kennedy
The Shining Moments
I Coulda Been a Contender
None of the Above
The Tara Treasury (with Harriet Modell Gardner)
The Way I Was (with Marvin Hamlisch)

OTHER BOOKS BY JIM BELLOWS

The Last Editor

EDITED BY JIM BELLOWS

The New York Herald Tribune
The Washington Star
The Los Angeles Herald Examiner

Age, you sneak
you pilfer blossoms
swipe cookies from the jar when our backs are turned
look innocent when you change our handwriting and forge our names
you're the commonest of thief
yet like a magpie you leave something in exchange for what you steal—
dollops of understanding
a shard or two of wisdom
remembrances of love
and now and then, for beauty taken
beauty given.
—Norman Corwin

"Old age is not for sissies."
—Bette Davis

CONTENTS

ACKNOWLEDGMENTS

OW DO YOU WRITE acknowledgments for a book in which everything is contributed by others? It is no easy task.

First among equals deserving acknowledgment is Keven Bellows, who contributed suggestions about whom to include, as well as creative ideas and editorial support. With humor and devotion, she undertook the immense logistical job of communicating with our far-flung company. The task of dealing with fourscore busy, talented, and inaccessible people—a Who's Who of the media, entertainment, and literary worlds—and doing so within a daunting time frame is difficult to imagine. Through it all, Keven supported the authors and contributors with unflagging good cheer and efficiency.

Pearl Morris Gardner, our resident lawyer, mixed admonitions with inventive suggestions and conceptual thinking, combining the best qualities of Clarence Darrow, Maxwell Perkins, and Sol Hurok.

In addition, our gratitude goes to the wonderful folks who served as conduits to our octogenarians by putting us in touch with friends and urging them to join our journey. They include Dick Wald, Saul Turtletaub, Norman Lear, Lennie and Debbie Green, Fred Hayman, Annie and Steve Arvin, Irv Zeiger, David Halberstam, Jimmy Breslin, Warren Cowan, Larry Gelbart, Judi Davidson, Ben Starr, Stewart Weiner, Art Stollnitz, Marcia Bullard, David Israel, Mitch Albom, Don Gregory, Sue Terry, Betty Goodwin, Mary Lou Luther, Edith Tolkin, Karl Fleming, Martin Bernheimer, Mary Anne Dolan, Greg and Sara Bernstein, Cokie Roberts, Leonard Maltin, and Lindsay Gardner.

The authors also offer their gratitude to Norman Zafman for his guidance in matters of consent and releases.

We also thank Stephanie Sills, who tracked down the often elusive folks behind the curtains that shield the world of the famous from the rest of us; Rachel Nelson, who kept her sanity while organizing a mailing program that would rival the operations of the Republican National Committee; Peter Bernstein, who was always there to provide succor and expertise when our computers threatened to crash; Sterling Lord, our eminent literary agent, who went beyond the call of duty in providing us access to some of his distinguished clients; and Hillel Black, our eminent editor at Sourcebooks, Inc., for his skill and guidance.

Most of all, however, we thank the Golden Eighty who interrupted their eventful lives to lend their thoughts, reflections, and anecdotes to this work. They recognized, sometimes more presciently than we ourselves, what a unique volume we were compiling. Through their participation, this project became something unique.

Our contributors have been on an incredible expedition, and as the enablers of their reflections, we have been on one, too. Touching their minds and hearts, however briefly, has provided us particular pleasure and our readers particular insight.

Life is, of course, a complex journey, with many side roads to be explored. There is no one route for the trip, as our variegated stories suggest. Nor is there a navigation device to map our path, or even pinpoint the destination. Every narrative on these pages glows with a love of life, and in sum they form a treasure. So we thank our contributors, most humbly, for sharing this journey with us.

INTRODUCTION

SCOTT FITZGERALD FAMOUSLY wrote that there are no second acts in American lives. If Fitzgerald knew any of the eighty famous people in their eighties whose words brighten this book, he would have had second thoughts. These luminous folks have had at least three or four acts in their lives. Some are at work on a fifth.

Born in or before what Fitzgerald called the Jazz Age, these people's lives have been passionate, resolute, and peripatetic. In these pages they share a road map to the landmarks along the way and a glimpse of the land in which they flourish today. Their personal accounts in their ninth decade are enriched by reflections and anecdotes about the past and paint an arresting picture of the present. We see some of the qualities that sustain their lengthy and productive lives. However, they are neither awed nor frightened nor sentimental about their age. In fact, a few of them are downright angry about getting old. Most, though, are witty, fascinating, and ultimately triumphant. Their words are personal, spirited, and unpretentious. And they inspire.

Many bookshelves groan under the weight of books on aging. But no man or woman knows a country until he or she has lived in it.

"I'm glad I'm not young anymore."
—Alan Jay Lerner in Gigi

Our awesome company *knows* the territory of the eighties because they have populated it—vibrantly. Indeed, they are the pioneers.

Our magnificent eighty look back and assess the ground they've covered, though many look eagerly forward as well. As with all journeys, their lives featured adventures, challenges, failures, and triumphs. Experiences with love, success, and career mark the way, sometimes with joy, sometimes with pain, always with growth.

And what a trip! If you reached "the big 8-0" last year, you were born in 1926, the year Valentino died, Gertrude Ederle swam the English Channel, Billy Mitchell was court martialed, Tunney beat Dempsey, and Hirohito became the Emperor of Japan.

You were ten years old in 1936, when the country was no longer keeping cool with Coolidge and was deep in the Great Depression. Liz Carpenter (p. 201) recalls that those who lived through that time didn't call it the Great Depression. "There was nothing great about it." Franklin Roosevelt was re-elected in a landslide, the Midwest was engulfed in dust storms, the Spanish Civil War broke out, and Lindbergh was impressed as he toured Germany.

You turned twenty in 1946, if you managed to survive World War II. The previous year, Norman Corwin (p. 21) wrote "On a Note of Triumph" at Franklin Roosevelt's request. In addition, the United Nations met for the first time in 1946. The world seemed a promising place. Betty Garrett (p.65) was in *Call Me Mister*, the Broadway review about the soldiers coming home. Harry Truman seized the coal mines, twelve Nazis were sentenced to death at Nuremberg, and Jane Russell (p. 127) outraged the censors with *The Outlaw*.

When you turned thirty in 1956, you had been through Herbert Hoover, Pearl Harbor, the Battle of the Bulge, and Roy Cohn. In 1956 you liked Ike. *McCall's* magazine touted "togetherness" and *Business Week* promoted the organization man. Adlai Stevenson lost the presidency to Eisenhower again, Grace Kelly married Prince Rainier, the *Andrea Doria* sank; Jonas Salk had announced to the world the invention of his polio vaccine, and *I Love Lucy* led the Nielsen ratings with Bob Schiller (p. 281) doing the writing.

By the time you reached forty in 1966, you still had half a lifetime ahead of you. What a decade that was. Kennedy beat Nixon, Jack Ruby shot Lee Harvey Oswald, Johnson wanted "no wider war," and students were killed on the Kent State campus by U.S. soldiers. Over 400,000 American soldiers were in Vietnam, with 6,000 already dead. Harold Robbins led the bestseller lists; *Hollywood Squares* debuted with host Peter Marshall (p. 219), and Bob

Hope toured our bases with his chief comedy writer Mort Lachman (p. 253) supplying his ad libs.

You hit fifty in 1976. Richard Nixon had beaten George McGovern (p. 273) for president in 1972. Three things beat McGovern: tapped phones, dirty tricks, and the forty-nine states that voted for Nixon. Herb Klein (p. 165) did a great job as Nixon's communications chief. But a year later Ben Bradlee (p. 9) would ride Nixon out of town. In 1976 Jimmy Carter ran against Gerald Ford and won the presidency. But soon enough, when Carter was greeted warmly by a cheering crowd, he would say, "It's nice to see people wavin' with all five fingers."

You were sixty in 1986, the year new Coke failed and Classic Coke prospered, the *Challenger* shuttle exploded, Chernobyl endangered Europe, and the DOW hit 1800.

You were seventy in 1996, the year Bill Clinton won a second term by defeating Bob Dole, Tiger Woods turned professional, and TV viewers embraced *ER*.

And in 2006 you turned eighty.

What a life!

Unsurprisingly, there seems to be a great deal of current interest in the subject of aging. Articles on the topic bubble up all over the media. In a 2005 poll conducted by *Parade* magazine and Research/America, a random sample of a thousand people revealed that 58 percent would like to reach the age of eighty-five, and 26 percent would like to reach ninety-five. Judging by the exhilaration displayed by this book's contributors, those percentages will be going up. In further results, 50 percent of respondents considered a person "young" if he or she was "active, busy, energetic," all of which appropriately describe our participants. And in answer to the question, "What makes a person seem old?" only 5 percent actually mentioned a person's age.

Whether or not the eighties is another country, as some of its inhabitants suggest, its population is certainly on the increase. It has grown by 1,117,873 in the first five years of the twenty-first century. (Predictably, the women outnumber the men 575,588 to 542,285.) Since the total population in the seventy-five to seventy-nine age group is 7.4 million, there are many more octogenarians on the way. Beyond the eighties, the national population is also growing. In the ninety to ninety-four age group, the growth is a robust 300,000, and in the ninety-five to ninety-nine category, the growth is 100,000.

Tom Brokaw's 1998 book, *The Greatest Generation,* recounted the stories of some extraordinary men and women. The people whose words fill our book are among the best of that generation. They fought in World War II, and following the war they built lives and careers that brought them fame the good old fashioned way—with hard work, courage, and resilience.

The authors have been gratefully surprised by the eminence of those who have taken the time to participate in this book, to speak of their sorrows and satisfactions. On a day in which we had spoken to Studs Terkel, Ben Bradlee, and Norman Lear before 1 p.m., we mentioned to editor Helen Gurley Brown, "We're surprised how these famous folks have taken the time to contribute their thoughts to this book."

"Don't be surprised," said Ms. Brown. "These people are *survivors.* And they're proud of it."

If our exemplary eighty showed one common thread, it was that in their eighties they still lead lives of passion and productivity. Theirs is an Aristocracy of Age. They told us they have never thought of getting old, and consequently never have. If they do not exactly support the hyperbole of Hugh Hefner, who said, "Today eighty is the new forty," they are still the youngest people in the room. Another quality they have in common is that they embrace life—they are deeply committed to causes, to careers, and to people.

Most of the book's narratives are based on phone conversations conducted during the winter of 2005/2006. Some of our questions were based on our subjects' individual careers. Others were asked of everyone, such as: How are you engaged in life? How do you deal with stress? What are the advantages of age? What is your advice to the young? A few notable contributors, like Ray Bradbury and Don Hewitt, sent us written thoughts on aging.

On these pages, you will find more famous men than women. That is society's fault, not ours. First, generally speaking, to be famous at eighty, you had to be famous at forty. Only movie stars, novelists, or perhaps a Washington madam could meet that requirement. The glass ceiling regarding women was firmly in place in the mid-twentieth century, except in show business.

Second, many women in their eighties today are still less willing than men to acknowledge their age. Some of the women who declined to join this illustrious company are working actresses, who no doubt fear that their careers would not be enhanced by spotlighting their age (though we doubt if anything could stand against their charm and invincible will). Still, you must forgive us a special affection for women like Elaine Stritch, Marge Champion, Nanette Fabray, and Betty Garrett who glory in their years, who continue to bite off more than they can chew, and then chew it. Indeed, there are some ladies among our contributors who are in their *nineties* and still full of energy and allure. Kitty Carlisle Hart, Lena Horne, June Havoc, and Rise Stevens are into their tenth decades, and the years have not diminished their magic. Consider Kitty Carlisle Hart, who never seemed to be at rest long enough for us to speak to her. We tracked her across the country on her concert tours before finally capturing fifteen minutes with her on a Sunday morning.

In addition, several men on these pages—like Studs Terkel, Budd Schulberg, and Norman Corwin—are also ninety-something and still thriving. Thus, our book's subtitle (*Our Most Famous Eighty Year Olds*) would be actionable under the Truth in Advertising laws. But as every author knows, precision is the enemy of brevity.

When President John F. Kennedy entertained a group of Nobel Prize winners in the Rose Garden, he said: "This is the greatest collection of talent we have seen at the White House since Thomas Jefferson dined alone." To which we might add, this book is the greatest collection of wit, experience, and insight since, well, the Nobel Prize winners gathered at the White House.

Wisdom and wit seem to be getting older. Today age seems to be where it's at. If the seniors aren't running the ship, they're often holding the compass. Our gray eminences are tenacious. They have the drive to excel, the ego to take the stage, and the sagacity to guide the young.

In their eighties and beyond, our valiant group still has the perspective and the stamina to make things happen. Look at Helen Gurley Brown, launching surrogate *Cosmopolitan* magazines in countries around the world…Paul Conrad still wielding his rapier pen, Helen Thomas still rattling President Bush with her questions while her younger colleagues doze, Norman Lear campus-hopping with the message to "get involved," Liz Smith remaining the indomitable goddess of gossip, and Gloria Stuart nearly stealing *Titanic* from Leonardo DiCaprio.

"Work hard, take chances, be very bold," says a character in the movie *Julia*. That command has seemed to direct the lives of our eighty/eighty subjects. And it is the advice they offer the coming generations, the recent under-grads and the baby boomers who are new to being old. Each of our contributors has always loved his or her work, and they are uniform in urging their juniors to "seek work that captures your passion."

"There are worse things than death," wrote Woody Allen. "I mean, if you've ever spent an evening with an insurance salesman." By which Mr. Allen undoubtedly meant that the most unendurable thing is boredom. Boredom short-ens life more surely than disease, and curiosity lengthens it more surely than exercise. None of our contributors seem troubled by boredom. We suspect it will never bother them very much.

Gerald Gardner
Jim Bellows

"Time, time, what is time?
The Swiss manufacture it,
the French hoard it,
the Italians want it,
the Americans say
it is money, and the Hindus
say it doesn't exist."
—Truman Capote

NORMAN LEAR

Norman Lear, one of America's most influential television producers, scored a string of hits with his partner, Bud Yorkin, that included Sanford and Son, Maude, *and* Diff'rent Strokes. *Their groundbreaking comedy* All in the Family *brought such issues as Vietnam, race, and sexuality to the small screen. In addition to his television credits, Norman founded People for the American Way, an organization that fought against the political right wing. He also bought a copy of the Declaration of Independence that he sends on nationwide tours aimed at encouraging the young to vote.*

THERE WAS AN ARTICLE in the *New York Times* recently about Don Hewitt, the creator and longtime producer of *60 Minutes*. He's eighty-one and has nothing to do. He was bemoaning the question—what is he going to do? What is he going to put his heart and soul into? Where will his passion go? I've been thinking about that since I read that article.

Look at Norman Corwin, the legendary radio writer. His father died at the age of 109.

When Norman's father was 105 or 106, Norman used to talk to him every Sunday morning. And the old man started every Sunday conversation the same way. He'd say: "Norman, are you keeping an active mind?"

When I turned eighty I had a party, and I had the last word. I had no idea I was going to say this, but after I did all the thank you's, I said: "I hate to tell you this, but for a few minutes I've been thinking about the taste of the coffee tomorrow morning. And I've got to tell you—

the two least understood little words in the English language are 'over' and 'next.' This evening is over, and I'm on the next." And that's exactly the way I feel.

I understand that I'm eighty-three. I understand that there are difficult years ahead. I understand that at some point the body is going to feel the years more than it does now. But this is the moment. This is the time. This morning I had a wonderful moment with my ten-year-old twins. And then I talked to one of my older children in New York. And I'm soon going into a couple of meetings that I'm really looking forward to..

I feel exactly the same way I did when I was producing and developing shows for television: Full of curiosity and joy in the moment. Today I see the world through the eyes of the youngest people in my life. I see it through the eyes of my grandchildren. The fight is to make the road ahead good for them.

There are a lot of advantages in age. The only reason I wouldn't trade "now" for "then" is there is too much that's lovely going on right now. And I wouldn't want to give up any of it.

In those earlier years, when I was asked "What about the stress?" I used to say: "There are two kinds of stress. There's stress and then there is *joyful* stress." And joyful stress adds time to your life. It's being involved in what's going on in the immediate moment.

"There is a real connection between humor and longevity."

You know the metaphor I love? The mountain climber who's always throwing a grappling hook ahead of him. And then he pulls himself up. With energy and passion, he pulls on the rope. And each time, when he gets to his goal, he throws the grappling hook ahead. It's a great metaphor for life.

The Lear Center in the Annenberg School at the University of Southern California was just created. They're exploring the effects of entertainment on every aspect of our culture. I love it and I support it.

I've been touring the Declaration of Independence for the last three years in a giant exhibit. It's part of a drive to encourage young people to vote. One of the reasons young people cite for not voting is that they "don't feel sufficiently informed." One of the things we want to do is encourage youngsters to know that they are far more informed than they think they are. And, more important, once they declare themselves a voter, automatically they will see more and they will hear more, because they will be sensitized to it.

There is a real connection between humor and longevity. Norman Cousins is a great example. He was in a hospital. They hadn't figured out what was ailing him. Then he heard two doctors discussing his case at his bedside. And they cast such a dark cloud of gloom on him that when his wife visited him a little later,

Cousins said, "I can't listen to this. I can't be in those doctors' company, I want to go to a hotel room." So they took a hotel room. And they rented medical equipment for the room. And he called his friend Allen Funt, the creator of the TV show *Candid Camera*, because Cousins enjoyed that show. And they screened a constant diet of *Candid Camera* and the Groucho Marx television show, *You Bet Your Life*. Then he wrote a book which came to the attention of the faculty at UCLA, and they invited him to come and teach his theory—the theory of the influence of laughter on your health.

When I had prostate cancer some years ago, Norman Cousins was at my bedside talking to me about his book. And I got videotapes of *Candid Camera*, and I called Lorne Michaels and I had him send me everything he could from *Saturday Night Live* of Dan Aykroyd and John Belushi. And I lay in bed and laughed my head off. So my experience is that laughter is a great therapy.

I have one bit of advice for my contemporaries. It is based on a fundamental piece of philosophy. I don't know whether it's from the Talmud, but it's Talmudic in spirit.

A man should have a garment with two pockets. In the first pocket should be a piece of paper on which is written: "I am but dust and ashes. I am but a grain of sand."

And in the other pocket is a piece of paper on which is written: "For me the world was created!" So there's no morning in my life when I don't open my eyes and think about that. And I think it's necessary to live with understanding, in the great scheme of the Creator—whatever you believe the Creator to be—the great scheme, the great plan, feeling that you are just a grain of sand—but at the same time feeling: What's the world doing here if not for you?

NORMAN LEAR was born on July 27, 1922, in New Haven, Connecticut.

HELEN GURLEY BROWN

If Helen Gurley Brown is any example, you can have it all. In 1965, she transformed the flagging Cosmopolitan magazine into a testament to the pleasures of womanhood and a goldmine for the Hearst organization. Thanks to the magazine, young women learned how to beguile men and promote their careers. Her best-selling guidebook to the joys of blessed singleness, Sex and the Single Girl, *liberated and redefined a generation of women.*

EVERYBODY, HE OR SHE, is lucky is get to be eighty or ninety and it always astonishes me that people make such a big whoop-de-doo about your being that age. I'm also astonished that people don't do everything they can to have a good time, to make those years palatable, sometimes pleasant—not unpleasant. So, my point about the eighties—you are just lucky to be there and you want to make the most of it and those people who have done so I think are pretty admirable.

Back in 1965 I took the helm at *Cosmopolitan* magazine. I transformed it to show the joys of women excelling at work, enjoying life's better things, and beguiling men.

The Hearst ownership wouldn't have had me there if they didn't decide to go ahead with it. After all, it was their magazine. They owned it. But it was hemorrhaging and I think they would have closed it down if I hadn't come along.

There were people, I'm sure, who were horrified that I had been allowed in there. A man named Richard Deems, who was president of Hearst Magazines, was the one who made the decision. They looked at my proposal, they looked at the magazine—they knew about the book I had written, *Sex and the Single Girl*. Then they looked at my comprehensive outline for a new magazine. They made the decision to go ahead.

My first issue sold more than 90 percent of its print order. That's a tremendous sell-through. Magazines nowadays sell 35 percent or 45 percent of their print order and figure they get along with that. To sell 90 percent of your print order is really sensational. I knew at once, they knew at once, that the buyers of magazines liked it immensely and it wasn't very long before the advertisers came in. Advertisers want to be where the readers are.

I don't think I would be capable of editing such a magazine anymore. Any editing job is not a barrel of fun. The biggest deal is to make it good so people will buy it. That's an hourly proposition; a minute-by-minute proposition. You have to work with writers, you have to work with your editors. You have to work terribly hard all the time.

I work for a wonderful company that has always rewarded me for making money for them. On my twenty-fifth anniversary they gave me a silver-gray Mercedes Benz 550 and a driver just as a little present. I didn't expect anything. I didn't even know what my anniversary was, but they kept track and they did that for me.

I was not privy to any of Hearst's financial statements. But they knew that *Cosmopolitan* was making money and that it immediately brought advertisers in. I came from that world. I had been an advertising copywriter. I knew how to respect and appreciate advertisers. Every Thursday, as long as I was the *Cosmo* editor, we had a luncheon at Twenty-One and we'd ask a big advertiser and his agency to have lunch with us. There'd be about twenty people and we'd all visit. I would sit at the table and I'd put the head guy next to me. I would say, "You know that your secretary, your wife, your girlfriend, your daughter—they all love the magazine. But I want to explain to you why they like it so much. Would you hold the pages for me?"

"My two favorite words today would be 'Hanging on.'"

At the end, when it was time to have a younger editor, they knew I would throw myself under a train if I didn't have a job. I worked all my life, ever since I was eighteen years old. They found a job for me to be the editor of *Cosmo*'s international editions.

There were about twenty of them when I took the job. Now we have fifty-six. We open them up in new countries every year.

I'm too old to be the editor of *Cosmopolitan*, that's for sure. Could I edit a magazine for a somewhat older woman? I might be able to do that, although it's a lot of hard work. I can do what I'm doing, and I don't miss the other, because I did it for thirty years.

I'm not smelling the flowers today. I tried a little flower smelling when I stopped being the editor-in-chief. I went to the Metropolitan Museum a couple of times. I took piano lessons because we have a baby grand that never gets played. I took a couple of French lessons because I do not speak a foreign language. I did all that. I don't know if you can call it "smelling the flowers." I did try doing something different than what I've been doing. Just to sit on the veranda with iced tea and listen to a CD. No, that's not for me. Everything good that's happened to me has come from my work. I can have lots of flowers if I want them.

I'm the luckiest person because I still have a husband, and he and I embrace life together. We're going to a fancy resort in the Caribbean. We'll be soaking up the sun, eating wonderful food, and enjoying ourselves.

David has a hit play on Broadway and that's the most life-embracing thing imaginable. It's called *Dirty Rotten Scoundrels*. I think I've seen it about seventeen times. We go nearly every week. Some say that's because David's the producer—I do it because I am just nuts about it and he likes it, too. We have to pay for our ticket each and every time. Producers don't get free tickets. They get good locations. David is a Tony member so we go to all the new shows. We'll be going to some that we haven't seen.

This past Sunday we went to City Hall to watch Mayor Bloomberg be inaugurated. That isn't something you have to do, but we're glad we did it. It was icy cold out. David came home and got a cold, but it was a very special experience to watch the ceremony. The emcee of the show was John Lithgow, who's David's star in *Dirty Rotten Scoundrels*. Mike Bloomberg is a good friend. It isn't convenient to go clear down there to 20th Street on a frosty afternoon and spend two hours outdoors, freezing to death. But we did it. That's embracing life.

We have been all over the world at this point. I can't think of any place I haven't been. We don't have to go to other countries to embrace life, but we go there. I'm involved with my work and we do go to Paris and London every year and usually to Tokyo.

There's a slight difference between the way I handle stress today and as a young woman. In those days, stress had a lot to do with making enough money to support my invalid sister and my mother. I had to start working when I was eighteen. A lot of my stress through the years came from taking care of my sister in a wheelchair. That was a specific kind of stress, which I met by being good at my work. Stress today has to do with not feeling as good as you did when you were fifteen years old. There is some stress in that.

I've done everything I'm capable of doing. I want to keep this job at *Cosmo*. There are two countries we haven't gone into yet that I feel we must. One of them is Singapore and the other is

Denmark. We are in Norway, Finland, Sweden, but we're not yet in Denmark. We did just get a commitment.

My two favorite words today would be: "Hanging on." Quite a lot of my last book was a memoir. It's called *I'm Wild Again*. That has considerable biographical material in it. I don't think I'll write another one. I don't think I have anything else to say. All I try to remember is to be grateful for how well off I am. My wonderful husband has been mine for forty-seven years. He had two previous wives. He finally got it right.

I can't think of any advantages to being older. David uses a cane sometimes and he gets on the airplane first. All I can do is to try to remember to be profoundly grateful for the things I have to be grateful about. I try not to be a dumbbell. I do regret that I can't do some of the things I used to do. I just try to appreciate what I've still got.

I do have some advice for the generations that are following me. I don't want to sound pontifical and I don't know whether I'd call it advice. All I can call it is what I've learned. And what I've learned is that if you do the best you can, no matter how bad the situation, you probably are going to come out okay. That's something to remember.

The important thing is you're lucky if you get to be eighty-three, so why don't you come to your senses and be thankful for that? You've got to get through it as you have the rest of your life. Do the best you can.

HELEN GURLEY BROWN was born on May 18, 1922, in rural Arkansas.

BEN BRADLEE

The motion picture All the President's Men *lifted Ben Bradlee from journalist icon to American icon. The movie painted a vivid picture of the charismatic editor of the* Washington Post. *Bradlee shepherded the publication of Woodward and Bernstein's stories that unraveled the Watergate scandal.*

IN MOVING ON FROM the *Washington Post* I began to wonder about the amount of time spent with problems I had no capacity to fix. I've spent an awful lot of time in my life trying to solve problems that I have no skills for or that probably were unsolvable. One of the glories of the newspaper business is that we have to get it up 365 days a year. A really great story—something that turns out to be a Watergate that is two years of your life—comes along rarely. The great fun of our business is that

it's every day, it's five editions a day and you have to be ready to move and change, to stay on top of a problem in a really unique way. I'm sure in the course of an operation a surgeon faces the same kinds of things.

I used to hang out as editor and I got to be fairly well known for it. I would just go make a tour of the newsroom twice a day. I would see three guys talking and I would have to know what they were talking about. I could stand two guys talking without knowing about it. I'd go into the various sections of the paper and just hang out—sit down and talk to whoever was at the desk. I consider that a very important function of an editor.

Leaving the *Post* left a vacuum for me. But how to fill the vacuum? You fill it but you don't fill it with the same things. I guess the vacuums get smaller as you careen toward eighty-five. I've got a lot of stuff on my plate. I have an office here at the *Post*. But I also have some other jobs—volunteer jobs. I work for Tony O'Reilly. He ran H. J. Heinz for years. He was a famous Irish rugby player. H. J. Heinz Company makes pickles, baked beans. It's one of the two or three biggest food companies in the world.

I'm on an advisory board for him. It's got nothing to do with Heinz. O'Reilly quit Heinz after he ran it for thirty years, and he now has a company that owns newspapers in Ireland. He owns *The Independent* in London, sixteen papers in South Africa, papers in New Zealand, Australia, and parts of India. It's a big multi-million-dollar company called Independent Publications. He has an advisory board and I'm chairman of it. Its original task was to sell the idea of the first big acquisition of newspapers by a white Irishman to a black South African government, to prevent blacks from raising hell with him, putting him in jail; just holding the

journalists to standards they obviously could never fulfill. That was largely done.

It's a very interesting board and it's filled with good people. We contemplate our navel, and we talk about business. We meet once a year in Ireland and once a year in either South Africa or New Zealand and Australia.

"I'm awfully interested, in my old age, in truth. The obstacles that society places in your path to try and learn what the hell the truth is."

If sources are the life blood of a journalist, John F. Kennedy was a pretty good source to have. I didn't know him long. I didn't meet him until 1958 and he was dead six years later. It was a wonderful chance to have a front row seat in a very interesting time in America and a very interesting administration.

I enjoyed his company. Whereas he had other friends that fulfilled other needs, we used to schmooze together and with our wives. I saw him almost all the time with his wife Jackie and my wife Toni.

I still very much embrace life. I really do. It's something that, obviously, occupies a lot of my thoughts. Eighty-four! Everyone in my family was long dead at eighty-four. My doctor tells me I'm in pretty good shape. I don't smoke, I exercise, I work out in the woods with my chainsaws—all my toys—I cut a lot of wood.

I don't know about what journalism contributes to longevity. I've always worked hard, which I think is important. I've never been bored. This business is fantastic for that. The amount of time you spend doing something that bores you is really almost non-existent. I think that's very important in longevity. I've always looked forward to getting up and going to work.

What starts my engine in the morning these days? It doesn't kick over the first time. I come to work probably at ten o'clock instead of nine. I prowl around this place quite a lot to learn what's happening, see if there's any place that has a need that I think I can fill. I talk to these new reporters. I talk to the old folks who should be moving on, getting out, doing something else. I still talk to advertisers from time to time.

I don't know if I smell the flowers. I have a place in the country in Southern Maryland. When I can get to it, I go out in the woods and pick a spot that seems to be a little seedy or that needs to be cleaned up or thinned out, and I get my saws and I cut trees and limbs and burn brush. In a period of a week or two or three, I have it looking the way I think it should and I move on. If there's been a very high tide or a big storm, I go down to the beach, and the beach always needs to be cleaned up. I love that kind of work—in the open air.

I used to have a leisurely breakfast, read the papers, and then go out at about 10:30. I would stay until I dropped. In twenty years that has probably gone from five hours to three. I still leave the house at the same time, but I often get back at 1:30 instead of after dark. I go to bed at nine o'clock. I go to sleep at 9:05. I get my ten hours.

I don't spend a whole hell of a lot of time thinking about when it's all going to end. Sally and I have our child together who's twenty-three now. He's taken an enormous amount of our attention. He's got some learning disabilities that have made life difficult for him. He's a wonderful child, bright as can be, but he processes information in an odd way. I've spent a lot of time with him, which I didn't have with my other children.

I have great pleasures today. Good God, I've got wonderful friends and I have a wife who seems to agree with the game plans we form together. I do regret missing with my other children the experiences I'm sharing with my youngest son. I can remember my first child. I hardly saw him. I had the night shift at the *Post* and I came home and went to bed, and when he woke up, I was in bed.

I'm awfully interested, in my old age, in truth: The obstacles that society places in your path to try and learn what the hell the truth is and what really happened.

As a result, I've gotten kind of interested in lying and I've even sort of outlined a book about lying. My days are full; my nights are too full. You can go out in this town as many nights as you want, and I think we still do it a little bit too much.

The turning point in my life was probably that lunch with Katharine Graham when I told her I'd give her my left one for the job as editor of the *Washington Post*. Her decision to go ahead with me at a time when it was not an easy decision for her changed my life. She had some establishmentarian figures at the head of the *Post*. I didn't fit that description.

I've always had people helping me. There was a guy called Russ Wiggins who was one of the most intelligent human beings I ever met. He never went to college but he was the editor of the *Post* for over twenty years. He was just fabulous to me. Lyndon Johnson made him U.S. Ambassador to the United Nations for the last four months of his term. That's how I was promoted to be editor.

I advise young people to work hard and I advise them to speak up. I always did.

I've never been accused of being a shrinking violet. You've got to be sure people know how you feel and why you feel that way, if you're going to lead.

BEN BRADLEE was born on August 26, 1921, in Boston, Massachusetts.

CARL REINER

Carl Reiner supported Sid Caesar on Your Show of Shows, *created* The Dick Van Dyke Show, *directed films like* Where's Papa *and* Oh God!, *collaborated with Mel Brooks on* The 2000 Year Old Man, *penned a few novels, memoirs…where does one stop?*

THESE DAYS, I DON'T get out of bed until I do fifteen or twenty minutes of stretching. A trainer once told me, "Do your stretches in bed, because you can't forget to do them if you don't get out of bed before you do them."

The pressure on you is different at eighty. I don't have as full a calendar as I used to. I do have things to do. I have a lunch or an interview, and from time to time, I'm asked to emcee some worthwhile event. Among them is hosting the Directors Guild Awards Show, which I've done every year for the last twenty. And I have my computer. I'm sitting at it right now working on a screenplay…an animated feature for Paramount Pictures.

I get more thrills out of writing a book. I have just finished a novel which was published by Simon & Schuster and I did the audio book for Random House. Its title is *NNNNN*; it makes sense when you read it. When I was writing it, I had no idea where it was going. It turned and twisted and seemingly went up blind alleys. But somehow, unbelievable pieces of gold turned up. That was a most exciting journey, and I can't wait to do it again.

I've been lucky to have a number of careers as an actor, a director, a novelist. Maybe diversity tends to promote longevity. Right now, directing is not an option, because at eighty-four it takes more energy and time than I have. A director is the first one there in the morning and the last one to leave at night. I'm happy I found the computer. Right now I'm sitting at one and feeding it ideas and paper. Writing makes it possible for me to stay interested. And if you stay interested, you stay alive.

If you don't have time to smell the flowers, it means you are doing something more challenging.

How does one deal with stress, you ask? Well, by being aware that you're a faulty human being and there are psychiatrists out there who can help you find the best you in you. When I was in my forties, I found the best me in me.

How did I get to be the original me? Coming from a family of normal neurotics helps. Having a father you admired and a mother who thought you were the "best one" in the play didn't hurt. I think getting your ethics from your parents just by observation is a big thing.

I don't have the urge to mentor. I have three kids and five grandchildren, and I think the best mentoring is done by behavior and example.

I don't know why I've always observed the world in a comic or ironic way. I think that coming from the Depression and being Jewish hasn't hurt. I found that when I was young I could get out of possible altercations by being funny. As a matter of fact, I wrote a book, *How Paul Robeson Saved My Life and Other Mainly Happy Stories*. I described how in the Army I was confronted by a bigot who, to settle a racial dispute, suggested carbines. And instead, I made everybody around me laugh, and the guy couldn't shoot me because everybody was on my side, laughing.

Appropriately, *Enter Laughing* was the title of a semi-autographical novel about my early career as an actor. I'm in the one business that people go into because as kids they dreamed and wanted to be part of it. Nobody in show business has ever said, "Boy! I wish I wasn't in show business."

"If you stay interested, you stay alive."

CARL REINER was born on March 29, 1922, in the Bronx, New York.

"When I was young there was no respect for the young, and now there is no respect for the old. I missed out coming and going."
—J. B. Preistley

HELEN THOMAS

Deploring the somnolence of the White House press corps of which she is the acknowledged First Lady, Helen Thomas has never been afraid to make a press secretary or a president squirm under her questions and follow-ups. Helen has been covering presidents since JFK, serving as the UPI White House correspondent for fifty-seven years. She recently switched to Hearst as a syndicated columnist. She's also been a trailblazer, shattering the barriers erected against female reporters.

I DON'T TRAVEL WITH the president anymore. At my age, it's too exhausting. When you work for a wire service as I did at United Press International, you're on the body watch—to see if he's alive. It was very, very demanding. Now I write a column for Hearst Newspapers.

I certainly engage life today. Eat, drink, and be merry. I like to be with my friends. I like to know what's going on. I'm really a news junkie in that respect.

I'll tell you how I handle stress. I say—This too shall pass. You've just got to try to stay cool and admit when you're wrong, and tell them when you're right.

When I'm outraged at some obfuscation by the press secretary or the press, I usually vent with my friends. They don't have to wire-tap me; I'm pretty loud. I express my opinions, and they get very unhappy. I can be heard giving these asides when they're speaking. I don't keep it pent up.

I have much more free time now that I'm not on the UPI beat. I have more time to read. I don't have the pressure. A wire service is the most demanding place in news. There's never a day without news. When it isn't happening, you fasten your seat belt because you're sure it's going to pop. The other shoe will fall. I always had that philosophy. You have to be on your toes. On the quietest days at the White House, I would go up and try to sniff around and figure out what was cooking. It was too quiet. Often times, it *was* cooking. Like on the day we started the Gulf War. They were deadly quiet. It was quiet at the White House; quiet at the Pentagon—too quiet.

Every day I observe the timidity of the White House press corps at the briefings of the presidential press secretary. Not only have I observed it, it's broken my heart. I honestly believe that if there had been real questioning, we would not be in this horrifying war and thousands of people would be alive today.

I've been around here a long time and I feel they should not be let off the hook. We learned a lot of lessons from Watergate. We were not inquiring enough. The press room became an arena. After Watergate we realized we were not skeptical enough. It is amazing, after 9/11 everyone went into a coma. The journalistic newcomers stayed in a coma for a long time. They're young, they're in television. I don't know if they're getting orders from their corpo-

"I feel that I can sleep when I die."

rate bosses in New York or what. The bosses turned the reporters loose on Katrina and said, "You can show some emotion now. You can ask some tough questions." But on the war, you're unpatriotic if you question it.

In all the years I was asking tough questions of presidents, I would get these calls from people, "Who in the hell are you? Who elected you? How dare you ask those questions? Fire her!" After 9/11, when they saw such a subdued press, the people said, "Where is the press? Where are the reporters?" The public watching on television can think of a follow-up question to Scott McClellan quicker than we can, or they're wondering why the questions aren't being asked.

But I'm optimistic about the long run. Hope springs eternal. There's nothing else in life. I think these Bush people were able to use the fear card and it certainly worked on the press and everybody else. But we won't always have a president who controls the news, who has press conferences and then sends people out to spin. They wouldn't know the truth if it hit them in the eye. It's unbelievable the robotic responses you get to your questions. And these are major issues that affect every man, woman, and child in the country.

I think the public is more alert than we think. The public is really astounded at the weakness of the press. The public is aware. After all, if the press feels so locked out and helpless, what can the public feel? We are privileged to be in the White House and to ask questions. When we default on that, we let the country down. Our silence is deafening.

A lot of reporters are afraid. I think they're honestly afraid that people will resent their challenges and feel they're being nagging and argumentative. I don't worry about it. I follow-up to the end, 'til he cuts me off. Scott McClellan always ends up turning away and saying, "Yes, Steve. Go ahead, Steve—."

I was moved out of the first row during Bush's presidential press conference. Ed Guthman, who was press secretary for Bobby Kennedy, said, "Boy, if we ever tried that in the Kennedy years, the whole press corps would have walked out." You don't have that kind of collective action today. It's everybody on their own. You can't blame them. Everybody's an individual. They come in with their own pet questions. You can't have a sense of collusion against a president. Every time someone asks a question and McClellan tries to cut them off at the knees, I try to follow-up. *Wait a minute! You didn't answer his question!*

I miss John F. Kennedy at press conferences. I miss his intellect, wit, and warmth. He knew how to deflect us and not answer a lot of questions, but he did it with great *joie de vivre* and a smile. He knew what you were talking about. He definitely had a sense of life, of people, and he knew he could not get away with just empty answers like, "I'm the president and I can do that."

Carter had all the facts and figures at his fingertips. He was truly brilliant in many ways, but a scientific mind. He never had wit when he needed it. He could have deflected a lot of stuff if he had just shown some wit. His news conferences were deadly serious.

What was impressive about Nixon—he really knew politics and he never used a podium where he could put his elbows up—you never caught Nixon off guard…except during Watergate, because we were going after him hammer and tong.

Reagan used to go to Camp David and prepare like for an oral PhD before a news conference. Then they'd have a rehearsal in the White House theater. I don't know who played me and who played Sam Donaldson. But Reagan got his training there. He was caught off guard a lot. Many times he didn't know the answer, but still he was delightful and gave you that big smile. It was morning in America.

There have been newswomen for 150 years. We had Dorothy Thompson. When I arrived, it was Doris Fleeson, May Craig—some fantastic women. They got their big break because Eleanor Roosevelt would hold news conferences only for women and every once in a while she would leak something that was on the national agenda, and they'd have a scoop.

When I came to town in the summer of 1942, women couldn't join the National Press Club. When Nikita Khrushchev was coming to town, we bitched and screamed and picketed. We got through to Jim Haggerty, Ike's press secretary. Then, for the first time in history, women were allowed in the National Press Club, to actually sit down with their colleagues and have lunch and listen to Khrushchev. I was at the head table. That's when Khrushchev made his speech saying, "We will bury you." It was historic. We didn't actually get taken in as members until 1971. Our progress has been slow, but now there are many more women in the media. Now, the journalism schools are more than half women, just like law. Those are great strides.

I do think that I'm lucky. When I look back, I'm lucky I picked a profession where you're learning every day, 'til the day you die. I can think of stories I could have done better. But I don't have any big regrets. No looking for my lost youth.

I would say to the kids just starting out, try to find out what makes you happy, especially in terms of work, because you spend a lot of time there. Try to find out what your best talents are and put them to the greatest use.

When I got out of college and came to Washington, that was a major turning point in my life. I was lucky because I always had a basic direction. I was in an English class and one of my stories got on the front page of the high school paper. I was hooked for life. The same thing in college. I always knew where I wanted to go, where I wanted to be. I never thought I'd end up in the White House, but I knew I wanted to be a reporter.

I do think the news is a profession where you grow and learn every day. I haven't met any newspaper person who hasn't looked back in longing when they've left their job. Whenever you get together, you get the war stories. It's not about how they became a great investment banker.

I feel that I can sleep when I die. I think when you're alive you have to be interested in everything around you, and you really can make a contribution to your country.

HELEN THOMAS was born on August 20, 1920, in Winchester, Kentucky.

NORMAN CORWIN

Norman Corwin has been called "the poet laureate of radio" for good reason. When President Franklin Roosevelt wanted to celebrate the Bill of Rights as World War II inflamed the world, he turned to Norman Corwin. When he wanted to reflect on the allied victory in Europe on VE Day, FDR again called on Corwin, who responded with the legendary "On a Note of Triumph." He continues to teach at the University of Southern California.

AT THIS WRITING, I am 94.25 years old, and walk with a walker because at ninety-two I stumbled into one hell of a fall. I lucked into virtuoso surgery which, however, left me with one leg a bit shorter than the other, so that I gimp enough in navigation to feel like an actor playing the part of an old man.

Of course, I *am* an old man, but there is a block in my head that doesn't accept that station. There are, of course, palpable signs and symp-toms of elderliness—increased impatience with red tape, an inability to work into the night as I did through most of my eighties, and a tendency to tire more quickly of the wit and wisdom of President Bush II. The hardest thing for me is not occasional losses of balance, or a tooth, or a few hairs, but of a friend and loved one.

One of the most important requirements of successful aging is dignity, by which I don't mean starchy proud-mindedness or anything high-nose, but the maintenance of self-respect and respect of others. There is not room in the ambits of successful seniority for whining, kvetching, bitching, or demanding—except that when, in the last of those protestations, one's entitlements or rights may be at stake. And for God's sake, as long as one can mark a figure X, VOTE! The ballot marked by each octogenarian, nonagenarian,

"One of the most important requirements of successful aging is dignity."

and centenarian makes up for one not cast by a clod-citizen of whatever age who never bothers to enter a polling booth.

Yes, aging can be tough and rough. As Bette Davis said, "Old age is not for sissies." But it is possible to approach the ultimate without staggering, and even with a kind of glow, like a radiant sunset.

NORMAN CORWIN was born on May 3, 1910, in Boston, Massachusetts.

P. D. JAMES

P. D. James's brilliant mystery novels have placed her among literary greats. Most of her nineteen books have been filmed or televised in Great Britain, North America, and around the world. She has received many honors including the Grand Master Award from the Mystery Writers of America. In 1991 she was made Baroness James of Holland Park by Queen Elizabeth II.

I THINK THAT WHETHER or not we have a long, healthy, and productive old age depends largely on whether we are lucky in the genes we inherit.

There is, however, much we can do to help ourselves. I believe in the importance of a sensible diet and regular exercise. But above all, in keeping my mind occupied and stimulated by living each day to the full and by retaining an interest in other people and in the fascinating variety, beauty, and opportunities of our human life.

"I believe in keeping my mind occupied and stimulated."

P. D. JAMES was born on August 3, 1920, in Oxford, England.

DON HEWITT

Don Hewitt tried to get Richard Nixon to use makeup to cover his stubble before the first televised Kennedy–Nixon debate. A more successful undertaking was 60 Minutes. *The television show has profited CBS beyond a billion dollars, and schooled its audience in the wages of sin and fraud.*

WHILE IT MAY, AND frequently does, come with afflictions, getting old is not—in and of itself—an affliction, and coping with it is no "big deal" if the only afflictions you're saddled with are, as mine are, a hearing loss I can live with but that drives my wife up the wall, wearing glasses to read small print, and having difficulty dredging up names I thought I knew as well as my own.

So, at eighty-three, over and above those minor annoyances, my mind rattles on not all that differently from the way it did when I was thirty-three.

Do I work out? I do, but not in the generally accepted sense of what people mean when they ask, "Do you work out?"

What I do are mind calisthenics which, I guess, are not a whole hell of a lot different from daydreaming—daydreaming about how to keep my life as satisfying as it was when the end-all and be-all of it was dreaming up and then producing (for thirty-five years) *60 Minutes*…the most watched, the most honored, and most profitable broadcast of its kind in television history.

Was I devastated when they replaced me as executive producer of *60 Minutes?* I was, until a friend told me to think of *60 Minutes* as Yankee Stadium, the place that, even though Babe Ruth hadn't swung a bat there in more than half a century, is still known as "The House that Ruth Built."

That did it. Devastation all gone.

So, you might well ask, "Isn't there anything about growing old that rankles you?" The answer is "Not much," although truth to tell, it does rankle me when people ask me, "Do you still go to work?" "No," I tell them. "I not only don't go to work, I haven't been to work in the

"I haven't been to work in the last more than half a century."

last more than half a century. It's not that I was unemployed. I wasn't, but I don't recall ever doing anything that even remotely resembled 'work.'"

It certainly wasn't "work" hanging out at Westminster Cathedral choosing the best nooks and crannies to hide cameras in to cover the coronation of Queen Elizabeth—so many years ago that the old girl recently celebrated her Golden Jubilee.

Neither was hanging out at the Palace in Monaco lining up the television coverage for Grace Kelly's wedding or hanging out at St. Peter's figuring out the best way to cover the coronation of [Pope] John XXIII.

And it sure as hell wasn't "work" hanging out at Cape Canaveral with Walter Cronkite watching astronauts get blasted into space.

So, a life like I've had leads me to the conclusion that the best way to deal with your age is to ask yourself the question Satchel Paige, the black baseball legend who pre-dated Jackie Robinson, asked contemporaries of his: "How old would you be if you didn't know how old you was?"

I know how old I'd be. I'd be thirty-three...completely ignoring the fact that I was born before ballpoint pens, credit cards, panty hose, gay rights, house husbands, computer-dating, group therapy, artificial insemination, word processors, and guys wearing earrings.

I'm sure there are some weighty, philosophical truths—over and above what I just said—to shed light on why I don't feel old. What they are I don't know and have no desire to find out. Just as I liked my life when I was a fifteen-dollar-a-week copy boy at the old *New York Herald Tribune,* I like it now.

DON HEWITT was born on December 14, 1922, in New York City.

MARGE CHAMPION

As successors to Fred Astaire and Ginger Rogers, Marge and Gower Champion were a hugely popular husband-and-wife dance team that created some of the most memorable dance scenes in movie and Broadway history. Marge was born in Hollywood, and her father, who was the first dance director in motion pictures, trained Gwen Verdun, Cyd Charisse, and his daughter, Marge

THERE ARE CERTAIN advantages to being over eighty. Everyone helps, whether you're lifting a suitcase or walking on some pebbles. Of course, I know some older people resent that. They snap, "I can do it!" I don't see any reason that I shouldn't be helped over cobblestones. They hurt the bottom of your feet. Your feet get tender as you get older.

One of the key things in survival is flexibility. I don't only mean the flexibility of adjusting to life's adversity, I mean *physical* flexibility. That's equally important. Physical flexibility helps because it keeps the joints and the arteries open so the blood can flow through all those places that want to close up because gravity is pulling you down.

I think stretching is the most important thing. And the next most important thing is to keep the lungs busy. You can do that with singing, dancing, walking, anything that makes you fill your lungs right down to the bottom.

I think the worst thing about smoking is that it cuts off the flow of blood to your veins and arteries. So, if you do have an accident and need to have those veins join hands again, they can't do it.

I have lived several lives, all of them very stimulating. I was a "movement model" for Mr. Disney in *Snow White* and *Fantasia*. Then I had a life in performing, and a life in mothering.

The 1980s were not good. That's when I turned to professional help. I'm probably one of the sunniest characters you'll ever meet. I've often been accused of being *too* positive. But in the 1980s I learned what it was to be clinically depressed.

I wouldn't have known that side of life unless I had to go through that period. Gower died in 1980. My second husband, Boris Sagal, died in 1981. My son Blake died in 1987. It was exactly six years to the day after Boris died that my son was killed in an automobile accident.

Today my primary address is New York City, where I have an apartment. And I have this wonderful country house in Stockbridge in the Berkshire Mountains that has put me in touch with the earth in a way that I never had in California. In Los Angeles, I was always too busy—dancing, or singing, or looking after the kids and their tennis lessons.

In those days, Gower was the gardener of this couple. But since I've lived here in the country, I've found what a joy it is. Of course, the gardening season is very short, so it doesn't take up my entire year. We only have about four months in the summer. You don't plant before Memorial Day, and there's not much to gather after the first of October. But it has become one of my passions.

My garden includes some youngsters that I mentor. And it keeps me in touch. I might add that gardens and children have similar needs.

I should mention the great joy I get from my son, Gregg Champion, who is a fine quality TV and movie director. He just received the Christopher Award for *14 Hours* and has directed Sidney Poitier in two films.

I have friends who are actually older than I am. They're my inspiration. One of those was Al Hirschfeld. I had come to New York when I was nineteen, and I was going with a friend of his. And that's how I had my twentieth birthday party in his apartment. And we remained friends until he died recently at ninety-nine.

He visited me here in the country with Louise, his last wife, every year that they were together. She's an art historian and she went off to the local museum. And Al liked to sort of dawdle in the morning, and as we were finishing breakfast I said, "Boy, Al, you really have it made. You've got a beautiful young wife, you've got your gorgeous house on 95th Street, you've got your work."

And he said, "Wrong! I never worked a day in my life. Every morning when I get up, there's this blank piece of paper in front of me. And filling it up is my passion."

I learned a lot from that statement. I learned that unless it's some drudgery you're doing around the house—and I think even that is good for you—you have to have a passion.

And today my days are like Al Hirschfeld's blank sheet of paper.

I don't have the incandescent gift that he had. The one I felt was my real gift was my ability to dance. And that doesn't quite come up to scratch at eighty-six. But I still dance.

I don't pursue choreography that much. My life today is mainly devoted to things I would call "passing the torch."

I've been on the executive board of the Williamstown Theatre Festival for almost twenty years. And I have the chance through my grants to help pick the grantees every year. And I've been fortunate in finding some who have successfully directed on stage.

It's gratifying to see that you can make a difference, by perhaps opening a door for some talented young people at the very beginning of their careers.

In the 1990s I saw every show on Broadway, in order to nominate shows for the Tonys. I recently finished an eight-year stint as a member of the nominating committee of the Antoinette Perry awards. I loved that. You are one of an extraordinarily interesting committee. The group included Oliver Smith and Brendan Gill and people from all parts of the theater.

"Today my days are like Al Hirschfeld's blank sheet of paper."

What I loved about the committee was that I was able to gain some intriguing insights into each phase of the theater. The lighting designer would tell me why a particular show, even if it was a simple one-character show, was challenging. I got to know some of the secrets that each department in the theater is confronted with every day.

I have some advice for younger people. It's something Gracie Allen taught me. When Gower and I first came out to Hollywood with MGM, we were at a party where we met George Burns and his wife. And Gracie and I sat in a corner talking, and she said, "You're going to be successful. Don't let anybody talk you into a house that's bigger than you can take care of." And I said "Why is that?" And she said, "I know the space seems to take a big load off your shoulders. It doesn't." And she said, "It's an old cliché, but everything you own, owns a part of you." And I never forgot that.

One more little secret. In the beginning, I was the daughter of a dancing teacher, and I helped him. During the Depression, he couldn't afford to have assistants with him when he went to the homes of his various students, like Shirley Temple and Harold Lloyd's daughters. And I got the feeling of how important it is to be there for other people, whether they're young or old.

And that has been an extremely rewarding part of my life—being there for those who need help: for younger people who don't know the way, and for older people who are having a hard patch.

MARGE CHAMPION was born on September 2, 1919, in Los Angeles, California.

RAY BRADBURY

Ray Bradbury's most celebrated work, Fahrenheit 451, *is a chilling cautionary fable, a story of totalitarianism and censorship in which all books are forbidden. Bradbury's title has recently been revived as a Broadway play, appropriated by Michael Moore in a documentary, and become a synonym for repression.*

MY ANSWER TO GROWING old at *any* age, whether you're growing to be twenty, or forty, or sixty, or eighty, is to fall in love and stay in love.

As you progress through life you pick up your various loves and you connect with them and solve them, one by one.

When I left high school I couldn't write short stories, I couldn't write poems, I couldn't write essays, I couldn't write plays, I couldn't write screenplays. I couldn't write *anything.* I couldn't do anything.

But, I was in love with libraries and in love with authors who influenced my life. By being in love and going into libraries and sitting there and letting the lives of all those people impinge upon me, as I sat reading and researching, slowly, over the years my first love came to be. When I was twenty-two I wrote my first decent short story.

My next love was poetry and I kept working at it and being in love with the great poets until I was forty-two. Finally, in my forty-second year, I wrote my first decent poems and then I was off and running with my great love.

Another of my loves was to one day write a screenplay. I finally had a chance to do that and solve the problem of my love for screenwriting and motion pictures.

I wanted to be a playwright and it took me until I was thirty-seven and remembered my love for Ireland to write my early Irish plays. So that was another of my loves that came to be.

I wanted to write a novel. I had a lot of short stories that I wrote over the years, but the problem with a novel didn't solve itself until my love caused me to write *The Martian Chronicles*.

"Love covers everything and impels you into the future and you arrive at the age of eighty-five a damned happy person."

So, you see there's been a succession of loves that have pulled me into the future. I was so in love with writing on so many different levels that I never noticed how bad a writer I was.

Love covers everything and impels you into the future and you arrive at the age of eighty-five a damned happy person.

RAY BRADBURY was born on August 22, 1920, in Waukegan, Illinois.

*"The old age of
an eagle is better than
the youth of a sparrow."*
—*Greek saying*

DICK VAN DYKE

Dick Van Dyke was chosen over Johnny Carson, as well as TV show creator Carl Reiner, to star in a TV show that was called, sensibly enough, The Dick Van Dyke Show. *The wisdom of this selection may be seen in the enduring success of the classic CBS situation comedy, as well as Dick Van Dyke's wide-ranging successes, from the Broadway stage in* Bye Bye Birdie *to the movie screen in* Mary Poppins.

AT EIGHTY I'VE COME to the conclusion that attitude is everything. It has nothing whatsoever to do with your environment or the situation you're in. It's the attitude you take toward it. By God, I can't think of anything else that works for me more than the way I look at the situation I'm in and at life generally.

The other thing I think, as a guy gets our age, we start to find out what our character faults and personality defects are, and we go to work on them.

I found that all my life, what has been eating away at me was procrastination. I was one of those people who put things off. I never got my homework in on time. I never was quite aware what that was doing to me subconsciously. It's just eroding inside when you've got something on your mind. The minute I went to work on that—I've overcome drinking and smoking and everything else, but I don't think anything has been harder than trying not to procrastinate.

When you procrastinate, these problems stay with you. When you act on them, they're gone. Your conscience is clear and you're content and serene. I don't think people realize how much unfinished tasks are eating away at them.

I think if you live this long and are reasonably content, you're comfortable in the world. That's the only phrase that comes to me. I'm quite comfortable in the world and with myself. I find other people's reaction to me somehow reflects that.

When Carl Reiner created what was to become *The Dick Van Dyke Show*, he originally saw it as a starring vehicle for himself. But a writer friend of mine, Aaron Rubin, alerted Carl to me in the musical *Bye Bye Birdie,* and said, "Why don't you check this kid out?" Carl came to see me perform. So did Sheldon Leonard, whose company was developing the TV show. I got the lead in the show—one of the biggest breaks of my life.

I haven't been back to the Broadway stage since *Birdie.* But I've done a number of shows on the road over the years—I did *The Music Man* and *Same Time, Next Year.* And before *Bye Bye Birdie,* I had been in a show called *The Girls against the Boys.* It was one of the last Broadway reviews. It had quite a cast—Bert Lahr, Nancy Walker, Shelley Berman, and me. It was pretty good. The audience liked it. We ran two weeks and went out of business.

"I think if you live this long and are reasonably content, you're comfortable in the world."

But *Bye Bye Birdie* lives on. It's one of the shows that's been a natural for high schools. I don't know how many high school performances I've seen over the years, but I've seen a lot of them, including productions with my own kids.

I think we have all said, Carl included, that the years of *The Dick Van Dyke Show* were the best years of our lives. We had the most fun and the most creative gratification that we've ever had. It was never like going to work, ever.

We didn't do well the first year. We were on opposite Perry Como, who was very big in television at the time. We got cancelled at the end of the season. Sheldon Leonard saved our butts by going to our sponsor, Procter & Gamble. He went to Cincinnati and talked them into giving us a shot the next year. They left us on over the summer and we picked up an audience, thank God.

I haven't done a regular series for almost five years now. I've been very, very busy. I've gotten into pro-bono work: fundraising and charities. I'm on the board of the Midnight Mission down on Skid Row—Chairman of the Fundraising Committee. We just built a brand new building down there. I did a lot of begging and pleading for money, but we got it done.

I have a little group—five young guys and myself. We sing mostly children's songs, but jazz versions, everything from *Sesame Street* to all the Disney stuff. We do a lot of benefits. We go to children's hospitals and that kind of thing. It's a lot of joy to me.

I'm also an amateur computer animator. It's a big hobby of mine. I've gotten so good that I've been offered a couple of jobs. I don't know the first thing about the technology of computers. I just make pretty pictures. I learned how to do that. So I do special effects, animation—everything.

I didn't really feel a lot of stress in my younger days. My main stress was having a family and continuing to work. That was my main problem in life—keeping working. Other than that, I just never suffered a lot from stress, even though I didn't know how to act or sing or dance. Every time I'd go out for one of these auditions, I'd lie and say I could sing, and I said I could dance. Somehow, God help me, I managed to do it.

I can remember onc big turning point in my life. I had come to CBS in 1955 under a seven-year contract. I was the anchorman on the morning show. Walter Cronkite was my newsman. I was twenty-nine years old. I had no idea what the hell I was doing. I was bad. They took me off. I did some game shows and some children's shows. Finally, at the end of three years, they dropped my contract.

So I'm stuck in New York with my family. I don't know what to do. ABC gave me a game show, which was broadcast out of the old Latin Quarter. But I realized this was not my cup of tea. This was not what I wanted to do. It was an income, but I was unhappy. On my own after work everyday, I ran out and auditioned for everything in sight—everything but opera and ballet—musicals, plays, everything. And I got a lot of callbacks. I auditioned for *Bye Bye Birdie*. I got up and did a little soft shoe for Gower Champion and he gave me the job. That was the turning point. I really found what I love to do.

Look at *Mary Poppins*. Can you believe that? I'm not a professional singer or a dancer. I think I get so much joy out of it that I don't stop to think about the fact that I can't do it.

And I managed to carry a tune in *Bye Bye Birdie* with Chita Rivera. She's on Broadway now in her one-woman show, *A Dancer's Life*. They gave me a call the other day. I guess it's traditional between January and February that ticket sales are low and they said Chita's birthday is this month and would I come in and speak on stage and do a number with her? I said, "My God! I would get the biggest kick out of that!"

My career has been a ball. I have been so lucky. Don't think that luck doesn't count. It's incredible how lucky I've been. I just turned eighty last month. I said on that occasion that I can't believe I've lived this long and feel this good. I'm very big on exercise. Always have been. I've maintained my weight. I'm still dancing, still jumping around.

How to account for my longevity? I smoked for years and years. I had a bout for a number of years with chronic alcoholism. Somehow, my vital organs survived all that. I think genes account for a lot. I've always danced and always moved and always exercised and thank God never had a weight problem, or heart or blood pressure.

My main advice to young folks would be based on my mistakes. Train! Train and learn everything you can. I had to pick up dancing and singing and everything else along the way, which is certainly stress-producing. The more prepared you are, the better off you're going to be.

DICK VAN DYKE was born on December 13, 1925, in West Plains, Missouri.

STUDS TERKEL

Studs Terkel is a master of oral history. In his book Hard Times *he tape-recorded Americans recalling their pains during the Great Depression; in* Working *he sought accounts of the lives of working people; and in* The Good War *(which won the Pulitzer Prize) he interviewed veterans of the Second World War. Studs is a historian, a sociologist, and an exemplary journalist.*

THE KEY THING IS to keep myself alive. I've broken my neck. I had heart surgery at ninety-three. I was born in 1912, the year the *Titanic* went down and I came up. I should be dead, but I'm not for some reason or other.

First of all, I like being called a "troublemaker." Put that in quotations. In other words, the older I get, the more questions I ask of those who are my public servants. My public servants—my alderman is the president of the United States.

That's what this country's all about. We asked questions of George III, and a commoner told a monarch sitting on the throne—bugger off! Now, that's how the country was founded—when we told a monarch to beat it. Unless we tell that to a chieftain, whoever he may be—president or whoever the hell it is—unless we tell him that when we disagree with him, we're not being an active citizen in a democracy.

The first important thing is to ask questions. Ask "Why?" Why are we in Iraq? Why have these thousands of young men died? Women and kids have died. We know it was a lie. We know that. Therefore, I'm indignant. I say, "Get the hell out! Now!"

Never mind this phony stuff that we never lost a war. That doesn't mean a damn thing. To have a war created out of an outrageous lie and get away with it thus far is appalling. That's what keeps me going, too. Righteous indignation.

What first drove me to the oral histories of talking to people? It was the excitement of discovering something about people who think they're not important. They're not celebrities. So here's the irony about me. I am celebrated in some quarters for celebrating the uncelebrated. I like that. This is a waitress, or this is the tool-and-dye maker, or this is the shoemaker, this is the storekeeper, this is the stenographer. They keep things going as much as anybody else does. What is their life like? What's their attitude morning to night?

I was talking to a woman some years ago, a young mother of four, living in a housing project. It was integrated. It was way back in the days when public housing projects went up as part of the New Deal of Franklin Roosevelt. They were considered a step upward. This woman with these four kids—I don't remember now if she was white or black—but she was pretty and very skinny. Probably didn't eat much. And her kids had bad teeth because of no

> *"Because you're getting older doesn't mean you're getting wiser."*

money for a dentist. She had never been asked about her life before and the kids are jumping around. They wanted to hear their mamma's voice. The tape recorder was not as ubiquitous as it is now. She's talking and for the first time in her life she was asked about her life. I told her kids to be quiet and I'll play it back. They're hearing their mamma's voice and they're jumping up and down. Suddenly, she hears her voice, which she had never heard before, and she puts her hand to her mouth and says, "Oh, my God!" I said, "What is it?" And she said, "I never knew I felt that way before."

That's some big moment. Wow! That's Bingo for her! And Bingo for me! That's the kind of stuff that excites me.

I just finished a book on music. I've had interviews with some classical artists—singers and pianists—as well as jazz men—Louis Armstrong and Dizzy Gillespie—as well as folk and spiritual and blues musicians.

Gotta make sure what century I'm in. The twenty-first century is what I fail to understand. I'm still using a typewriter. I'm excited. I'm just starting to use the electric typewriter. That's where I am right now. Think of Caruso. Every immigrant family owned one of his records. It was two bucks a record, which is closer to fifty bucks today. But they've got to have Caruso records in the house because in his singing he did something no other singer ever did. He reached a certain note and then he'd go *higher*. He was telling us there's something more in us to be explored—more potentialities, no matter who we are.

One thing that keeps me going is curiosity. I spoke of being a troublemaker and being indignant when things are wrong—to speak out and say it. The other quality is *curiosity*.

Norman Lear and I were both in a film about Norman Corwin—he's ninety-five. People don't know who he is. It's not the fault of this generation; it's my generation's fault, too, that there's less and less memory span. Corwin was the greatest writer in the history of radio. He wrote the greatest radio programs ever written, like on VE Day. Now Norman Lear and I are in this movie about him. So are Walter Cronkite and Robert Altman. And it's a tribute to Norman Corwin.

Because you're getting older doesn't mean you're getting wiser. In many cases it doesn't work that way. Woody Allen was recently asked about age and wisdom. He said, "That's a lot of crap." He said he's learned nothing in all his later years that he didn't know before. And he commits the same errors as he did before.

To a great extent, he's right. Don't equate age and wisdom. Sometimes, that narrowness that you may have nurtured all your life becomes even more narrow and you become even more attuned to the narrowness, and you become just an old geezer complaining that the younger generation has gone to hell.

To some extent it has. Something's happening with technology. The speed.

I should be dead. But you know what saved me? I had a new heart valve put in about four months ago at the age of ninety-three. I think I was the oldest one at the Rush Medical Center who had that done. You know what saved me? The skilled hands of the surgeon, of course—but the machinery, the technology.

It's the technology itself that's running away. It's good in that it saved my life. It's good when it advances cures. But, in the meantime, that same species that built that machine has also given us Hiroshima and Nagasaki: machines of destruction.

We have a choice right now that we never had in all the history of the human race. Never has the human race had this choice of machines for advancement, or for the *destruction* of the species. It's jumped exponentially, leaped like a house on fire. Right now we know that all countries, not just North Korea, are working on nuclear stuff as a knock-off. We are the most powerful country in the world—once the most loved and now the most disliked—and with good reason.

That's what keeps me going. My anger right now, at this moment, has my blood coursing through my veins. That's great medication for me—wrath.

The greatest mind of the twentieth century was Albert Einstein. He's the guy responsible for this. That's the irony of it. His equation led one thing to another, from Enrico Fermi in Chicago to Oppenheimer in Los Alamos, to a guy on a plane named after his mother, *The Enola Gay*, one Sunday morning in August 1945, who destroyed a city called Hiroshima.

I believe the average American, the average person everywhere in the world, has a certain major intelligence that has not been called upon. So, fear is played upon. Franklin Delano Roosevelt was my favorite president by miles. Even he was guilty of using fear in establishing the Japanese internment camps. Horrendous thing. Even my favorite president.

So you have to keep on watching, all the time. That's what a citizen does. There's an assault on our intelligence. They talk about "the liberal media."

And then you start naming Rush Limbaugh and hundreds of talk radio stations. You've got Bill O'Reilly. You've got the Fox News Network. You've got Rupert Murdoch. Who the hell is kidding who? And they accept that phrase: liberal media. But bit by bit, people do catch on. At least I hope they do.

Hope is the other big thing. Without hope, if I were to say, "The world is going to pot, the hell with it," I'd be dead now. You have to have hope. Hope dies last. That's the key thing. You've got to have hope, as well as indignation. The two go together—Indignation without hope is useless. If the world's going to hell, it's going to hell. But I don't feel that. I feel there's still that special something in the human spirit to be called upon.

Right now we live in a key moment in human history. I know I'm melodramatic, but it's true, because of technology. Technology that came out of our species. Einstein never dreamed of Hiroshima when he approached Roosevelt and convinced him to build the atom bomb. When Einstein heard it was dropped on humans, he pulled out his hair and said, "I don't know what the weapons of World War III will be. But I know the weapons of World War IV—sticks and stones."

So today we have a chance for a new era of greatness, or the end. Think of the Stone Age. Our ancestors—living in caves. But now we're talking about our children! Regressing to sticks and stones. Imagine our children's children's children coming out of caves and not knowing who Shakespeare was.

It's a danger. It's a danger unless, of course, as many democracies as possible can talk and speak their minds. We here in the most powerful one in the world, if we don't speak our minds now, when will we? That's pretty much how I maintain my sanity, as well as my physical well-being.

That's one of my medications: indignation with hope. Don't forget that word "hope." That's being a *troublemaker*. I like that. I'm an American citizen. I question authority!

You've gotta get mad. You don't get mad, you're not alive. But with hope—that's the thing. That's pretty much the ticket.

STUDS TERKEL was born on May 12, 1912, in New York City.

MIKE WALLACE

Sitting beneath a shelf crowded with Emmy Awards, Mike Wallace can reflect on the hard-hitting brand of journalism he brought to 60 Minutes *since the show's debut in 1968. His no-holds-barred interviewing approach has always held the public's attention. His reportage extends from Eleanor Roosevelt to George Bush, from the Reagans to the Carters, from Kennedy to Arafat, from Haldeman to Baryshnikov. In a remarkable sixty-year career, he has been a confidant to the famous and the infamous.*

TELEVISION IS A COLLABORATIVE medium and when I retired last March after thirty-eight years on *60 Minutes,* I was working with people who were at least twenty years younger.

60 Minutes was great. You could come across a piece you'd like to do and if it was sufficiently interesting, you knew you were going to have an audience that was large, civilized, and curious. And you knew you were going to have enough time on the air to report it adequately.

If my style is different than it used to be, I can see it as a signal of the passage of time. And perhaps a sign of greater compassion. If you've been through enough challenges in your life—and everybody goes through some of them—you begin to understand that it's not as simple a process as you started out believing.

Certain tragedies take place in your life. I adored my oldest son Peter. He was nineteen. I was on a trip around the world and Peter was on a trip in Greece when he was killed in an accident. I decided to quit everything that I had been doing, which wasn't very interesting. It was honest work but it didn't make me proud. I had enough money saved for a period of a year, and I said, "I'm going to do what would make Peter proud." It was the best decision I ever made.

My father died at seventy-three of what was then called a coronary thrombosis, and my mother passed away at eighty-six. I've been pretty healthy except for three episodes of serious depression along the way. Luckily I have a very wise psychiatrist, Dr. Marvin Kaplan, who was very helpful to me during one of the worst experiences I had as a journalist.

CBS and I were being sued for $120 million by General William Westmoreland. I was sitting in a drafty federal courtroom hearing myself called a cheat, a liar, a fraud by Westmoreland's attorney.

Dr. Kaplan said, "You know something, Mr. Wallace? What you must understand is, you're going to have to testify, and you're going to have to answer the kind of questions that you like to ask the people that you interview."

A couple of years ago, shortly before May 9th, on the sixtieth anniversary of the end of World War II, the Kremlin decided to talk to the CBS News Bureau in Moscow. They wanted me to come and do an interview with Vladimir Putin about the celebration. I was astonished. I was the sole reporter that was asked to come, and the reason was that I was still working and it was a birthday gift to me on my eighty-seventh birthday—May 9th. That was the day the celebration was going to begin. Reporters from all around the world came to Moscow for the event.

"If you've been through enough challenges in your life … you begin to understand that it's not as simple a process as you started out believing."

This is what my book, *Between You and Me,* is about—the opportunity to talk to all kinds of people over a period of half a century. I've talked to Eleanor Roosevelt, Margaret Sanger, Salvador Dali. I dedicated the book to Dick Salant, who back in 1962 was president of CBS News and gave me the job and the life he knew I yearned for.

And of course the most fortunate thing of all was the fact that I've been able to spend the last twenty-two years with Mary Yates, the widow of my long-time reporting associate Ted Yates, who was killed in Jerusalem on the first day of the Six Day War. He was the bravest man I have ever known.

It took me a long time to find out who I was. I was thirty-eight before I knew what to discard and what to hold on to.

I was surprised when Eleanor Roosevelt agreed to do an interview. I remember her walking into our studio. She was such a wonderful woman. People don't think of her as beautiful, but she was such a beautiful individual in herself. She was not a traditional beauty—the beauty came from inside. And she was the eyes and ears and legs for FDR. And in our household, Franklin Delano Roosevelt meant America.

The only advice I have to the young and to the baby boomers who are turning sixty is—keep at it. Keep at it because you don't know when all of a sudden something is going to occur to you, some opportunity is going to come along.

America remains an extraordinary place in which to grow up and grow old if you have the patience *and* if you achieve the wisdom to understand that it's out there for you if you keep looking.

MIKE WALLACE was born on May 9, 1918, in Brookline, Massachusetts.

*"The longer I live
the more I see that
I am never wrong
about anything."*
—*George Bernard Shaw*

BUDD SCHULBERG

*"What Makes Sammy Run?" Budd Schulberg's classic novel about power and corruption in Hollywood, earned him the animus of the filmmaking community. He went on to other triumphs—*The Harder They Fall, A Face in the Crowd, *and the Oscar-winning classic* On the Waterfront, *in which Marlon Brando famously complained, "I could've been a contender." He helped found the Watts Writers Workshop in Los Angeles and the Frederick Douglass Creative Arts Workshop in New York. His memoir is called* Moving Pictures: Memories of a Hollywood Prince.

I T'S MY FEELING THAT in your eighties it's essential to embrace life. I'm not great on my diet or exercise. But I'm a strong believer in being actively engaged. When you build up obligations, you can't really think about your age. All you think about is: Hello. You've got to keep up with different things…deadlines!

Like what I'm worried about right this very moment. I really think that the answer is that you've got to keep going and keep very busy. I go to college reunions and see the people that stayed active. They are in so much better mental health than the ones that retired. At the next reunion half the ones that retired are gone.

I don't think I "smell too many flowers" today. In fact, my days are very much the same as they've always been. I start a bit later. I used to work nine to five. Now, very often, I work from ten to six. I try to go to sleep every night thinking about what my work schedule is for the next day.

I hear that Norman Lear's favorite word these days is "Next." I think that's very well said. The only difference with me might be that I know what my "next" is, even 'til the next year, or the year after. Right now, along with all the articles I'm writing, I'm putting a new book together and I'm working on my memoir and I'm also working on a screen-play with Spike Lee about Joe Louis and Max Schmelling. As you can see, I've sort of overdone it now. I'm wondering how I can do it all.

"I give the same advice to the young that I give to myself—put more into life than you take out of it."

I find today's younger generation has no curiosity about the past, so they know nothing. They don't know Franklin Roosevelt from Teddy Roosevelt—if they know them at all. It seems that the world just started the day they were born. I really think you need some sense of the history that you're part of. I give the same advice to the young that I give myself—put more into life than you take out of it. Be sure that you've added more than you've subtracted.

I once wrote a movie called *Winter Carnival* with F. Scott Fitzgerald and I learned a few things from the experience, some negative, some positive. One thing I learned is how difficult it is to get back on track again. It helped me keep my eye on my career and not get pulled off on tangents the way Scott was. Scott regretted the wasted time and then realized he had to make up for it.

I wrote a novel about my collaboration with Fitzgerald called *The Disenchanted* in which I said the worst part of writing movies was the waiting—waiting for the studio to make up its mind. There were other problems in writing movies. One was the cavalier way the producers treated the writers. The movie producer completely chopped up the work, which gave the producer something to do. He would sometimes have two or three different writers working on the same script. There were all kinds of indignities. I hated the system. I guess I was looking for a way out.

When they re-released my novel *What Makes Sammy Run?* several years ago, I visited some American colleges. I was shocked to learn that Sammy Glick, the amoral, opportunistic subject of the book, was now a hero and a role model for too many students. I was speaking at Hofstra College, and after I got through a young man rushed up to me. He was all excited and he congratulated me, shook my hand, and said, "I was worried about whether I would be able to function after I got out of school but now, having read your book, I see the way to go."

It's very sad. And it's very telling about the atmosphere today.

I've enjoyed helping young writers get started. I helped found the Watts Writers Workshop in Los Angeles in 1965, and I was there recently when we celebrated the fortieth anniversary of the Workshop, along with other original writers. They read from their work, and it was a great afternoon. I'm still very active with a similar group in New York that I started in 1970. We have a faculty of twenty and about two hundred students.

To be frank, I've always been stressed. I have a bad habit of thinking I can do things faster than I can and so I take on too many different things and then they start to pile up and I get nervous about them.

I'm not sure that I'm handling stress better today than in my younger days. I just do it in different ways. I'm a sports nut, so I watch football. I watch a lot of games in the baseball season. It takes my mind off my worries. I find myself worrying about the Mets.

The Eureka moments in my life? I can think of several. I think one was my battle with the Communist Party. I was a young enthusiast when I realized that I had to leave the party. That was one of the turning points. I think when I went to Watts was another. Going down there the day the curfew was lifted after the 1965 riots really affected my life. And meeting filmmaker Spike Lee. At that time I thought I would never write a film again.

BUDD SCHULBERG was born on March 27, 1914, in New York City.

KITTY CARLISLE HART

Well into her nineties, Kitty Carlisle Hart must be tracked down with cross-country phone calls, as she is on tour. Thus continues the saga of the still young and beautiful Kitty, widow of dazzling playwright Moss Hart, longtime panelist on To Tell the Truth, *ingénue in the Marx Brothers'* A Night at the Opera, *author of the refreshing memoir* Kitty, *and chair of the New York State Council of the Arts.*

I'M LUCKY. I WAKE UP every morning and I say, "What's for today?" I find wonderful things for today. I just got back from doing my show in San Francisco and Palm Springs. I'm off to points west and south. I'm busy. It's interesting to me—my career has taken off now that I'm ninety-five. It's totally taken off. I had to wait 'til I was ninety-five to be this popular. I've been doing my show for about eleven years with my conductor and pianist. I had a big party here the other day for Sloane

Kettering. I often lend my house to charities when they want to throw parties. I said to the head of Sloane Kettering, "Why can I not remember anybody's name and I can remember lyrics?" He said, "Because it's a different part of the brain."

In my show, I sing five songs written by the five great composers I sang with at the piano in my own home or in the theater—including George Gershwin, Irving Berlin, and Dick Rodgers. Since I had the privilege of singing their songs with them accompanying me at the keyboard, I think I know how their songs should sound.

I used to go dancing at El Morocco with George Gershwin and we would bet each other on which composer's song would be played first. George was a good dancer.

In my show, I tell funny stories and I make people laugh. I tell a story about the Marx Brothers, with whom I appeared in *A Night at the Opera*. I tell a story about Harpo Marx. Moss had a big house in Bucks County that he was very proud of. He invited Harpo to come for the weekend and when Harpo arrived, Moss said to him, "The local minister is coming to call and I don't have that much to say to the local minister. So why don't you interrupt us for some reason after ten minutes?"

"Why can I not remember anybody's name and I can remember lyrics?"

Harpo said, "Sure. What should I say?" And Moss said, "You'll think of something." So, after ten minutes, Harpo rushed into the room. He was dressed only in a towel. And he had a big shaving brush and a straight razor in his hands. And he shouted, "Come on, Moss—*it's time to shave the cat!*" The minister fled.

I remember when Moss was writing his wonderful memoir, *Act One*. Every night he read me what he had written that day. He would say, "We're not going to make any money from this. We're going to be impoverished." And I would say to him, "You finish this book and

I'll sell ribbons at Macy's." That's why he dedicated the book to me. I knew it was a great book. It was the best theatrical autobiography ever written.

I'm surprised at how young I continue to feel. I'm surprised and thrilled. I'm so happy. I go to the piano every day and I practice. I know how to play the piano and I do my scales. I feel if I do the work, I deserve the applause.

Once I did a summer tour of one of Kaufman and Hart's great comedies, *The Man Who Came to Dinner*. I did it with Moss. He played Jonathan Whiteside and I played his secretary. He thought I was pretty good.

Moss directed *My Fair Lady*, the legendary musical by Lerner and Loewe based on the Shaw play *Pygmalion*. He let me come to the first rehearsal of the show, and we were there for three days. We were arriving at the theater in a taxi and he said to me, "How do you think Julie Andrews is?" I wasn't very enthusiastic. And Moss said, "If I were Belasco, I would take her into a place downtown and I would *paste* the performance on her." I said, "Why don't you?" Well, he dismissed the company, and he coached Julie for a day and a half, and after that, for the first ten days of the show, I could hear Moss's every inflection in her voice. And then she made the role her own. She's wonderful.

I don't know whether laughter promotes longevity, but I laugh a lot. And I work. I care about my children and my grandchildren. I worry about them. And they're wonderful to me. I have a wonderful life. I have a nice apartment and good health. The only problem is that when it's so cold, I can't walk, and I like to walk. I've realized why older people go to Florida, because in New York you can't walk in this weather.

KITTY CARLISLE HART was born on September 3, 1910, in New Orleans, Louisiana.

HUGH HEFNER

Editor Hugh Hefner became the sexual revolution's spokesman when he founded Playboy *magazine in 1953. "Hef" had the courage and wit to celebrate sex in an era when folks still blanched at the subject. The magazine featured marginally clothed young women, along with the words of some very famous writers. The ladies were also to be found in Playboy Clubs and on a TV show called* Playboy's Penthouse.

WHAT SURPRISES ME ABOUT getting older is that I remain so young. It is not uncommon for people who enjoy their lives to feel as if there is a young person inside. That is certainly true of me. If you do it right, the only thing that really changes is the outer shell.

The last two years have been the best of my life. Part of that is connected to a life well lived, looking back over the adventures of my life, but feeling connected to the boyhood dreams.

I had a stroke in 1985 and it was produced, in part, by stress, and indeed I did change. I took better care of myself. Stopped smoking the pipe, started exercising more, and changed my diet and regimen. I'm not driven as I used to be. Part of that was the ability to pass off some of the business end to my daughter and focus on the part of the *Playboy* company that I really cared about, which is the magazine and the creative end of it.

After I had the stroke, I called it a "stroke of luck." I said, "Life is like a train trip. You're looking out the window and everything is whipping past and you're not really seeing anything, and you need to get off the train and walk around a bit and smell the flowers." The home that I live in now, Playboy Mansion West, is ideally suited for that. It's five and a half acres of forest, with birds and flowers. It's in the middle of Los Angeles, a block from Sunset Boulevard, but it's very much like an English estate.

As I say, I'm not as driven as I used to be. I take great satisfaction in the impact that we've had. At the same time, the last half dozen years have really been the most rewarding. I was in a marriage—my second marriage—and I was devoted to it, faithful to it, for eight and a half years. When it failed I was emotionally beat up and bruised. That was the beginning of 1998. I discovered a whole new generation that had grown up and was waiting for me to come out and play. As a result of all that, it made the brand, the magazine, the company hotter than ever before. That combined with the fact that we've done a reality TV show, *The Girls Next Door,* that turned out to be a big hit. Some of the things that come along unexpectedly add to the pleasure.

I do think that the key to a good life, particularly in the latter portion of it, is remaining young in heart. That is particularly true for me. I grew up in a typically conservative puritan home, but it was a home filled with life. When I was young, I was filled with dreams and I really enjoyed my childhood and adolescence.

Memories connected to that are touchstones for me, never more than in the most recent years. One thing I know—if you don't have a sense of humor about yourself, then you're old. I think a sense of humor is key to your humanity. My mother was a very good woman but was locked in the constraints of that earlier time. In an interview later in life, she said she didn't think sex was funny. Well, I think that if you remove the humor in the human condition, you lose the humanity.

Everyone wants to be attractive. But I think most of it doesn't have to do with physical attraction. It has to do with who you are. Humor is a good part of it. The people who are well liked are by and large the people who like others. It's part of what being alive is all about.

I said once that when you're in a position to *not* be a nice person, that's when you learn who you are. Power corrupts. I have been very sensitive to that in my life. Not losing one's sensitivity to those around you has always been very important to me.

I wake up every day knowing I'm a very lucky guy. I like sleeping late, so getting up is not as easy as it used to be. I look forward to the day and what lies ahead. But it is nice sleeping in, too. I've always been to some extent a night person, but less so now than before. When I was younger, I used to work around the clock and do most of my work and play in the evening hours.

My mother lived to be 101, but I think longevity goes beyond genes. The cliché is, "If you want to live a long time, pick your parents well." Of course that's true. But I also think that mind and body are intimately connected and so is attitude. A joy in living promotes longevity.

My views have evolved from when I was younger, but I haven't changed my mind in a very significant way. In other words, when I was younger, particularly in the early days of the magazine and before, I was very determined and driven. There were things I wanted to prove to myself and to the world. I'm a much more easygoing guy now. With all the very special moments in my life, I say quite sincerely that this is the best time of my life. Part of that is being able to look back over a life well lived and the satisfaction of that and the romantic connections of it all.

My search has been for a life where the lyrics to the love songs are true—

I mean the romantic ballads of Cole Porter and Ira Gershwin and the rest. What's the point and purpose of it all if you don't create the dreams? I've always been fascinated

"I say quite sincerely that this is the best time of my life."

with trying to understand the why of it all. Why we do the things we do. Why we hurt one another in the ways we do. Why are we so hypocritical? It's the reason why I pursued psychology as a major in college, because I wanted to understand more about the human condition. I think that came from the fact that I was raised in a typical Midwestern Methodist home. My folks were farm people in Nebraska. I'm a tenth generation, direct descendant of William Bradford, the original governor of Massachusetts, who came over on the *Mayflower*. So those puritan roots run deep.

I see the hypocrisy in it. And I saw it when I was very young. I think I saw it at a simplistic level back then because there was no display of affection in my home. There was no hugging and kissing. I think I identified that, early on, with repression, and escaped at an early age into the dreams and fantasies of the movies and the music.

My daughter and I established First Amendment Awards to honor those who have contributed to protecting those rights. Today, I think it is unfortunate that in so many ways we move forward two steps, and then we fall one back. I think that it is ironic and sad.

It began for me right after World War II. There were a lot of dreams about fighting a war for democracy. Then in the post-war era they gave us FBI surveillance and the McCarthy Era and the House Un-American Activities Committee. I felt as if a part of what we had fought had rubbed off on us. Of course, a part of that feeling was simply growing up and maturing and seeing things I didn't see when I was younger. Bigotry has always been there, and then we go through periods that promise great change. And indeed, I do think that over the last fifty years there have been tremendous changes in a more humanistic kind of world. But right now, we have an administration that has lost sight of some of that.

The only advantage to growing old is that it's better than the alternative. It's nice to be young but, at the same time, I wouldn't trade away the years and the memories that I have.

To the young I say—hold on to your dreams, whatever your dreams may be. When you're young, you do dream impossible dreams and there are many forces in society that urge you to compromise and give up on those yearnings. I think the dreams are what make it all worthwhile.

HUGH HEFNER was born on April 9, 1926, in Chicago, Illinois.

ART BUCHWALD

To say that Art Buchwald is a humorist is like saying the Ferrari is a car. Art Buchwald's delicious columns appeared for decades in the Washington Post *and 300 other papers. His satire on the political scene earned him two Pulitzer Prizes plus the fierce adulation of millions on both sides of the Atlantic and both sides of the aisle.*

I'M GLAD TO BE considered one of the eighty famous people in their eighties.

The thing that's keeping me going is writing, just like the authors of this book. If you don't play golf, you have four hours each time you don't play to do other things.

> **"I also spend time giving my thoughts for other people's books."**

I am also still flirting with pretty girls, and that keeps me young. I also spend time giving my thoughts for other people's books. It's very important for me because it means I'm not dead.

ART BUCHWALD was born on October 20, 1925, in Queens, New York.

ELAINE STRITCH

Elaine Stritch's caustic charm and charisma have won her audiences' admiration and love for decades. She's an absolute phenomenon, whether in her Tony Award-winning musical memoir, Elaine Stritch at Liberty; *her cabaret acts at the Carlyle Hotel; or in shows like Steve Sondheim's* Company *where she turned "The Ladies Who Lunch" into searing social comment. She is brash, incorrigible, a one-of-a kind theatrical force, and a legendary performer.*

I WAS ASKED TO PUT down on paper my thoughts about "getting old," in quotes. Well, if we must put a label on this "time of my life," in quotes, can we please say, in quotes, "getting older," not "getting old"? It sounds more ongoing. Which is encouraging.

Okay?

I think Jerry Lewis said it best—"I wake up. I'm a hit."

Here's another idea. Keep moving. That was advice from my husband. And it worked.

Everything about my husband worked, until his time was up. You see, he never enjoyed the luxury of *getting older,* so I'm never going to knock it. I'm going to try to enjoy it. I'm thinking about what's next. Now, that's good noodling. It enlivens me and fills me with anxiety at times, but most times healthy useful ambitions.

Now, what's next for me is the Carlyle Café in the fall. And that creates a certain amount of anxiety, sure, but good *healthy* anxiety. It's hard work but it's fun putting it together. And keeping in the limelight keeps you on your toes. And there's nothing healthier than that, providing you take your toe shoes off once in a while and put your feet up.

One thing while we're on this subject that I am absolutely sure about: I don't want to go back. I want to look *forward*—whatever decade I happen to be in.

Advice to this generation comin' up? Oh, I know—before I forget. Get the word "like" out of your vocabulary. Stop using "like" as a prefix to every bloody thing you say. "Like, y'know?" "Like, ya think it's cool?" Like, it's not. Like, it's boring. Like, believe me!

"There's no such thing as easier. Just do it. And wear comfortable shoes."

Another thing. Don't take anything to make your ambitions easier to come true. Just plain work hard. There's no such thing as easier. Just do it. And wear comfortable shoes.

So, gang, suit up, show up, put one foot in front of the other, and try to do the next right thing.

On the subject of age discrepancy, I just did a reading of a one-act play by Frank Gilroy about a female movie critic who has an affair with a man in his, oh, say, late forties. The movie critic was played by me. So there! I was having an affair—at my age—with a man in his late forties. And nobody batted an eyelash. I guess I'm still foolin' 'em.

ELAINE STRITCH was born on February 2, 1925, in Detroit, Michigan.

"What the retired need
isn't leisure, it's occupation.
Two weeks is about
the ideal time to retire."
—Alex Comfort

BETTY GARRETT

She sang "South America, Take It Away" in Call Me Mister, *the great World War II review; she seduced Frank Sinatra, one of the three sailors in the screen version of* On the Town; *she married Larry Parks, the unforgettable Al Jolson in* The Jolson Story; *and in recent years, now in her eighties, she is busier than ever as a performer, author, composer, and little theater producer. Her memoir is called* Betty Garrett and Other Songs, *its title taken from a musical review she performed across the country.*

INEVER THINK OF myself as old. I figure I've been young a long time. I feel my face and I don't feel wrinkled. I think my mirror is wrinkled. I realize I do have wrinkles because I see them on my body. It's in good shape. It just needs a good pressing. Come to think of it, if all my wrinkles were ironed out I'd be seven feet tall. There are some good things about growing older—at least wrinkles don't hurt.

You notice that I say "growing older," not "growing old." There are other advantages to growing older, if I can just remember them. Oh, yes. The world is so quiet and peaceful when you take out your hearing aid. You can't drive anymore, so everyone else drives you and you can enjoy the scenery; that is, if you can see. You can tell dirty jokes and use all kinds of obscenities. People just say, "What a cute old lady." You don't grow hair under your arms anymore. If you were a dancer, a high kick was expected. Now you do a time step and you get thunderous applause.

You get a lot of appreciation and compliments if you just keep on "keeping on." Then again, there's Cary Grant's comment, "When people tell you how good you look, they're just thinking how old you are." Well, when all is said and done, as long as I can put my underwear on standing up, I'm still young.

A lot of people remember me singing "South America Take It Away" in *Call Me Mister*. That was a thrilling opening night, one of the best I've ever gone through. There was something about it, the minute the curtain went up. The audience was just with us. Of course, that whole theme of soldiers coming back made it the perfect show for the period. Every song and every sketch related to soldiers returning from the war. I don't think any of us

"There are other advantages to growing older, if I can just remember them."

realized how big a smash it was going to be. Although, after that opening night, I think we all looked at each other and said, "We've got a hit."

In 1949 I played an aggressive taxi driver named Brunhilde Esterhazy in the movie version of *On the Town*. I was under one of those seven-year contracts. They came up every year for the actors. The actor had no way of getting out of the seven years, but the studio could dump you every year if they wanted to. I loved working at MGM, but I used to chafe under the contract. The studio controlled our lives. They could tell us who to go out with and whether we could leave town on a vacation. However, looking back, it was a very safe thing. You got paid every week of your life, except for thirteen weeks, which was supposedly your vacation. You had classes available to you. You had coaches to help you. It was lovely to walk on the lot and have the gate man say, "Good morning, Miss Garrett," and have a place to park your car and your own dressing room. It was a very lovely time, actually. We all got to know one another. And the big place was the commissary where you went to lunch every day and all your friends were there.

I've done a number of Broadway musicals since my Metro days. I went back to do *Meet Me in St. Louis*. Then I went back a few years ago to do Stephen Sondheim's *Follies*. I got to sing "Broadway Baby." I'm one of the founding members of a group here in L.A. called Theater West—and we've been going for forty-four years. I run a musical comedy workshop every Wednesday night.

Right now I'm working on a musical review of the songs that I've written over a long period of time, coming out of my musical comedy workshop. I've done benefits down at the McCallum Theater in Palm Desert. I do a show every year for an AIDS benefit called S.T.A.G.E. (Southland Theatre Artists Good Will Event). I'm one of the chairpersons and I also perform in it.

I don't stop singing and dancing. I just finished doing *Nunsense* at Theater West. It's hysterical. It's about a convent of nuns who put on a benefit. In that show I get to sing a song and do a tap dance in full nun's habit.

I'm very active. I think that's the secret. I'm teaching. I'm performing. I have three scripts for which I'm doing staged readings. One of them is a wonderful old play called *Mornings at Seven.* The other two are original plays written by Theater West members.

I don't really know how I deal with stress. Probably the same way that I always tell actors to deal with stage fright. You don't concentrate on the stage fright. You concentrate on the task at hand. What do you have to do *right now?* What's the scene about? What are you doing and what are you feeling at that point? If your concentration is completely on something else, the stage fright will leave you.

I imagine that's probably what I do in my life. I just do what I have to do and concentrate on it. Not that I'm free of stress. I think I have quite a bit of that. You're talking to somebody who's interested in geriatrics—I was on a panel with a bunch of women who were studying geriatrics, people who were ninety years old or over. They said certain things they had in common. One of the top things was *involvement.* The other one was *a sense of humor.* If you can't look at things from the funny side, that's when you get lost and get stressed out. I grew up in a boarding school. I think I found out very early that I could make people laugh. I suppose that made me start to see the funny side of life.

Whatever I'm doing now, I get deeply involved in it. My husband used to say to my kids when they were younger, "Don't disturb your mother. She's in her ivory tower." I was usually thinking about something I was planning to do.

My advice to young people is to be involved and be passionate about what you're involved in. I had to give a speech for graduating students at the Idyllwild High School for the Arts. All the kids there were creative. My advice to them was: Be creative all your life. Even if you don't use them, always keep those creative juices flowing. That will give you life and joy and energy and all the things you need as you get older. I think that's the best advice. To be involved and *don't smoke!*

BETTY GARRETT was born on May 23, 1919, in St. Joseph, Missouri.

JACK VALENTI

In 1969, Jack Valenti took the big bad Hays Office, home of movie censorship for thirty-four repressive years, and replaced it with the MPAA ratings system. But his most exhilarating time was when he followed Lyndon B. Johnson into the White House. Within an hour of John F. Kennedy's death, Jack Valenti was a witness to history, watching LBJ take the presidential oath on Air Force One while it was carrying them back to Washington.

I THINK WHAT ENHANCES longevity is first, superb physical condition. When I got out of the White House I was forty-four and I was in terrible shape. I began a regimen of physical fitness that I've continued now for forty years. Today I feel like I'm in pretty good physical shape.

The second thing is to never take a job or do anything just for money, but do something that is so much fun that you can't wait to get out of bed every morning to be about your chores. I had that exhilaration at age twenty-nine. I decided with a partner to form an advertising agency and start from scratch. For twelve years we built it. It was just unbelievable fun to do that.

Then I was in the White House, and I never had so much fun as I had working at the White House for Lyndon Johnson. Then, I got into the movie business. I have been able to spend my entire working career in two of life's classic fascinations—politics and Hollywood.

The White House was the summertime of my life—a 10.5. The movie industry is a 9.9. I always figure if you leave the White House, I don't know of any landscape you can enter and make your life as fascinating as the movie industry.

The turning point for me was when I met Lyndon Johnson. Most people who rise to prominence in jobs that are almost Olympian in nature are chosen for that work. I didn't run for office. Johnson plucked me out of obscurity and let me perform on the largest stage in the world. If Johnson hadn't chosen me, I would still be living in Texas, probably living a pleasant life. The operative word is "chose."

And every one of the presidential assistants who went on to become famous were chosen by Johnson. If it hadn't been for Johnson, I'd never have met any movie moguls, I'd never have met Lew Wasserman, and he would have never asked me to become a leader of the Hollywood film industry. So the Eureka moment for me was in 1955 when I met the majority leader of the United States Senate—though I didn't know it at the time. It totally reshaped my life.

I think about the guys working in the White House now, knowing what they're going through. The president calls them in and they're sitting in the Oval Office. I went into the Oval Office maybe twenty times a day, and I never went in there without feeling a sense of excitement. I miss it. But it's nostalgia rather than a burning desire. I would never go back and work in the White House again. I would never have the intimate relationship that I had with President Johnson and therefore it wouldn't be the same. I could never duplicate it. I think about it now and then, but I don't clamor to be back there.

The White House does have a burnout factor. After three years, I felt the abrasion—to my body and my mind. You don't use a watch at the White House, you use a calendar. I would never have left the White House if this new vista hadn't opened up for me when Lew Wasserman came to see me. If I'd gone into land development or oil production, as some of my Texas friends suggested, I would have become a full-time millionaire. But I don't think I would have had near the fun I did in the movie industry. I'm always around creative people. They sometimes get a little wacky and off the wall, but they're never dull and I've loved every hour of it.

I have finished my memoir. It takes me from my birth in Houston to where I am right now. Random House through its Harmony Books/Crown Publishing Company has bought

"The past is always more pleasant because it isn't here."

it. Its title: *An American Saga: A Memoir of War, Assassination in Dallas, the White House and 38 Years in Hollywood.*

I've always embraced life and I embrace it today. I embraced life when I was twenty years old and was a young combat pilot. Not only do I embrace life, I love it. And that's true in my elder years—my afternoon years. When you're having fun in what you're doing, you're embracing life. You're rising with it. You're riding a rising tide. I don't think that's restricted to older people. (I'm still embracing life, but I did that sixty years ago, too.)

I'll tell you how I feel about stress. I'm kind of like old General Patton, played by George C. Scott, when he was on the battlefield with General Omar Bradley and he says, "Oh God, I love it! I just love it!" He loved the sounds and the shocks of battle. I really think that when you're under stress the adrenaline is flowing so that at flood tide, you're really at your best.

I think retirement and "smelling the flowers" is a synonym for decay. I smell flowers, but I only want to smell them for a time. I want to keep busy. I'm involved in a number of things now. I could go away for weeks, but who needs it? I'm involved in a number of projects that command my presence.

I loved Barry Diller's remark when he was contesting with Sumner Redstone to buy Paramount and finally Sumner got the price up high, and Barry bowed out. The press said, "What's your comment?" Barry said, "He won. We lost. Next." To me, I'm a Barry Diller man

in that sense. Next. Always reaching for tomorrow and never indulging in the past. I talk about the past when I tell stories about Lyndon Johnson, but I never live in the past. The past is always more pleasant because it isn't here. That's a dangerous brew that you mix when you're always living in the past.

I talk a lot to university students and I tell them—never take a job for the money. Take a job doing something you're having fun doing. Because if you have fun doing it, you'll probably do it very well and if it's money you seek, once people know you're doing something very well, they'll offer barrels full of money to do it with them or with some company they're forming. So you always come out ahead. Otherwise, suppose you take a job for more money than you get on the job you love. After a while you're going to be, in the words of Thoreau, "living a life of quiet desperation." You're not going to like what you do even though you're making a lot of money.

I can't get in the heads of young people. I know I tell them that. I say I'm a glaring example of what you can do if you just do what you love to do. I've had careers—an advertising agency, a career in the White House, a career in Hollywood—and I've never had a dull day.

I don't think that there's anything that you do well in life, or any achievement, without two words: *hard work.* I make a lot of speeches, and often now I don't use notes anymore. I've become kind of a professional. People come up and say, "God! That was magnificent. How did you do that?" I say, "It's not magic. It's just hard work." I wrote out what I was going to say. I must have gone over that speech a hundred times. Over and over and over and over and over.

I think that for every minute that I speak, I probably spend an hour preparing for it. Edward Bennett Williams, the legendary trial lawyer, once told me something intriguing. I had congratulated him on a closing argument to a jury without a note in front of him, and he said, "Jack, it's easy. For every hour in the courtroom, I spend ten hours in preparation."

Unless you've got a rich father or a rich wife, I don't think anything comes to you without hard, hard mental exertion, and sometimes physical exertion, too.

JACK VALENTI was born on September 5, 1921, in Houston, Texas.

AL NEUHARTH

When Al Neuharth launched USA Today, *the first national daily newspaper, there were doubters. Skeptics were as wrong as the Hollywood executive who turned down "sound." Neuharth wanted short reads on major stories, great coverage of weather and sports, snappy writing, and colorful graphics. He got them all. Small wonder publications around the country now crib the style. Small wonder too that* USA Today *currently boasts the largest circulation of any U.S. daily.*

LET ME TALK TO YOU about aging—both personally and professionally. Personally, I am married to a third wife who is considerably younger than I—some twenty-five years or so. She and I have six adopted children that range in age from six to fifteen. We adopted our last set of twins when I was seventy-six. I'm now eighty-two.

From a personal standpoint, I am pretty well occupied with very important family matters and there is no question that having a teenag-er—a fifteen-year-old beautiful blonde sopho-more in high school—gives you a certain per-spective. Having six-year-old twins in first grade gives you another perspective. And then three in between. That's a heck of an incentive to get up in the morning and do a lot of things, person-ally, during the day.

Professionally, I decided several times to retire from any key executive positions but I also decided so long as I was mentally and physically in reasonably good shape, I would continue to express opinions, so I write a weekly column for *USA Today* and that forces me to stay in touch with everything from politics to sports to other things. To be able to comment on them forces me to study and form opinions.

Both personally and professionally, I think the more active you are the better—your mind, certainly, but your body also. I think it's very important, as you get into your sixties and seventies and eighties, that you keep a sharp edge mentally as well as stay in reasonably good shape physically.

In my younger days, when I encountered problems or frustrations, I was much more likely to explode and be dejected if not depressed—pissed off more easily. I'm inclined now to take a deep breath and a second look to see whether things are really as bad as they seem to be.

"At eighty-two I don't want to put off until next year or next month what maybe I ought to do this week or today."

Yet I find that, in many ways, I'm more impatient at eighty-two than I was at sixty, because I'm not sure how much time I have left to get the job done. But I think I'm much less inclined to go off half-cocked. I'm more inclined to thoughtfully work problems through. I often say—for Chrissake—at eighty-two I don't want to put off until next year or next month what maybe I ought to do this week or today. I'm not smelling as many flowers as some people do but I'm enjoying a hell of a lot of other things.

I see many, many advantages to being older. But it depends on your situation. If you're in pretty good health and if you can pay the rent and pay for the groceries each month. and if you have family or friends that you feel warmly about—I think those are all positives that are much stronger than what most of us had twenty, or twenty-five, or thirty, or forty years ago.

The baby boomers are now approaching the sixty age range. My suggestion to them is that they try to figure out "what kind of retirement" they want and to think about it pretty carefully. There are a lot of different kinds of retirement. I don't have a rocking chair. I've never played golf, so I don't have a golf club and I don't have a fishing pole. I think for a lot of people, a fishing pole or a rocking chair or a golf club become the only things that they lean on or that are meaningful to them after that "retirement" age hits them.

I don't think that's enough. I know a lot of people in that age bracket, or even close to my age bracket, who love to fish or golf or sit in their rocking chair. But I don't think that's as fulfilling as having somewhat more demanding and rewarding personal and professional activity.

Twenty-five years ago, the television generation, as we called it then—people who were in their late teens and twenties—wanted a maximum of information with a minimum of time and hassle, and they were used to TV and they wanted it quicker. Their attention span was shorter but their hunger for lots of stuff in a hurry was great.

There was no particular moment when the idea for *USA Today* seized me. I realized over a period of time that we in the newspaper business in the late 1970s were not hooking the younger generation. I had an advantage. I was the head of the Gannett Company, and we had eighty-seven newspapers around the country in thirty states. As I moved about and as we did our individual surveys, I realized that for younger readers particularly, those newspapers weren't as good as our editors and publishers thought they were.

We did a hell of a lot of extensive, expensive research. Lou Harris was a great pollster of that era. Kennedy credited Harris with having won West Virginia for him in the 1960 presidential campaign. I was with the Knight organization, then. We had Lou Harris do his first newspaper survey for us and Jack Knight said, "If he can get votes for Jack Kennedy, why can't he get readers for us?" And Harris was effective. When we decided to take a hard look at a new national paper, we had him do some expensive research. (It was so expensive, we ended up buying his company, so we could make a profit from it.)

Lou Harris sat down with our Gannett board of directors in the early stages of the research. He sat at a long table and he had the *New York Times* and the *Wall Street Journal* in front of him. He leafed through the *Times* slowly, page by page, and he said, "Ladies and gentlemen, the television generation simply is not going to fight its way through dull, gray newspapers no matter how good they are. Here are two very good ones. And the TV generation is not going to fight its way through them."

I'm not sure about the future of newspapers. I don't want to make the mistake that railroad folks did—believing they'd be here forever. But I do think that news and information companies, and that's what newspaper companies are, will not only survive but thrive, because the hunger for news and information and entertainment is greater than ever.

Nobody can gather news like trained newspaper journalists—nobody in TV or radio, nobody on the Internet, nobody at Microsoft can do it! Newspaper-trained journalists are the key to the future in the news and information business.

Now, will we be able to continue to deliver that in print as effectively as we have in the past? I'm not sure. I think there are some strong advantages that the newspaper has over other forms of media, including the Internet. If newspapers market themselves as the news, information, entertainment, and advertising shopping business, I think they have a lot going for them that other media do not.

I wouldn't want to predict whether circulation will continue to show a gradual decline. I do think it's important to observe that while most of the major metropolitan newspapers have been showing slight annual declines in circulation, many of the smaller dailies and nearly all of the weekly newspapers show gains. I think there's a message of some kind there.

I think the big turning point in my life was when I went broke at age twenty-nine in my first business venture. I started a little sports paper out in my native South Dakota and begged and borrowed all the money I could—about $50,000—and lost it all in two years because of mismanagement. So I ran away from home at age twenty-nine, all the way to Florida, and got a job on the *Miami Herald* as a reporter.

The more I thought about what had happened, the more I realized that I had screwed it up but, damn it, I was lucky I screwed up when I was old enough to learn something from it and yet young enough to start over.

I have often said to my older children—I have a son fifty-four and a daughter fifty-two—that one of my concerns about them is that they're over fifty years old and they haven't failed yet! A really big failure. Failures in your twenties and thirties teach you much more than a string of successes.

AL NEUHARTH was born on March 22, 1924, in Eureka, South Dakota.

RHONDA FLEMING

She was one of the most beautiful actresses in Hollywood when she starred opposite Bing Crosby in A Connecticut Yankee. *But she was more beautiful still in later years when she founded the Rhonda Fleming Mann Resource Center for Women with Cancer at UCLA. Seeing her sister's unmet emotional needs while battling cancer, Rhonda Fleming created a center where women and their families could receive this kind of support.*

I THINK WE'D ALL like to be able to go back and know what we know now. I'd like to go back to my thirties and have the wisdom I have today—the wisdom that comes with getting to your eighties. I'm a lot wiser now in every way.

I don't waste valuable time anymore. I have learned to say "no" when necessary. I love being a mentor to younger women. I'm also reminded of what my mother told me. She lived to be ninety-four and said, "What happened to my eighties? My seventies? How did I get here so fast?"

That's how I feel today. I'm blessed to be healthy and active. I spend a lot of precious time with family and friends. I've learned to be grateful for my blessings. Time is getting shorter and I still have much to do and to accomplish.

My life as a movie actress was truly a fairy tale. One day I was spotted by an agent as I ran to school—his car circling around the block several times before he blocked my path, asking if I'd ever thought of being in movies. That was the beginning of my career, eventually meeting David O. Selznick and being cast in my first top featured role in the film *Spellbound* with Gregory Peck and Ingrid Bergman. I was cast in the role of a nymphomaniac in a mental institution, and Ingrid Bergman was my doctor. When I told my mother, a devout Mormon, the character I would be playing, we had to look up the word in the dictionary, having no idea what a nymphomaniac was.

My career continued to flourish afterward—and having been an untrained talent with no aspirations of being an actress, I was in complete disbelief. I went on to star in over forty films, with some of the greats like Bing Crosby in *A Connecticut Yankee in King Arthur's Court, The Great Lover* with Bob Hope, *Gunfight at the OK Corral* with Burt Lancaster and Kirk Douglas, and even starring in four films with our late president, Ronald Reagan.

And now, in my eighties, my career is in doing what I love most, helping others.

I'm not in show business anymore, so now I'm free to do what I want to do. My desire now is to use what name value I have to reach out and help those less fortunate. I've never been busier—establishing the Rhonda Fleming Family Center at P.A.T.H. (People Assisting the

"Time is getting shorter and I still have much to do."

Homeless) that houses men, women, and children; the Clinic Resource Center for Women with Cancer at UCLA, a dream fulfilled that was very near to my heart after the passing of my sister, Beverly. It's taken me years to learn that life is a school of learning. We're meant to experience everything, including suffering—to be able to grow in mind, body, and spirit. Every heartache and disappointment makes us tougher, wiser, and stronger.

I lost both of my parents at the time my only sibling, Beverly, was diagnosed with ovarian cancer. When she began going through her cancer treatment, it became blatantly clear that she was not receiving the loving care she needed. It was then that I realized that I had to do something that would make things better for women suffering with this dreadful disease. With my late husband, Ted Mann, we established a clinic at UCLA for women with cancer, and when I told Beverly of our plan, she said, "Oh honey, make it a place of hope!" And that's what we did—the clinic is filled with warmth and love, with beautiful paintings and lovely plants, and it's an environment that is welcoming where there is not a trace of stress or fear. It was exactly what I had envisioned, and it is an example to me of what can be accomplished with good, healthy anger—the kind that can motivate working for good. And that's what it took for me to fulfill my dreams.

Of course, some stress in our lives can be very difficult to overcome. The best way I've found to deal with it is through meditation, long walks, laughing more, and above all, through prayer.

What starts my engine in the morning these days? Well, a good night's sleep is a must! Then a prayer for the day—and stretching, a morning walk, and a healthy breakfast. I'm always thankful for a new day and a new beginning, especially in my eighties.

RHONDA FLEMING was born on August 10, 1923, in Hollywood, California.

*"No wise man ever wished
to be younger."*
—*Jonathan Swift*

JACK GERMOND

The unadorned prose of Jack Germond's journalism reflects what he sees as the beautiful simplicity of the news business— "find out what happened and put it in the paper." The public seems to like his intellectual modesty. The self-effacing titles of his last two books are Fat Man in a Middle Seat *and* Fat Man Fed Up, *both about his many years covering politics in Washington, D.C. He was with TV's choleric* The McLaughlin Report *from the beginning, and says he quit when he couldn't stand the embarrassment.*

I'M ALMOST TOTALLY RETIRED. I just finished a new book, and I have a couple of hobbies, which are really the same hobby— gambling. I go to the track two or three days a week and I play poker once a week. I go into town, see people, have dinner, and so forth, so there's little danger of my atrophying.

I don't have much stress anymore, and to tell you the truth, I haven't really felt a lot of stress in my life. During my days on *The McLaughlin Report,* I was never intimidated by television. It was just another medium, and the fact that there were a lot of people watching didn't bother me in the least. I wasn't worried about making a mistake.

The most stress I felt in my professional life was when I was at the *Washington Star* and we were competing with the *Washington Post.* That would get your blood flowing every day. The *Post* was so good and we were trying to compete with the massive resources they had. And of course, it was very stressful when the *Star* finally went under.

But I didn't worry about it. I had two daughters. The older daughter died at fourteen of leukemia, and I knew for five years that she wasn't going to make it. It does give you a new perspective on life.

After that, nothing was important to me. Not that nothing else was important, but nothing was *as* important. I didn't worry about stories too much. And I didn't worry about people who worked for me and would come in and complain about the things that were going wrong. I never spoke about it, but I said to myself, "This is not a problem."

Journalism was the kind of business that was especially well suited to somebody like me, in the sense that you get your product out there every day, and if it's screwed up, you can come back the next day and make up for it.

I thought newspaper work was quite easy. No, the word isn't easy—it's *enjoyable*. I enjoyed the work, so I was not stressed terribly.

Of course, the newspaper business doesn't always promote longevity. It's tough on the body. In my generation, we drank so damn much, and we kept long hours and we smoked.

"My well-considered advice is to ignore most people's advice."

I smoked for fifty-five years and I quit only when I had to, six years ago.

Journalists are very much caught up in life. If you're in newspaper work, you're dealing with politics, and you're always engaged in something. Today I'm not covering the political world on a daily basis, but I'm still fascinated to see the developments. I watch the news every night, check the nightline, read the papers.

One of the things you learn as you get as old as I am is that you've seen everything before. And I often stop to think, "How many times have I written that lead?" I would hate to find out.

I have some advice for my contemporaries. My well-considered advice is to ignore most people's advice.

And my advice to young people just starting out is equally simple. The most important thing in my life—aside from my family—is having a job that I enjoyed doing, never considering anything else. I had a great time. I've got all sorts of great memories.

And also—I'm glad to be finished with it.

JACK GERMOND was born on January 30, 1928, in Boston, Massachusetts.

LIZ SMITH

In the tradition of Walter Winchell, Earl Wilson, and Ed Sullivan, today there is Liz Smith, America's most beloved gossip columnist. People who read Liz's column in the New York Daily News *and elsewhere say "Great dish!" by which they mean the inside talk of Broadway and Hollywood, not recipes—though Liz did write a succulent book called* Dishing *that covered both. She recently reported on a bash attended by such famous octogenarians as Mike Wallace, Ben Bradlee, and Elaine Stritch.*

I THINK IT'S A VERY GOOD philosophy not to be worrying that you're probably going to be dead in another ten or fifteen years—if you're lucky. I think it's better to have the other attitude.

Some people in their eighties insist that they continue to feel very young. I think they're being a little disingenuous. I'm not sure everyone in their eighties feels that way. I shouldn't generalize. I don't know that I feel young, but I certainly still feel adventuresome and curious, and I want to make the day count just like I always did. Once, I wanted to make enough money to live on. Then I wanted to make money to be comfortable on. Then I wanted success and all of that. But having gotten all of that, I still want to make the day count.

I never look back and think what other thing I might have done with my life. I don't do that. What's the point? That's like thinking about dying all the time. It's a dead end.

I went to a party recently at which a lot of famous octogenarians were present—Lauren Bacall, Elaine Stritch, Eli Wallach, Mike Wallace,

Carol Channing, Ben Bradlee. And I saw something they all had in common. They're not done yet. They're not finished. They just move a little slower.

Look at me. I get out of bed every morning with the same ambitions and the same anxieties that I had when I was young and didn't know what I was doing. And now I'm old and don't know what I'm doing! I'm still trying to decide what I'm going to be when I grow up.

A lot of writers and authors and reporters have influenced me, every great one I've ever read. But nobody influenced me to keep living longer. That was just a fact.

Right now, I'm trying to get my newspapers to extend my contract for three or four more years. They're all up in about a year, and I don't want to quit working. If I'm healthy, I don't want to quit.

My life is stress—people yelling, screaming, calling, and writing nasty letters. And I have to be somewhere all the time, all dressed up with my hair done, made up, and trying not to look like I'm half dead. I just have normal stress like anyone living in New York who is in a successful position where much is demanded. Occasionally I just quit, go take a bath, go to bed at 6:30, read, and watch the evening news and something on tape or television. I drop out now and then, but not for long.

"I'm still trying to decide what I'm going to be when I grow up."

I've some advice for the kids just starting out. Success is loving your work. If you're not doing something you love, you need to get out of that and get into something else. You have to want something, to educate yourself about it, to succeed. You have to *want* it. For the young, they have to learn to use computers and all the technology that's available to them. I'm all for people who have artistic bents going to college and taking all the English literature and art history that they can. If they want to be some other kind of person, then they need to study mathematics and science. You've got to go one way or another. You need to decide. And the sooner you do, the better it'll be for you.

Right now, I'm trying to figure out what I'll do with this weekend when I don't have to do anything. That's rare for me. I've got forty-five movies scheduled that I might go to, and people to call for dinner, and I'm going to take my godchild tomorrow and buy him a PlayStation and take him to the movies. I'm always planning and working like I'm going to live forever. I think I *am* going to live forever. As far as I know, I'll drop dead and not know I'm not living forever.

I'm glad I'm not young anymore. I wouldn't like to be young because I can remember my insecurities and seeking romance, and trying to find the right guy and all that stuff. It never worked out the way I wanted it to.

LIZ SMITH was born on February 2, 1923, in Fort Worth, Texas.

CY FEUER

Cy Feuer was the celebrated producer who gave theatergoers some of Broadway's most enduring musicals, including Guys and Dolls, Can-Can, *and* The Boy Friend. *For half a century, Cy Feuer and his partner, Ernie Martin, were virtually a brand name for hit musicals. He was at his peak during the heyday of the American musical stage, and had an unparalleled string of Broadway smashes, working with stellar composers like Cole Porter and Frank Loesser.*

WHEN YOU GET OLDER there's a natural compensation for age. You become inactive and you don't desire to do it anymore. It's a matter of desire. Diminishing desire. Let me put it that way.

People think about the exhilaration of great theatrical events, the opening nights, the shows, the hits. Well, what I was doing was my job. To me, you get up and go to work. There was no eulogy involved in it as far as I was concerned.

Of course, there was that string of five musical smashes, one right after the other. That was great.

Three of those hits were the work of Frank Loesser—*Guys and Dolls, Where's Charlie?,* and *How to Succeed in Business without Really Trying.*

My memory is a little gone about this stuff. I think the first I remember was in Hollywood where Frank wrote a song about the Army: "What Do You Do in the Infantry?" That was when we both got out of the Army. That's the first thing I remember of his.

Frank wrote my first Broadway musical, *Where's Charlie?* That was the beginning. I knew him at first as a lyricist. As a matter of fact, when I was the head of the music department at Republic Studios, he was working under contract at Paramount. A lot of this is foggy, but I do remember. I had Jule Styne under contract. He was my piano player and we worked on these B pictures.

Jule said, "Let me write the score for them." The reason I let him write the score was because I bought him a lyricist by the name of Eddie Cherkos who I paid thirty-five bucks to do the picture. There'd be four or five songs in the movie. Jule was under contract as the piano player, so he didn't get anything. He got his salary.

Jule didn't compose the underscoring, just the songs. The underscoring I used to do. We were doing these great B musicals and we had auditions and Jule would play the piano and he also would help the singers. If they were singing too high, he was able to transpose on the piano. He'd say, "Try it a half-tone lower."

I was very glad to get out of the music writing business, because I had no talent. I went to Julliard and survived there by sheer perspiration. My classmates could just sit there. They didn't even have to go to Julliard. They could just do it by instinct.

"I bound out of bed in the morning. Every now and then I fall down, but I still bound."

The only talent I ever had in music was conducting. That was easy, it was transferable to directing theater.

I had played the trumpet at the Roxy Music Hall, but that was a struggle. I went to Julliard on a trumpet with great effort. As soon as I could give up the trumpet, I did. I knew I had no talent for it and it was too much of an effort. I gave it up for orchestrating, which also was a struggle.

I had dreams of being the musician that I wasn't.

I came to New York and started producing shows for the musical stage.

I found it was a great experience. It was tough, but tough is wonderful. You're out there and you have a timetable. You have to be finished with your rehearsals out of town in time for your date to come into Broadway. It was exhilarating and it was difficult.

They've made movies out of most of my shows. But to tell you the truth, I can't remember them. I know that Sam Goldwyn made a film of *Guys and Dolls* and screwed it up with his casting. He had the casting backwards. Sky Masterson should have been Frank Sinatra. That thing was just a matter of trying to cater to public taste in terms of billing. He wrecked the show with that.

I'm ninety-four years old. There isn't much activity. My interests are still there. First of all, the business as I knew it no longer exists. It was a much more personal, one-to-one thing at the time.

The Broadway musical was wonderful. It was like working in a little bar. Today, I haven't any concept of what a musical is. My first musical cost $150,000. The same thing would cost over a million today. It's very hard for me to understand the financing today. I think anybody who puts money in a musical these days is out of his mind. They're sure losers.

I had a partner who was tough—Ernie Martin. I used to do the creative work and he used to handle the business end. He was also great at firing people.

Once I made a tremendous mistake—the greatest costume designer at the time was Irene Sharoff. She did all these great MGM musicals. And I said for this show we're going to get Irene Sharoff. We hired her and when she brought in her first sketches, I took a look at them I said, "Oy! We got the wrong person." We needed somebody who understood the street, not the fashion world. I said, "We gotta fire her." Ernie looked at me and he said, "This one is on you."

So I called her in, we sat down, and I started to hem and haw. Finally, she said to me, "Are you firing me?" I looked at her and I said, "Yes." She burst into tears. "Oh," I said to myself, "Jesus!" She said, "This has never happened to me before. No one has ever done this to me." And I said to myself, "Should I un-fire her?"

I'm kind of energetic for my age. I bound out of bed in the morning. Every now and then, I fall down but I still bound.

Looking back, I'm very satisfied. I don't have any regrets.

I remember working with Sid Caesar on *Little Me.* There was something about Sid. He could display a terrible temper at times. I was directing the show. We were rehearsing out of town and I came into his hotel room.

I said something about the pace. I said, "Pick it up…pick up the pace."

He said, "The pace, huh?"

After I left, he turned to Neil Simon, who had written the show. Sid was a great big guy. He went to the wall and he tore the sink out of the wall and threw it out the window.

"How about that for picking up the pace?" he said.

I'm no longer constantly looking for the next project. I still have the energy but not the desire. But are there any advantages to being my age? I'm trying to think. I don't deplore it. It's acceptable to me. The reason it is acceptable is because I still have all my marbles. I've witnessed the diminishing of that in some others. That I find sad. So I'm satisfied with my age.

I think it's important to have a positive attitude. I don't consider aging a threat. That sums it up. It doesn't seem to be a threat to me. Of course, I can't really champion this for everybody because I'm not sick. I don't hurt. I think that those who hurt have an entirely different perspective. I think that really dominates their thinking.

There was a turning point in my life that I remember very vividly. I was a conductor and a composer at Republic Studios in Hollywood.

I had to write a score for some picture. I can't remember what it was. I think it was called *Women in War.* I decided to write the score myself. It was about fifty minutes of music, which is the length of a symphony. I did the entire thing. I did all the orchestrations—everything. Then we came onto the recording stage with about sixty musicians. We had three days to record it. And after the second day, I was sitting there, really physically tired. We played back the last cue and I gave the orchestra a break. Republic had this magnificent soundstage that they had built for some ridiculous reason. Their soundstage was better than their pictures. I was sitting there alone and I was listening to a playback of this music. I was tired enough to step aside to listen to it objectively.

As I listened, I said to myself, "This stuff is no good. It's second rate." And while sitting there I said, "This is the best I can do." So I decided on the spot—I'm not going to do this anymore. And I didn't.

That was a deciding moment for me to get the hell out of that business.

CY FEUER was born on January 15, 1911, in Brooklyn, New York.

LENA HORNE

Elegant, glamorous, wise, and raging against the racial injustice and color barriers of an earlier Hollywood, Lena Horne has captured millions of adoring fans with her brazen performances and uncompromising principles. She has, in short, grown into a legend. Lena Horne continues to engage our hearts and minds with her talent and her passionate conscience.

I NEVER PAID MUCH ATTENTION to film work, except when I was working with Vincent Minnelli. My film work was so truncated and limited because of the prevailing racism. I preferred cabaret work because I could communicate directly with the audience. I realized it first at Café Society in 1940. I felt that I was in control as a performer for the first time.

At the age of two, I became the youngest lifetime member of the NAACP. Naturally, I didn't know what it was all about at the age of two, but I have horrible memories of being in the South with my mother, who toured as an actress.

I grew up attending integrated schools in Brooklyn with mostly white teachers. I liked some of them so much—Mrs. LeBaron, my art teacher, and Mr. Young, my tough Latin teacher—that I wanted to be a teacher. My grandmother had been a teacher so she encouraged my ambition. She stressed education above all. She died before I went into show business—she would have been horrified! But teaching and show business aren't necessarily that far apart. We remember great teachers the way we remember great performers. I've forgotten most of the names I knew, but not the names of my favorite teachers.

As an adult, Café Society became my civil rights training ground. Barney Josephson, who ran the place, wouldn't let me sing "Sleepy Time Down South," for example. And I met Paul Robeson and Walter White, who had been friends of my grandmother. They both explained to me that I couldn't work just for myself, but for so many other people. They told me I didn't have the luxury of white performers, of working for my personal success alone—but I had to think about sharecroppers and Pullman porters.

I didn't rebel, because the family lesson had already been instilled in me. I was used to being obedient. It hit me hard during the Second World War, when I saw for myself how horribly black GIs were treated—worse than the enemy. I was kicked out of the USO for refusing to sing at a camp in Arkansas where black GIs were forced to sit behind German POWs to see the show. That was a big moment for me, because it made me wonder what we were fighting for.

Blacklisting after the war was another difficult time. It seemed to me that civil rights activists were being targeted—that it was "subversive" and "un-American" to want black people to be treated like human beings and citizens.

The civil rights movement of the 1960s was only another part of the process, though certainly the most powerful. I was with Medgar Evers in Mississippi two days before he was murdered. I must say, after that I almost gave up hope. Obviously, many things have changed for the better. But entrenched inequality still exists—especially in economic and educational opportunities.

I believe that the whole anti-affirmative action movement is a way to return to racism and Jim Crow. Racism is imbedded in America. Alabama just voted to keep its Jim Crow laws on the books.

Unfortunately, I am no longer optimistic about things getting better for the people that Paul Robeson and Walter White told me I was really working for. The saddest thing is that there are no more great civil rights leaders, because it seems the people really can't do it by themselves.

The advantages in old age? I could have answered that in my sixties, when I was most happy as a performer, and when my grandchildren recognized me as a performer.

Am I looking for something new? Yes, I'm always looking to see new things in people—especially politicians.

> *"If there is a 'lioness' inside it's because not everybody had a grandmother like mine."*

90

Advice for the young? Realize that you will live several lifetimes in one life. You may be one person at twenty, another at sixty, another at eighty.

Nancy Wilson said, "Everyone sees Lena Horne as a beautiful, sophisticated lady, but there is a fierce lioness in this woman." Well, I'm old and I'm still angry. And if there is a "lioness" inside it's because not everybody had a grandmother like mine.

LENA HORNE was born on June 30, 1917, in Brooklyn, New York.

DICK FRANCIS

When age and injury grounded champion steeplechase jockey Dick Francis, the readers of mystery novels greatly profited. The former jockey began writing a string of thrillers set in the world of horse racing. He has been named Grand Master by the Mystery Writers of America and lives in the Cayman Islands, where he contemplates the waves assaulting his oceanside home as he reflects on the plot of a new Dick Francis novel. His racing silks have always been pure gold.

I HAVEN'T WRITTEN A NOVEL since I was eighty, which was five years ago. I am writing one at the moment. My wife Mary was a great partner for fifty-three years. She unfortunately died five-and-a-half years ago, and life has been lonely. It's because of her death that I haven't written anymore until now.

She was a great help. She loved researching different subjects for the various settings of my books. She had a better education than me. She learned to fly and she became a first-class pho-tographer and she did a lot of pharmacology. Now my youngest son Felix is doing research for me. He and I are spending a lot of time on the phone, while I'm writing this current novel.

I live in the Cayman Islands and it's lovely here. At the moment, the sea is very rough. I'm watching the waves breaking in front of this window where I'm sitting.

I see no great advantages to the advancing years. I would prefer to be thirty-something and doing the job which I absolutely loved, being a jockey. That was the plum time of my life. There's nothing more thrilling than riding good horses and winning, too.

I had spent six years in the Royal Air Force during the Second World War, piloting fighter and bomber aircraft. I was a jockey for ten or eleven years after that. After I gave up being a jockey, I became a newspaperman—the racing correspondent for the *London Sunday Express,* a job I held for sixteen years.

I published my first thriller in 1952, set in the world of racing. And I produced a novel a year for the next thirty-eight years. *Dead Cert* was first, *Nerve* was second, *Odds Against* was third, and *Kicks* was fourth. Though my books are all set against a background of horse racing, the heroes hold a variety of jobs, from artist to private investigator. I like to have a different character in each book, a different environment.

Here in the Caymans I am miles from anywhere, but I have lots of people coming to stay with me. I've got my author's agent and his wife here at the moment. Also my son and his wife. They're leaving tomorrow, but the following day my other son and his wife arrive. Winter is the time of year when people like to come to this climate.

I've never felt under any stress at all. I loved my life as a jockey. I loved my time in the Royal Air Force, especially when I was in the air. I didn't like it very much when I was on the ground.

If I have any advice to younger people it would be to do a job you enjoy. There are lots of office people who hate their work. I think doing a job which you love is half the battle of longevity.

I don't feel that I want to give up writing. I'm getting old. Actually, yesterday I fell and bruised myself a bit, but I'm still all right. I'll do a little bit of writing today....

"I think doing a job which you love is half the battle of longevity."

DICK FRANCIS was born on October 31, 1920, in Pembrokeshire, Wales.

*"The essence of age
is intellect."*
—Ralph Waldo Emerson

DOMINICK DUNNE

America's leading celebrity journalist writes in the tradition of Scott Fitzgerald and Truman Capote. No one knows the dark side of the rich and famous better than Dominick Dunne as he writes of the rich who believe they are above the law. He has carved out an incredible career as a bestselling novelist and a special correspondent for Vanity Fair *magazine, covering the criminal entanglements of the rich and famous.*

I AM EIGHTY AND I'VE NEVER worked harder. I have a monthly diary in *Vanity Fair* magazine that is widely read. I am shortly to finish my next novel, called *The Solo Act,* and I have a weekly television series called *Dominick Dunne's Power, Privilege and Justice.* I'm doing them all. There are two documentaries being made about my life for French Television and Australian Television.

Now that I'm eighty I don't care about a lot of things that used to bother me. I used to always back down to male authority figures, because my father was so mean to me as a kid. It's women like Tina Brown who have helped me find myself. But I'm unafraid now that I hold my own—totally. I say to myself—"Screw it! I'm eighty!"

There's something very freeing about being eighty.

I'll tell you what shocks me the most today. I think the reason I've stayed so young is that I have a lot of young friends. I encourage young writers. I learn from them and they learn from me, but it shocks me that even successful young people—I'm talking people in their thirties—don't read newspapers. Reading newspapers is an hour and a half of every morning for me. That's a very important time for me. I read three newspapers. I always have, all my life, every single morning. It stuns me that people get all their information from television. There's nothing wrong with that, but I think they're kind of missing out.

In 1983, the night before I left for the trial of the man who murdered my daughter, a journalist friend, Marie Brenner, invited me to her house for a Tex-Mex Sunday dinner. There were about eight or ten of us in the kitchen. I sat next to this young English lady and an English gentleman. The English lady was not *quite* the glamorous Tina Brown that we now see, and I had a wonderful time with her at dinner—just a terrific time. She was fascinated by Hollywood. The next day, which was the day I was leaving, I got a call from Marie Brenner saying, "Tina Brown wants to have lunch with you." I said, "Oh, Marie, I can't." Marie said to me, "Do it!" I believe in these orders in life. I met Tina, without a clue as to what she wanted to see me about. We didn't have a minute of pleasantries. I sat down and she said, "You know you shouldn't waste all those Hollywood stories that you have at dinner par-

"Now that I'm eighty, I don't care about a lot of things that used to bother me."

ties. You should be writing that for a magazine." I said, "Tina! I just wrote my first novel and it was dumped on in the *New York Times* and they made fun of it. I wouldn't know what to write." She said, "I could teach you." Then she told me that she had just set the deal with Sy Newhouse to become the editor of *Vanity Fair.* She said, "Last night, we all knew where you're going today." At that time in my life, I was so raw that if anybody mentioned my daughter's murder I would start to cry. Tina said, "I've read a lot about trials, but I've never read about a trial written by a participant." She said, "Keep a journal and when it's over, you come and see me."

I did exactly that, and writing the journal helped me get through the worst experience of my life. When it was over, I gave her my journal, and she turned me over to an editor. That was my first magazine piece ever, called "Justice." The week before the issue came out—the first, all-her-own issue—Tina Brown took me out to lunch again, and she said, "Next week, when this issue hits the stand, every magazine in New York is going to be after you, but you're mine." I had been down and out for a lot of years after Hollywood. It was the first time anyone had shown the slightest interest in me. I owe Tina everything. She worked with me. I love her. I had lost confidence in myself—had totally lost it and never expected to get it back and she gave it back to me, or made it possible for me to find it again. Then she would say to me, "Put yourself in the story. I want you *in* the story."

Graydon Carter, the current editor of *Vanity Fair,* is a great editor, too. He can read an article and say, "It lacks this. You've got to get this. You've got to build up this area." He can give you overall notes like that, and he's invariably right.

On my tenth wedding anniversary, Lenny, my late ex-wife, and I gave a dance. It was a black-and-white ball. It started at ten o'clock at night, and we had a set designer redo the whole inside of our Beverly Hills home. It was like the Ascot scene in *My Fair Lady* that Cecil Beaton had done. We had backdrops outside of the windows, lights in the house, and everything. There was a kind of a rule... the fire people had come and told us how many people we could have, and we had to say no house guests. Truman Capote called—of course we had invited him— and he said, "I have to bring these two people from Kansas. He's the D.A." It was Alvin Dewey, but Truman's book *In Cold Blood* hadn't come out yet, and Alvin Dewey was not yet famous for solving the murder of the Clutter family. Anyway, he brought them and they were great. Truman was like a star. He was at the peak of his fame. It was before the drinking got to him and everything. What people don't know about him is that he was a great dancer. He danced with all the movie stars...wrote us the most wonderful note. And then he gave his own black-and-white ball for Kay Graham at the Plaza Hotel and didn't invite us.

My first successful novel was the second novel that I ever wrote and it was called *The Two Mrs. Grenvilles.* My agent and my editor both had said, "This is wonderful." I had been down for so many years, I didn't expect anything. Then one night, I had been at the magazine late and the elevators were closed and I took the freight elevator down. A young woman I didn't know got on the elevator, and she said, "You're Dominick Dunne." I said, "Yes." And she whispered, "I loved your book." Then I thought, "Hell!" Her comment meant so much to me, because your friends rally around. Your agent and your editor praise you. But what she said was so real.

"I loved your book." I thought, "My God. I did it."

The turning point in my life? I was producing an Elizabeth Taylor movie called *Ash Wednesday* in the Dolamites of Italy. I was over there for a year. Elizabeth Taylor took a dislike to the writer and he got sent home. I used to drink in those days and do more than drink. When I was loaded at a party in Italy, I said something that was funny at the time, but was mean. It was repeated in the *Hollywood Reporter* two weeks later. I had made a joke at the expense of the writer's wife. She was a very powerful agent. It hurt her feelings when it was repeated. Sometimes you can say something that's funny, but it doesn't work on paper. When I got back to America, I knew it was over for me. I stopped getting invited to dinner parties and all that stuff.

So I just left Los Angeles. I drove up to Oregon. I got a flat tire in a little town called Camp Sherman in the Cascade Mountains, and I took a one-room cabin for the night and I stayed six months—with no telephone, no television. It was the most incredible experience of coming to terms with yourself—the silence. I'd always been a party person—going out to parties constantly, and there I was in total isolation. That is where I started to write, in that little cabin. You can't bullshit anymore. I used to say, "Oh, she ruined my career because she's...." Baloney! I picked her to ruin my career. It was an incredible experience.

When I was up there, Truman Capote wrote me a letter. I was stunned to get this grand letter from 870 United Nations Plaza on this great Tiffany stationery. It was sent to the general store. It was amazing what Truman had done. He heard that I had dropped out of my own life, and it was a letter of encouragement and admiration for what I had done. He ended it by saying, "But remember this. That is not where you belong. When you get what you went there to get, you must return to your life." At that time when I'd begun to feel peace for the first time in quite a few years, I really was thinking of living there forever. What he pointed out was there was a purpose in going there. When I went to Truman's funeral, two years later, I thought if he'd only done what I did, he wouldn't be dead. His alcoholism killed him.

I think about age. I have two sons and a granddaughter, and I think about their lives after me. I'm in that phase now where I hope I have a wonderful, big funeral. Jerry Wald was at the funeral of a man he detested and they said, "Jerry, why are you here?" And he said, "I just wanted to be sure the son of a bitch was dead."

I'm an active participant. I'm not a bystander. I used to be a bystander in life. Today, every day is full for me. I don't know how to relax. I write every day. I'm about to go to France for the Cannes Film Festival and I'm going up to Monte Carlo while I'm there to check on a celebrated murder case. The Safra murder utterly fascinates me—that billionaire who was murdered. And the male nurse is coming up for another trial. I'm going to try to see him in prison. When you're working like that, of course you embrace life. I see these guys who are even younger than me and they're all on walkers and they've got a maid in attendance. I think, "I don't want to live like that." I want to drop dead on the tarmac.

DOMINICK DUNNE was born on October 29, 1925, in Hartford, Connecticut.

ALAN BERGMAN

Gilbert squabbled with Sullivan. Rodgers bickered with Hart. But Alan and Marilyn Bergman, the famous lyric-writing team, are ever equable and much in love. The Bergmans, who wrote "The Way We Were," "The Windmills of Your Mind," and "What Are You Doing the Rest of Your Life?" have won an Oscar, Emmys, Grammys, and the esteem of their collaborators.

THE ADVANTAGE OF WRITING lyrics with my wife Marilyn is we love what we do and when you do something you love with somebody you love, it's the best thing in the world. It's really paradise. People always ask if there are any problems. Why would there be problems?

We have a lot of fun. We love to write. We don't write out of pain—we write out of enjoyment and love. And we're fortunate enough to have great composers as collaborators.

Marilyn and I had each worked independently with the same composer. That's how we met. I was writing with him in the morning and she was writing with him in the afternoon.

Johnny Mercer was my mentor. He spent quite a bit of time with me over a period of about three years. He was not only an inspiration but a marvelous teacher. I learned a lot about the craft from Johnny Mercer. I was in my early twenties and I was a student of the popular song. I really knew everything he had written. And I knew the work of wonderful lyricists like Ira Gershwin, Yip Harburg, Larry Hart. Their work inspired me. I knew I was one of the lucky people. When I was eleven years old I wanted to be a songwriter. I dreamed of writing songs for movies or for the Broadway theater. When you write a song for a film, it should be part of the fabric of the movie, and an extension of the screenplay. When the lyrics, the music, and the image come together and create a fourth entity, there's great satisfaction. The challenge is how the song functions in the movie, like "The Way We Were," like "The Windmills of Your Mind," like "What Are You Doing the Rest of Your Life?" We've been lucky to have wonderful directors who understand the role played by songs in movies—directors like Sydney Pollack, Norman Jewison, and Richard Brooks.

Very early in our careers we wrote a song called "Nice 'n' Easy" for Frank Sinatra. He asked us to write an easy, swinging love song for an album he was about to make. Creating a song especially for a personality like Sinatra is like creating a piece of theater, like tailoring a custom-made suit. The success of that song led to our first film assignment.

I play tennis every day at 8 o'clock. Then Marilyn and I go to work. We're constantly working. We wrote a show that played at the Mark Taper Theater in Los Angeles for eight

"If I wasn't the age I am now, I'm not sure I could write the kind of songs I write now."

weeks—it was called *Like Jazz*. It started with a phone call from Dr. Billy Taylor, who is in charge of jazz at the Kennedy Center. He asked if we would write a jazz song cycle for the Center.

We said, "We'd be delighted. What's a jazz cycle?"

He said, "Anything you want."

We said, "With whom would you like us to write it?"

He said, "Anybody you like."

So we asked Cy Coleman, a great composer with whom we always wanted to write.

We asked, "Cy, would you like to write a jazz song cycle with us?"

Cy said, "Sure. What's a jazz song cycle?"

We wrote about fifteen songs that were performed one night at the Kennedy Center for 2,000 people. The audience response was wonderful. Cy said, "Let's make a theater piece out of it." So we called Larry Gelbart. Larry heard the songs and said, "Let's do it."

Like Jazz worked well at the Taper. It's now called *Up Close and Musical,* and will be on Broadway soon.

If there's occasional stress, the enthusiasm for what you're doing sees you through, and you learn to say, "Next." There's always another empty page, there's always another street to go down, another tennis ball to hit.

I've always enjoyed singing. Lately I've been appearing at clubs in New York singing our songs—the Algonquin, Michael Feinstein's at the Regency, concerts at the 92nd Street Y. It's fun to be doing something new. I have a CD coming out with a sixty-piece orchestra that everyone seems to like.

If I wasn't the age I am now, I'm not sure I could write the kind of songs that I write now. I like to think that I'm following in the tradition of the great writers I grew up learning from and trying to emulate—Oscar Hammerstein, Larry Hart, Ira Gershwin, and of course Johnny Mercer. When asked for advice by young songwriters, I tell them to listen to the work of the masters who came before them.

Richard Brooks told a wonderful story: During the Depression he ran away from home and rode the rails. One night he jumped off the train and found himself in a hobo camp, joining them in the proverbial can of soup. An old guy with a scruffy beard—Richard was sixteen so the guy may have been forty—said, "Kid, what do you do?"

Richard said, "I'm a writer."

The old guy said, "Oh, you're a writer! Have you ever read Dostoyevsky? Have you ever read O'Neill?" The old hobo went on, "Kid, if you want to be a writer, let me give you some advice. For every word you write, read a thousand."

If you want to be a songwriter, listen to a thousand by Berlin and Mercer, Alan Jay Lerner, and Stephen Sondheim. That's my advice.

ALAN BERGMAN was born on September 11, 1925, in Brooklyn, New York.

NANETTE FABRAY

Nanette Fabray went into vaudeville at age three, did some Our Gang *shorts with Jackie Cooper, and hit the Broadway stage running in 1940. She enlivened such musicals as* High Button Shoes, Mr. President, *and* Love Life. *She also won three Emmys for her inspired comedy antics with Sid Caesar. Because she once suffered from a hearing disorder, she has fought for the rights of the handicapped most of her life.*

I WOULDN'T GO BACK to being young for anything. The only thing I would like is if my body could do what my ten-year-old granddaughter's can do. But I love being where I am. I really do.

Advice for the coming generations? Be more observant and more patient with a little more admiration for older people. They've survived. They deserve your admiration and your attention. But the young don't get it. I didn't get it either when I was younger. In the show *Bloomer Girl,* there were a couple of older people in the cast and I thought, "Oh, God, those poor old souls. What have they got to live for?" They must have been all of fifty.

When you're young, you're immortal and you know everything. That same philosophy is passed along forever. It's never going to change.

What gets me out of bed each morning these days is my two cats. I have to take care of them. They don't let me stay in bed. I get up in the morning and go outside about six o'clock and get the paper. I love to read the paper from cover to cover. I've got nearly two hundred books to read. I love to read.

Sid Caesar had a photographic memory. He could look at a script and know everybody's part. He was at his most creative and his funniest when he did it the first or second time. Working with Sid was half my life. We did a lot of operas on his show. We loved doing those, and all of them in faux language. Sid was brilliant at doing double-talk language. We had to sort of mime what he was doing. Carl Reiner was wonderful at it, too. But I stumbled through.

I did a Broadway musical called *High Button Shoes.* The script wasn't very good. The first day of rehearsals we sat in our chairs facing the director, George Abbott, with our scripts in our hands, and Mr. Abbott said, "Now everyone cover up your scripts, because we're not going to do that show. Everybody go home and write a new script." Everybody went home and wrote better parts for themselves.

I miss Broadway. I really miss the musicals. Those shows, and my television work with Sid Caesar, was where I belonged, really and truly. I was happiest doing Broadway shows. I loved the feel of the audience. Noel Coward once came backstage and said to me, "Nan, you have no idea what impact you have on the audience." He said, "One of these days you're going to find

"Between age 80 and 120 isn't enough time for all I want to do."

out that you have this wonderful interaction between you and the audience. And that's very rare. You can't learn that or buy it, but you have it." I knew it was a great compliment if I could figure out what he meant.

I did a show called *Mr. President* for which Irving Berlin wrote the songs. He was a nonstop, creative genius. The show was in terrible trouble because it had a weak script, and the authors refused to change a word. But Irving Berlin was marvelous. If something new would come up, he would write nine songs for the scene.

I was born with a genetic condition called Oto—meaning ear—sclerosis. The little bones in your ear that conduct sound solidify. It's a hereditary disease. In school, I didn't realize that I was missing a lot of what was going on. When the teacher would turn to the chalkboard, I would not hear what she was saying. I flunked my way through high school. I didn't realize what my problem was.

It wasn't until I was in the show *Bloomer Girl* and we took the show on the road to Chicago that I realized I couldn't hear the orchestra. I went to an ear doctor in town. He gave me a cursory examination and said, "I'm sorry to tell you—within five years you're going to lose your hearing. And when you lose your hearing, you lose your speech." That was the diagnosis I was given: "deaf and dumb."

I had a nervous breakdown. I went in the hospital for seven months because I could not cope with this prognosis of degeneration of my hearing and my speech. What would I do? I earn my living on the stage. So I had a complete breakdown. It broke up my first marriage. I couldn't tell this darling man I was married to that I was going to be deaf. I just receded from our marriage and we got divorced.

Then I learned that it was not true. I was *not* going to lose my hearing. There was a radical new operation that might help me, and it did. My hearing was restored.

I became a spokesperson for the deaf and hard of hearing. I spoke out at a New Orleans convention about what the government should do to help people with hearing loss. I was swept up into the inner workings of Congress and the federal hierarchy. The head of the rehabilitation program, Mary Switzer, said, "Nan, I'm going to use you. You're the first celebrity that's acknowledged this problem. You're going to talk about how we need to help the hearing-impaired."

I spoke before Congress. I was put on the board of several committees. I was elected the chairman of the National Council on Deafness. I was appointed by President Truman and then by President Reagan to the National Council on Disabilities. We wrote the Americans with Disabilities Act.

I fought to get cut curbs and ramps to accommodate wheelchairs, which are now on all streets. Professional real estate people didn't want that because it would cost them some money. I went before Congress with a 6x6 board on the floor, and a man in a wheelchair. I said to him, "Can you get over this?" He tried and couldn't. I said, "Well, that's the size of a curb." That was a dramatic display of the problem. We had to do something for the handicapped. We got the cut curbs, ramps, and wider doors for bathroom facilities.

When television came in, there was no way the hearing impaired could understand what they saw. I tried to get sign language on TV. One of the first things I got signing on was the little bubble on religious programs showing people signing the words. Then I was a founding member of the National Captioning Institute—captioning on television. It was a twenty-year fight to get that on television. When you turn your sound off now, captioning will come up on the screen.

I loved working with Sid Caesar and it was tragic how I lost that. It was a terrible, terrible blow. Ed Traubner (now dead) called himself a business manager, but he was only my accountant and did my income taxes. One day near the end of my second year with Sid, Ed called me and asked if I had a contract for the following season. I said I guessed so, and he said, "Would you mind if I went to find out if you have a new contract?" I said, "Sure." He went to the Caesar office and began making demands—like equal billing with Sid, equal salary with Sid, he demanded this and that. All this without my authorization. Sid was hurt and upset that I would make these kinds of demands. From what Ed told me of his meetings with Sid, I was hurt that Sid didn't seem to want me anymore. Sid and I didn't reconcile over this terrible mistake until about three or four years later.

In the 1950s I appeared in a movie musical called *The Bandwagon* with Fred Astaire and Oscar Levant. Oscar had just gotten out of a mental facility. He was obsessed about his health. He was an extreme hypochondriac and pretended to have a heart attack every second. There was nobody for Oscar to pick on during filming, because everybody else was a bigger star than he was. So whenever anything went wrong, he picked on me. I hated making that film, except the "Triplets" number which I loved. The song was original, challenging, and very funny.

Lucille Ball, a good friend, and I were on a television program early in both our careers. She was adamant. "Nan," she said, "you *can* have it all. Career *and* family." I said, "You can't. One or the other must come first, and I say family must come first." We continued to argue, with her insisting one can devote full time to a career and still have a successful family life. "You *can* have it all!" I guess Lucy got what she wanted, a huge career, but her marriage ended in divorce. I had a lasting, great marriage, and a career that was wonderful.

Between age 80 and 120 isn't enough time for all I want to do. I'll soon start building my ninth new house. While watching TV, I crochet caps for newborn babies. I need quality time with friends, family, grandkids. I continue writing the book, for family only, of my life and family history. (Of course, this means more lessons to learn how to better use my computer.) And de-nesting. We spend half our lives acquiring stuff; now it's time to try to get rid of it.

NANETTE FABRAY was born on October 27, 1920, in San Diego, California.

PAUL CONRAD

Among the favorite years for editorial cartoon lovers are 1964, 1971, and 1984, since those are the years when Paul Conrad won the Pulitzer Prize. His wit entertains and instructs readers of the Los Angeles Times *and many other newspapers. More problematic is whether the various presidents and public officials who have felt "Con's" lash feel as warmly toward him. In recent years Paul has become a celebrated sculptor.*

I DEAL WITH STRESS TODAY about the same way I always did: Searching for an idea, throwing out the bad ones, re-adapting and getting another one that says something. It's not as easy as it used to be.

Finding the idea for the editorial cartoon, that's what's tough. The rest is easy. The only problem I've got is now and then I can't draw until I take a Propanol. It's a beta-blocker to stabilize my hands—and it seems to be only the right one. You wait about half an hour and then go.

Are there any advantages to being my age? I don't see any. I'm really in good shape, but I've taken pills, pills, pills 'til I'm blue. That seems to be where the story is—to stay in good shape, physically and mentally, and that hasn't changed at all.

Some people in their eighties never thought about age and they never did get old. That's kind of true of me. I was eighty before I realized it. Here he is! In fact, I'm eighty-one now. And there'll be another one coming up in June.

I've never gotten mellow with age. Oh, no. I'll never mellow out. That's not me. Though I don't think I'm doing as well as I can. I mean, my ideas aren't as good. And I'm trying my damnedest.

Cartoonist Doug Marlette said about me that in the world of journalism, I was the designated feeler. Meaning, I suppose, that I felt a deep sense of injustice.

But God, you have to be unconscious not to. It's just an absolute disgrace.

Anger is a necessity. People should get furious.

As long as I keep that feeling going, I'll be all right.

When Otis Chandler brought me to the *Los Angeles Times*, he and I got along great. We really did. The same thing held with Tom Johnson when he became the publisher.

But during the Vietnam War it was something else. Jim Bellows, who was Associate Editor, and Ed Guthman, who was the National News Editor, would come to my office after the daily editorial board meetings in Otis Chandler's room. I never did go there. We would talk about what was in the news. They were very good. We talked about what worked and what didn't. Boy, did I need that. But even during Vietnam, things weren't screwed up as they are now. This Iraq thing beats everything!

George Bush is the end!

Used to be I could throw the pencil down and there they were. Nothing to it. That's not true anymore. Sometimes I have to sit and wait for the beta-blocker to take over. It's hell to get old.

What starts my engine in the morning is reading the paper. I don't look at the morning news on TV. I listen to it while I'm lying in bed. They never get around to saying what I want to hear about.

"It's hell to get old."

I still embrace life. I just thoroughly enjoy it. I still work. Still turn out the bronzes. I do four cartoons a week for the *L.A. Times*. The Tribune Media Services in Chicago bought the *Times* and the *Times* buys me for a very good price. They buy them but don't run them.

I looked forward to Tuesdays because Robert Scheer's column would be there. Now he's gone.

I once said, "It takes a big man to laugh at himself and not many members of the establishment are big men." It's absolutely true. Laughter is the greatest thing God gave us. Unfortunately, not enough people laugh at themselves.

I got sued twice: Once by Fred Hartley and the other time by Los Angeles Mayor Sam Yorty. Hartley didn't like a cartoon that I had done of him. The nice thing was, each time I got sued, they also sued Otis Chandler and my editor, too. The Mayor sued because he thought I defamed him, but they didn't win.

There have been some collections of my work in several books. But I don't like to go back and look at cartoons I've done. I'm afraid I'll swipe one.

PAUL CONRAD was born on June 27, 1923, in Cedar Rapids, Iowa.

"Only young people worry about getting old. I don't believe in dying. It's been done. I'm working on a new exit. I can't die now. I'm booked."
—George Burns

FRANK MANKIEWICZ

Under President Frank Mankiewicz, the programming, staff, and budget of National Public Radio thrived eight-fold, and its audience doubled. He served as Bobby Kennedy's press secretary during his Senate years, and his political friends include Ted Kennedy and Gary Hart. His creative gene pool has been sound—his father wrote Citizen Kane *and his Uncle Joe wrote* All about Eve.

I DON'T KNOW FROM STRESS. I don't do stress.

I hear people talk about it and write about [it] and I read what they say. People say, "Wow!! Stress can cause impotence or mental disease," but I'm not aware of it. In fact, I'd be hard pressed to describe it.

I think perhaps it's because I live day to day. That would seem to be the best explanation. I don't have far, far-reaching concerns. I don't worry about what I'm going to be doing three years from now.

Maybe it's a fake immunity. Maybe I don't really have it. Maybe I'm terribly concerned and just concealing it. I don't know. I've never thought seriously about stress.

I know what gets me out of bed in the morning. It's work. It's something to do. I've always worked. I expect to start writing a book very soon. I've been collecting a lot of stuff. When I wrote books, that was always a challenge. Get up, have breakfast, sit down, and write.

The Mankiewicz family is famous for writing

movies, but I've never considered doing that. Every time I've tried even the mildest kind of fiction, I'm embarrassed. Also, I think it may be because my father hated it so much.

My father didn't really like the movies. He didn't like the industry. He didn't like the people. He welcomed outsiders. But I guess the money was too much for him, so he stayed.

It was interesting growing up with Herman Mankiewicz as your father. But if I hadn't known what he did for a living, I wouldn't have guessed. You couldn't tell from his conversation. He would never come home at the end of a day and say to my mother, "Well, I think I've licked that second act," or "We're going to get Joan Crawford for the girl." Nothing. Never talked about movies ever in his life. I don't think he ever went to see any of the movies he wrote. I'm not sure he went to very many movies at all, except he did go to see *Citizen Kane*. He really died before he fully grasped where it stood in movie history. He was fifty-five.

I regard it as a very significant day when you realize you are older than your father was.

My mother died at eighty-nine. There were good genes on her side. She had a sister who died a couple of years ago at 102 and a brother who died well into his nineties. Eastern European Jews from Lithuania seem to live long.

I've had a lot of careers—I've anchored a TV news show, written books, run for Congress, managed George McGovern's 1972 presidential campaign. I'm not sure that changing careers promotes longevity, but it certainly promotes a continuance of interest that dwindles when you stay in one place too long.

In the early 1970s, I wrote four books. Two of them were about Richard Nixon. (One was about his career and one about his impeachment.) One of my books was about Fidel Castro. I went down to Cuba and interviewed him on TV and spent a lot of time with him. And one book was about how television was changing our lives. That was fun. I gave up writing books to go to work as president of National Public Radio.

Before that, I was Robert Kennedy's press secretary when he was in the U.S. Senate.

"There's very little in being a sage."

And there was one important thing I thought I learned from him. I forget what the occasion was, but Bob had said something disparaging about Canada. He always liked to quote Dante, who wrote about the evil of not taking sides. "The hottest places in Hell are reserved for those who, in time of great moral crisis, maintain their neutrality."

For days the Canadian media were attacking him. I went in to see him about it and I said, "We've got to do something." And Bob said, "Well, I don't think so. I never like to look back. Never try to think about making something look better than it was, because it ain't going to work. Let's look ahead. Let's look at something that may bridge over time. Look over your invitations. See what I've been invited to in Canada and let's accept." Never say, "Well, I didn't say that" or "I didn't mean it" or "I'm sorry I said it."

I found that instructive.

Even in my own life, I don't like to dwell on how I remedy this or that.

I don't see any advantages to the advancing years. I think of things I want to do and then the immediate thought is: Nobody's going to want me to do it because I'm eighty-one. Or by the time I get around to that I'll be eighty-four. It's a sudden realization that you're just not an active participant in a lot of things. Like taking part in another campaign or taking over the editorship of something, or whatever it is that comes along. And then I immediately think: No, I can't do that. Nobody's gonna want me. I think there's very little in being a sage. On the other hand, I've got a lot of interesting clients at Hill & Knowlton and a few more books to write, and the velocity of my tennis serves is only slightly diminished, if at all.

If you asked me for one bit of advice for those generations that are following us, I think I'd say: stay healthy. That means don't abuse your body. As I look back on my life, I think the best thing I ever did was quit smoking. Not only did it keep me healthy, but my wife says she never would have married me if I had not. And that would have been a great loss.

Recently I was thinking: Is there any significant part of my life that I think was more important than anything else? A part that I would have added to, or sustained, or done more? I think, honest to God, it's the three years I spent in the Army.

I was an infantryman. I was in Europe. I wasn't in the goddamn Navy, an officer or something or other that so many guys in college got into. I didn't do anything special. I volunteered at the age of eighteen, and went in. Did infantryman basic training and went to Mississippi and then went overseas, and fought in the Battle of the Bulge.

That was during World War II, our war. I really learned a lot about my country, and my countrymen. As I look back on it now, it's the one part of my life I wouldn't want to give up. Suppose somebody says to me, "You didn't have to go in the Peace Corps. You could have done something else in those three years." Yeah, but I wouldn't have met Robert Kennedy. And, like the Army, that experience really shaped my life.

Because when Bob got elected to the Senate, one of the first things he did was make a trip to Latin America. I had been the Peace Corps Director in Peru and I was then the Latin American Regional Director in Washington and he called me up. I was just amazed. I pick up the phone and a voice says, "This is Senator Kennedy."

He called me because he was going to Latin America and the State Department had given him a schedule for Peru, and somebody said to him, "Call Frank Mankiewicz because he was in Peru for two or three years with the Peace Corps and he knows that country."

He called me up and he read me the schedule the State Department had given him. He was going to spend the morning at the American School for the kids of the Foreign Service. Then he was going to have lunch with the businessmen in the Peruvian-American Chamber of Commerce in Lima. Then a reception in the evening at the embassy.

I said to him—probably the smartest thing I ever said—"Senator, why are you going to Peru? You don't have to go to Lima to meet those people. You can do that right here." He laughed and said, "That's what I thought. Tell me what I should do." I gave him a different schedule.

Then one morning, two weeks later, I was in Panama for a meeting of some kind, and he was coming through on this trip to Latin America. I thought: Well, I'll go down to the airport and say hello. (In those days, you had to stop in Panama for a couple of hours to refuel—there were no jets and you couldn't fly all the way to Lima.) I went down to the airport and I met him on the plane. Pan American had fixed up the aircraft with berths up front. He was in one and Ethel was in the other, in pajamas, and

before I got on the plane there were two reporters down at the gate and they said, "When is he coming for his press conference?" I said, "I don't know anything about a press conference. I'll ask." I went up to him and I said, "Senator, are you coming down for a press conference? There are two reporters there who think you are." Everybody laughed and said, "No. There's no press conference scheduled." He said to me, "If I don't go to that press conference, who gets hurt the most—the reporters or the publishers? Or the paper?" I said, "I think the reporters." He said, "Yeah. I think so, too. Let's go."

He got out of bed and one of the people with him said, "Well, Senator, why don't you stay in bed in the berth and we'll bring the reporters on the airplane. You can have the press conference right here. You don't have to get dressed." He looked at me and said, "What do you say to that?" I thought—hell! There's a test here. And to my eternal credit I said, "I think that's what General de Gaulle would do."

He laughed. And he said, "You're right. Let's go." Got up and got dressed and we went down and had a press conference.

When he came back from Peru he called and asked me if I'd be his press secretary.

FRANK MANKIEWICZ was born on May 16. 1924, in New York City.

SID CAESAR

There was Julius Caesar, and there was Caesar Cardini, the Mexican chef who invented the Caesar salad. But in terms of entertainment, the greatest Caesar of them all was unquestionably Sid. As the incomparable star of Your Show of Shows, *Sid Caesar dominated television during its formative era, sent his viewers into convulsions with his spontaneous talents, and launched a generation of young comedy writers into orbit.*

I'VE LEARNED THAT IF you control your attitude, you can control your life.

If you can't control your feelings, you can't control your life. If you can control your feelings, you don't have to be depressed all the time. You can talk yourself out of it. You should talk to yourself. *Really* talk to yourself and *listen.* Everybody knows what's right and what's wrong. You've got to understand what's going on around you.

I was used to working hard on *[Your] Show of Shows*—an hour and a half—and we had to write it every week. I had the best writers in the world. I spent more time there than I did at my home. You've got to learn how to cut back a bit. It was difficult to do because live television is very demanding.

The world of comedy has changed. Today they feel they have to use four-letter words to make a point. It's not making a point. I think people laugh because they get embarrassed.

I can't engage life today as I did as a

younger man. You've got to settle for what you can do. You don't have to say, "Oh, those were the days! Boy, I used to...." Because, *these* are the days. Enjoy what you have.

I'm engaged in life. I read. I watch a little television. I go out and see some people. I exchange ideas and thoughts in conversations. It keeps you going.

In the old days, I handled stress with alcohol. It was a quick fix and I didn't have any hangovers until I was about thirty-five. Then you wake up one day and you say, "The hell with it!"

Today, I have very little stress. Sometimes health-wise you get a little worried about this or that. But if you keep yourself healthy, watch your diet, and get a little exercise, you're in command.

I wrote a memoir a few years ago and I said that I've learned how to deal with my fears and insecurities. Once you talk about something and the heavens don't split open, you're okay. Usually, there are certain things that people never say and try not to think about. But there's nothing to be afraid of. You talk to yourself and you get answers.

I still have the curiosity to wonder what's next. What's around the corner?

The secret is to take it easy. Relax. Enjoy life. Next, next, next, next.

You know the big advantage to being my age? Experience. You handle things better.

Make up your mind what you want to do. If you really, really, really know what that is, then put out all your strength and do it.

The only way you're going to reach your goal is through work.

"You don't have to say, 'Those were the days.'... These are the days!"

SID CAESAR was born on September 8, 1922, in Yonkers, New York.

LINDY BOGGS

Corinne Claiborne (Lindy) Boggs is a great American institution. The wife of House Majority Leader Hale Boggs from Louisiana, she won a special election to fill his seat in Congress after he died in an Alaskan plane crash. She was reelected to eight terms. Lindy Boggs is a descendent of the Claibornes and the Brewsters. She was a regent of the Smithsonian Institution and served as the U.S. ambassador to the Vatican. Another distinction she holds is being the mother of ABC News correspondent Cokie Roberts.

THE ADVANTAGES OF AGE? When you're older, your foibles are more tolerated. Each time of your life is special. And I've gotten into a second childhood, which is pretty good. But it's horribly frustrating to be a patient. Let's hope that will be one of the scientific explosions—pushing back aging.

What gets me out of bed in the morning? Chicory coffee.

What keeps me going during the day? Tabasco sauce.

After I retired from Congress, I served as the U.S. ambassador to the Vatican. I protested that I was too old, but President Clinton refused to take no for an answer. I'm so glad I had that magnificent experience.

My children have been very supportive of me. Cokie is my Pooh Bear. She held my skirt when she was very little, and she wouldn't let go. She and my daughter Barbara and three of my granddaughters are products of the Sacred Heart School in New Orleans where they received a wonderful education. When Cokie enrolled there, she started holding the skirt of the Mother Superior, and very early in life she got into some very interesting conferences.

I'm a descendent of William Brewster, who came over on the *Mayflower*. When Cokie was little, I used to drag her with me everywhere. Hale was the Majority Leader in the House of Representatives. I didn't have anyone to leave Cokie with at home so I'd take her around the Capitol with me. And in the Rotunda there are these huge paintings. One of them is of the *Mayflower*, and the Brewsters are in the center of the canvas in this storm-tossed vessel. They all looked as though they were ready to heave. And next to that painting is another one that pictures the baptism of Pocahontas, with Pocahontas in a lovely white dress and with beautiful long black hair. And I pointed to the Brewsters and said, "Cokie, these are your ancestors." And Cokie said, "*They're* not my ancestors. *She* is!" And she pointed to Pocahontas. She's always been a very selective journalist.

I think it's important to embrace life, and I embrace life by having a full schedule. Right now I'm scribbling in and reading from my journal. Tuesday, May 9th: Go to Washington for Lindy Boggs Movie Festival. They're screening a documentary about my life. May 10th: I arrive at 2 p.m. for a Nancy Pelosi event at Statuary Hall. Then I go to the reception and the Lindy

"I embrace life by having a full schedule."

Boggs movie and a conversation at the National Archives. I was vice president of the Archives before I went to Rome. I have a tremendous admiration for the work that is done at the Archives. They have charge of all the presidential archives. That was one of the most enchanting periods of my life.

When my husband Hale Boggs perished in a tragic plane crash, I won his seat in Congress and served for seventeen years. Today there is a Lindy Claiborne Boggs Room in the Capitol— it's a reading and restroom for Congresswomen.

The women who were in Congress were few in number for a good while. And so they shared the restroom of the congressional wives. And then as their number grew, it became uncomfortable for them. The lounges for the Congressmen are on either side of the House of Representatives: the Republicans have theirs and the Democrats have theirs. And there are a couple of sofas and some very soft chairs in them. The restrooms that the Congresswomen shared with the congressional wives were on another floor and rather inconvenient.

Finally we were able to secure rooms. And they turned out to be very historical. John Quincy Adams was the only president who ever came back to serve in the House after he was president. He was stricken on the House floor, and he was brought into the Speaker's office, laid out on the couch, and that couch is still there. And today, that's the Lindy Claiborne Boggs Room.

I helped found a literacy center at Loyola University in New Orleans. Even though we were in the process of making schools equal—quote, unquote—so many of the people in the workforce had not had as good an education as others, and they were embarrassed by it. So we set up an adult literacy center at the graduate school of Loyola University. Loyola is a very special place. It's right next door to Tulane. It's a dreadful thing to say, but there's a beautiful statue of Jesus standing in front of Loyola with his hands outstretched. And we Tulanians used to joke and say, "He's saying 'Better school—go next door.'"

LINDY BOGGS was born on March 13, 1916, in Pointe Coupee Parish, Louisiana.

JUNE WAYNE

June Wayne almost single-handedly restored the moribund art of lithography. She was named Woman of the Year for Meritorious Achievement in Modern Art by the Los Angeles Times, *and her work can be seen in most major U.S. collections. June has written numerous books and articles. She is a teacher, lecturer, illustrator, critic, and inventor, an extraordinary activist and advocate for artists.*

IN RETROSPECT MY LIFE looks glamorous and purposeful. Fortunately nobody asks for a list of failures.

My greatest challenge was, still is, transforming a new idea into a work of art. I would need five hundred years to complete what I've already thought of.

Because I created Tamarind Lithography Workshop, the art world has typecast my impact on the printmaking arts. But my "biggest accomplishment" is the art I made and am making, for which everything else has been a warm-up. Ageism handicaps artists (like every other calling). The art world sneered at the late works of Picasso and DeKooning; now they can't get enough of it.

"Inspiration" is a flaky word. I never use it. I prefer "intrigued, sparked, energized, stimulated…."

My life resembles a Napoleon pastry— "Milles Feuilles" layers of custard on soggy dollar bills.

My Valhalla is a library where Juno is the head librarian. (Juno is my nickname.)

Right now I am intrigued by a crazy-sounding scientific term—APOPTOSIS: *to trick cancer cells into committing suicide in a timely manner.* Does Apoptosis have a social parallel? Who commits it? Who decides "timely"? Is it a word we eighty-folk should take to heart?

Contemporary artists are making (and leaving) too much art for future generations to take care of. As a thoughtful citizen, I prune my inventory from time to time.

Right now, two phenomena are at the top of my fret list:

(1) the arrogance of the Executive branch of government

(2) the perforation of the wall between church and state

Creativity needs freedom the way fire needs oxygen. With fundamentalists raging across the globe, civil rights have more to fear from religionists than from local skinheads. To get elected, Jack Kennedy assured the American people that he would put the Constitution ahead of his church. Today Kennedy couldn't run for dogcatcher without weekly photo-ops of himself and Jackie taking communion.

As I see it, fundamentalism is a man's game, soccer to the nth degree. Those are *men* on television, shooting Uzis into the air when they are happy, or into people when they are crabby. They blow themselves to bits just to claim a personal covey of virgins. (Where do the girls go when they aren't virgins anymore?) What is Dubya's (George W. Bush's) testosterone level these days? Maybe premarin should be piped into the White House, into 10 Downing Street, into mosques and synagogues and gymnasiums—wherever men need some tamping down. Is war a hormonal imbalance?

If scientists are going to have the planet (already near the "tipping point"), neocons will have to keep their deities out of research labs.

Where has political talent gone? My generation had Winston Churchill, Franklin Roosevelt, Charles de Gaulle, Harry Truman during World War II. Even General MacArthur and Dwight Eisenhower had some credibility. And there were orators on Capitol Hill. Now we've got the Iraq War from Dubya. As for Tony Blair's Iraq, how does a British debater rebut a fatwa? And where are the talented Democrats? I can only think of one politician who seems to mean what he says: Russ Feingold. (A few of the women on the Hill seem to be firming up but not fast enough.)

The times don't always produce great leaders, but a bit of luck can make a difference.

"People you don't know assume you're a little old lady and you're kind of dumb. So they say indiscreet things, thinking we are deaf as well."

Katrina may have taken down the Republicans and a shotgun may have clipped the stony bust of Cheney Halliburton. I hate to rely on accidents, but luck seems to be all we've got going at the moment. If preemptive strike becomes our permanent foreign policy, Hitler was right.

What has any of this to do with being an artist? Nothing. A lot.

JUNE WAYNE was born on March 7, 1918, in Chicago, Illinois.

JANE RUSSELL

Howard Hughes' titillating western The Outlaw *outraged the censors and captivated the country. So did his on-screen discovery, Jane Russell, who portrayed a screen image of an irresistible sex goddess. She gained additional notoriety from a photo that showed her glowering with sulky beauty from a haystack. Bob Hope, her co-star in the film* The Paleface, *once introduced her as "the two and only Jane Russell."*

I LOVE TO SING. I've been singing for years. I performed in a lot of nightclubs—in Australia, all over the United States, in New York, in Chicago. For me, singing is more fun than acting. There are a couple of young guys that have really been helping me and we're having fun. People want to know if they're my sons. We're just good friends. There's no romance going on. I started a thing up here in Santa Maria because there was very little for older people to do, and I'm so sick of the damn music they're playing today that I could croak.

We found a piano man. First we performed in a restaurant, then in a hotel. We call it "The Swinging 40s." They are fabulous songs. These are the songs everybody remembers from the Second World War. Ten or twelve singers join us, and everybody gets up and takes turns singing songs of the 1940s. We do "Bye Bye Baby," the hit song from *Gentlemen Prefer Blondes*, which everybody knows, to close. And we start with "Seems Like Old Times."

Today I have a lady, Mary, who lives with me. She does the cooking and I do the dishes. I have been doing a lot of reading. But I have macular degeneration, and the reading is getting tough unless I have a really good light. I never read fiction. I like biographies. I read a lot of the Bible. We have a Bible class going on up here in my house. There are times when it's quiet and good, but then I get bored sometimes. I have four brothers. We were raised in a fabulous way. My mother was the best Bible teacher in the world. She had been a stage actress before she had the five kids, so she made the characters in the Bible come to life for us: the bad ones and the good ones. We got Bible stories from as far back as I can remember. It was a big, wonderful family. My mother had twenty-one grandchildren running around the place. My brothers each built a house in a different corner of the property.

I had a great childhood. I think that really helps. I had one girl cousin who was my age and we were surrounded by twelve boys. She had six brothers and I had four. Aunt Ruth had two more boys. We had a lot of fun. Many of them are now living up in Washington State, so I bought a home up there. I go up there in the summer time. I don't think I can face the

"Everybody gets up and takes turns singing songs of the 1940s."

snow all winter long. I'm sure that's where I'm going to end up, though.

I liked a lot of the movie about Howard Hughes, *The Aviator*. The only strange thing about it was how they had Howard behaving at the end of the film. They had him repeating the same words over and over. He'd say something like, "We won't go Wednesday. We won't go Wednesday. We won't go Wednesday...." He'd be walking away saying, "We won't go Wednesday." I never saw him do that. Neither had Terry Moore, who had lived with him for a long time, or anybody else I've talked to.

When they finally took Howard out of the country, because of the crashes he had been in and the pain killers they had been giving him, he never got to see anybody that had ever known him. The people who worked for him just adored him. They called him "The Boss." Anything you wanted was done for you.

Leonardo DiCaprio had wanted to know what Howard was like before he made *The Aviator*, so he came to see me. I told him Howard was very polite. He didn't like to fight face-to-face with people. The only time I really saw him angry was in a TV hearing when the senator had asked him if he would do something—and Howard looked up and said, "No. I don't think I will." That's as mad as I ever saw him.

I did a movie called *The Paleface* with Bob Hope. The big song from the movie, "Buttons and Bows," won an Academy Award. I never sang it in the picture, but I sang it at the Oscars.

When I got to do that movie, I thought I had gone to heaven! Bob did one or two takes of each scene . . . period. It was lots of fun. It was the first picture that I ever got to do that was normal and quick. They had to let Bob go every day at a certain time. Once, it was earlier than that time, and Bob looked around the stage and saw that they had to do a lot of lighting, and he said, "Well, I think this will get done just in time for us to do the scene tomorrow. I think maybe I could get in nine holes if I leave now." He walked across the stage and as the door was about to close behind him, the director whined: "Bob! You come back here!" We all burst out laughing.

Then there was *The Outlaw*. Howard had this struggle with the Hays Office and the censorship code. Frankly, I liked the good old Hays Office and I wish we still had it. There actually was nothing wrong with *The Outlaw*. I think it was the publicity that scared everybody, and the photos of me. They had me posing for pictures from nine in the morning 'til five at night until the picture was released. It was nuts. The Catholic Church was screaming that if you went to the picture you would be excommunicated. When I had to do another picture that also got bad reviews and the same kind of publicity, I said to Howard, "Listen, I do not want to go through this nonsense anymore." He promised me that I would never have to do it again. But, he added, "If you tell anyone, I'll deny it!" The publicity for *The Outlaw* was incredible. Up in San Francisco, they were screening the movie all day long. And after each showing, I would go onstage as straight man for a comedian. I'd ask him questions and he'd do the punch line. I had to make nine personal appearances a day. Finally, after eight weeks of this, I left and signed a document that said I wouldn't do any movie anywhere else, and I went home and got married. My husband, Bob Waterfield, had to go to Fort Benning, Georgia, and I went down there with him. I just stayed down there for the next eighteen months. Then there was the movie I did with Frank Sinatra and Groucho Marx called *Double Dynamite*. Ava Gardner and Frank had just started going together. Since he and his wife Nancy had broken up, Frank and Ava weren't very popular. Ava would be sitting up in the sound booth a lot of the time. Making that movie was no fun at all. Boring!

In 1968 I got married to a beautiful guy named Roger Barrett, and he died three months after we were married. That's how I learned what depression was about. I was that way for about five years. But I conquered my depression. I went to New York to appear in the Broadway musical *Company*. I remember the first time I had to go out and do that show. The producers had filled the audience with all the kids that were working in the theater in New York, so you knew you had a lot of other actors sitting out there. It was very nerve-wracking.

I wrote a memoir back in 1985: *Jane Russell: My Path and My Detour*. And since then, I have wanted to do a small book called *The Lord's Accident*. The Lord has it all planned but, to you, many things look like accidents. In my life, it's been one accident after another. I start going in one direction and suddenly I'm going in another.

JANE RUSSELL was born on June 21, 1921, in Bermidji, Minnesota.

"Old age is like flying a plane through a storm. Once you are aboard there is nothing you can do."
—Golda Meir

MEL DURSLAG

Some of America's most gifted writers, like Damon Runyon, Jimmy Breslin, and Ring Lardner, started out writing about sports. Another gifted writer in that company is Mel Durslag. His work has brightened the pages of the Los Angeles Herald Examiner, TV Guide, *and America's leading periodicals for fifty years.*

I EMBRACE LIFE. I try very hard to keep showing a pulse. I work at it. But I'm not very active, professionally.

I suffered plenty of stress in my life. I had a tough routine for a long time. I never had one job. I always had two. In the old days, if you were a daily columnist, you wrote seven days a week. I started out writing seven and, in a big concession, they let me cut down to six. I went six for God knows how many years before I finally cut down to five. All the time, I also did magazine writing.

I wrote for the good magazines—*Colliers* in the 1950s, while it was still alive; *Saturday Evening Post; Look; Sports Illustrated;* then I had a long-term deal with *TV Guide.* All the time I was also working for Hearst on the *Herald Examiner.* I worked there for fifty years. I retired at the age of seventy in 1991. I was tired. I didn't think I was going to live this long.

I don't miss the exhilaration of the newsroom, but I miss a lot of the people. Writing was hard for me. I never found it easy. Some guys claim it's easy. I've always doubted them. I had a very, very tough time when I was doing magazines and columns at the same time. I would get up in the morning, write a column, take it down to the office or send it in, do some interviewing for the next day's column, and then start working late afternoon or early evening on my magazine assignments. I did all my magazine stuff at night. It was a long day.

For *TV Guide,* I did a lot of non-sports. I did entertainment pieces and features—mostly on the light side. I tried to keep my column rather light, too. I didn't find it any harder to write about entertainment than about sports. Writing is writing. You've got to research it, you've got to put it together, and so forth.

I don't see any advantages in age. I've got to say it's better to be young. The biggest counterfeit I know is "The Golden Years."

I always consider myself very lucky. I had a very good job. I traveled in good style. I saw everything, and more than once. I went everywhere, met an awful lot of interesting people. My wife was along with me on a lot of it. I can never claim that I was shorted. I was lucky.

As you go along, I feel, you face a dilemma. Should you work yourself half to death, as a lot of us did in the process of growing older? Or should you take it easy and spend more time with the kids and picnics and so forth? Health-wise and mental health-wise, there's something to be said for

easing up. But, if you're trying to accomplish anything at all, you've got to do it.

In my case, I didn't want to be just a local sports writer. I tried like hell, right from the beginning. And I didn't have any money, either—no back-up. That's another thing that drives you. If you don't make it, there's no one who's going to come through for you. You're driven: (1) by a lack of back-up, and (2) by your own desire to do something. A lot of the kids today have back-up. It makes it a lot easier.

But some say too much back-up inhibits you, robs you of incentive. Well, there are a few that make it even with all the back-up in the world. Look at Alan Jay Lerner. He came from a wealthy family. You have to make a choice as you go along if you want to try and accomplish at least a little something.

Sometimes I ask myself why I'm still around and alert and a lot of my contemporaries aren't. And the explanation is a four-letter word: L-U-C-K.

> *"You have to take care of your health and just hope to be lucky. Luck with an asterisk."*

Let me qualify that. Luck with an asterisk. You have to try to live intelligently. You have to take care of your health as you go along and then just hope to be lucky. I know guys who had marvelous luck and then all of a sudden, out—with a heart attack. That can happen. It's sort of a combination of the two. Luck is very, very important in a person's life.

Someone said, "The harder I work, the luckier I get."

Frank Leahy used to say, "Prayers work better when the players are big."

I had been at the paper since 1939, except for three years during the war. When I started there it was the *L.A. Examiner*. In 1961, the Hearsts and the Chandlers got together—did something that would get them thrown in jail today. They made two papers out of four. The paper became the *Herald Examiner* and the *Times* became the *Times-Mirror*.

The *Herald Examiner* was quite a paper. We had two bookmakers. One was a guy downstairs in the circulation alley. That's where the trucks would pick up the papers to be distributed. When you wanted to make a bet, you wrote it on a piece of paper, wrapped it around the money, put it in a bucket, and lowered the bucket down to the alley.

The second bookmaker was a copy cutter. In those days we did stuff by linotype. You sent a story down, the copy cutter down in the print shop would cut it up in pieces, and he'd pass it out to the linotypers. You wrote out your bet and put the money in the pneumatic tube and shot it from the editorial floor down to the copy cutter. One day, I answered the doorbell in my house and two FBI guys were there....

But I worked very hard. I had a stress attack in 1981. I was only out about a week, and I was going up the wall. So I got some therapy. I didn't go on Prozac, then, but I did years later, after I had a heart attack. I've had two heart attacks and I've had heart surgery twice. I don't know if you ascribe it to my work. I tend to doubt it. If you want to do anything that's half decent, you have to suffer.

I never found it easy. I knew the novelist Jim Bishop rather well. He was a Hearst syndicated columnist for a long time. He used to boast to me that he never took more than forty-five minutes to write a column. I always questioned that—how you can write a column in forty-five minutes that makes any sense, anyway? He always claimed writing was easy for him. I didn't run across too many guys who thought it was.

MEL DURSLAG was born on April 29, 1921, in Chicago, Illinois.

*"Certainly old age has
a great sense of calm and
freedom. When the passions
relax their hold,
then you have escaped from
the control not of one
master, but of many."*
—Plato

JACKIE COOPER

At MGM in the 1930s there was Mickey Rooney, there was Judy Garland, and there was Jackie Cooper. Jackie was the only child star to go on to head a major Hollywood studio. There is no evidence to suggest that as a studio chief, Jackie displayed any of the qualities the young Jackie found so vexing in MGM's resident mogul, Louis B. Mayer.

WHEN I WAS AT MGM, I remember a couple of times my mother and I were sitting across from Louis B. Mayer, behind his desk, giving orders on this and that. And it was always about some disagreement.

One day, he yelled at my mother about something and it brought tears to her eyes. I was a kid, so seeing her tears, I started to cry. Somehow, Mr. Mayer and my mother got me settled down and they reached an agreement.

Then, as we were leaving the office, L. B. grabbed me by my shirt under my chin with his fist. And he said, "Don't you ever come in here and cry again! You hear me?" I was seven years old. Nobody had ever grabbed me or treated me like that. It was just terrible. From then on, my mother kept me away from him as much as possible. I really didn't like the guy.

I started out in *The Little Rascals.* That was the name of the *Our Gang* comedies in the early days. I was going to the school on the lot with those kids and it was very uncomfortable for me. That was my first school. I had never been to a school. My mother took me out of that school. We were getting good money at MGM, so she hired a tutor—and the tutor was with me clear up to the beginning of my high school days. When I wasn't working she came to the house for three or four hours a day, five days a week. If I was making a movie, the tutor was on the set. It was easier because she didn't have to worry about reporting my progress to the studio, because she worked for my mother.

That was so many years ago. I'm eighty-three now. I'll be eighty-four in September. It's hard to remember a lot of it.

When I became a teenager, MGM used me a little too much, and the pictures started making less and less money. Wallace Berry was sick and tired of me. He didn't want to work with the kid anymore. I think he was a little jealous of all the reviews. Very often the reviewers liked me a little better than him.

I didn't like him. He was mean to me. He didn't like kids. If I was on his lap in a scene, the minute the director said, "Cut," he'd push me right off, even if it made me fall on the floor. "Get the hell off me!"

At that age, I was more interested in my personal life, and at age thirteen or fourteen I found Judy Garland, Mickey Rooney, Freddy Bartholomew. There was a lot of publicity using us all together. We got along. I didn't have to see any of them too much. Judy and I felt like real buddies—boyfriend-girlfriend kind of thing.

"All of a sudden, these jobs that were held by mature men in their forties and fifties were being held by guys in their twenties and thirties. I was too old."

My mother was more like my sister. She had been making money on the road, playing piano for performers in vaudeville. When MGM bought me from Hal Roach, my mother came home and stayed home. And, as I said, as I was growing up, she was more like a sister to me. We had that kind of relationship. She didn't raise me to be afraid of her. She raised me to respect her.

When I had made some kind of a name for myself, after *The Champ* and *Treasure Island,* our agent got me booked into some theaters. My mother would play the piano for me and I would tap dance and sing and talk to the audience. We were buddies, working together. She made it fun.

A mutual friend was handling Bobby Darin and he wanted to become a producer. His name was Steve Blowner. He said I ought to be at Screen Gems. That was the TV arm of Columbia Pictures. Steve said that the guy who was running the place wanted to be an independent producer. So when the guy was ready to leave and the people in New York asked Steve, he suggested me. And they said,

"Okay, let's put Jackie in the job and see what happens."

I was one of the few former actors that got into that kind of job. I knew what they were talking about on the set—an electric bill, or too much overtime, or whatever the hell it was.

I enjoyed running a studio. I was in charge of making their television series. I enjoyed improving things and making so many of the people smile. That was very pleasant for me. I missed the acting and I missed the directing, but that didn't make me do less work.

I was well into my sixties and finding it very difficult as an independent director or actor for hire. All of a sudden, these jobs that were held by mature men in their forties and fifties were being handled by guys in their twenties and early thirties.

I was too old for any studio. A lot of us suffered that. It wasn't just me. I talked to a number of people, directors especially. The age thing was really rough. I was about sixty-eight. I said to myself, "What am I doing?" I finally quit trying.

At a certain point I didn't want to work anymore. My agent was very surprised, but he and my business manager understood it.

Retirement is a pleasure. I'm with my wife. We can go down to the races at Delmar, and stay on the beach for as long as we want. Our son is working in New York. We go back there if we feel like it for two, three weeks. There is no rush to get back because I don't have to get home to work. I had been under the pressure of work since I was five years old.

As a studio executive, I didn't have any great pressure. That was because my mother had taught me well. If I had a problem then of some kind—"What do I say to this director?"—I would go home and instead of saying, "Keep your mouth shut!" she would say, "Do you think he would do so-and-so if you said such-and-such?"

But it was a pleasure getting away from being concerned with all of that, and not having that kind of pressure, and enjoying my wife and me being together. We've been married more than fifty years.

I have a habit—it started when I was mostly working steadily. Having breakfast. I don't want to cook in the morning and I don't want to ask my wife to cook, and I don't want a housekeeper (we have a housekeeper three days a week, but not to cook). I've gotten up early all my life. I get up about 5:45 or 6:00. They've already delivered the *L.A. Times,* and I've turned on the coffee. I wash up and I sit down. I have a half cup of coffee in a big cup...I'd call it a cup of coffee. I read a bit of the *Times,* the front page and the sports page. Then I go to Nate & Al's, because I want to have a nice breakfast. I drive to Nate & Al's, I eat, and I come home. By now it's 9:30 and I'm relaxed. I see how my wife's feeling, what she'd like to do. My wife and I enjoy being together. Does she want to go shopping? Today I've got something else to do. I want to look for a new car.

My advice to youngsters is—If you're not going to go to school and if you don't want to earn degrees and get into universities, then be sure to learn something where you can go out and make a living.

If you want to be in the entertainment business, you don't need much of an education unless you're talking about running a company. If you want to be an actor, look at a specific actor. Look at George Clooney. How did he get there? Say to yourself: What did he do? What does he know? Investigate a bit. Did he quit college to do this, because some people said he's real good at his work? Some of that information could help a lot.

In thinking about the future, a young person should look to a relative—someone a little older and wiser and more successful. Ask a doctor or a psychologist. You might get some wonderful advice.

I was married twice before. The first time I got married, I had said to myself, "If I don't get married to this girl and I go overseas, nobody will care if I live or die. Who will I leave my money to? Not those relatives who mistreated my mother." We had a son, a wonderful guy. He's now sixty.

The second marriage was, "Well, I'm going to play with this girl, I'm seeing her every day and I think I'm madly in love." Fortunately with that marriage, I didn't have any children.

Barbara and I have three children. We lost one. She was a good girl, but she got involved with drugs and she passed away when she was barely twenty. Our other daughter is forty, and our son is fifty.

I learned long ago that if you want to stay married and you want to be happy and you want to keep this lady you like, you better be a good guy.

JACKIE COOPER was born on September 15, 1922, in Los Angeles, California.

MARIA TALLCHIEF

Maria Tallchief was born on an Indian reservation, where her father was a member of the Osage tribe. It was dance that captured the young girl's heart. George Balanchine saw her, fell in love with her, and she became his wife and the inspiration for many of his finest works. Her dedication was complete, and her legend has grown. She has passed her love for her art on to younger dancers.

IN THE FIRST PLACE, I'm a Catholic. In fact, I just received communion this morning. That's very important to me. I say my prayers every night. That's, perhaps, the most important thing of all for me today—except for my daughter and my grandchildren.

I'm living in a protected place and there are nurses here, and if there's any problem, the nurse comes. She gives me my pills for the morning and for the night. She takes my blood pressure and such as that. I have very little stress in here.

Being married to Balanchine was a blessing. It couldn't have been better. He created the most beautiful roles in the world for me in "Swan Lake," "Sugar Plum Fairy," and "Firebird," of course.

I was in the right place at the right time, and I knew it. When I met Balanchine, I knew ballet was what I wanted to do. I also studied the piano. In fact, I have perfect pitch, which was nurtured when I was very young. My mother was determined I grow up learning the arts.

I prefer not to go out if I don't have to, so I try to stay here and do plays and things. Some children are coming to see me here. They come to see me and they chat. I encourage the children to appreciate ballet. I feel that's good.

I had to fight against people wanting to exploit me because I was an American Indian. I didn't want to be known as an American Indian ballerina. I wanted to be known as a *ballerina*. They tried to exploit the unlikely name of Tallchief. Well, I'm very proud of my name. They tried to change it when I first went into ballet—The Ballet Russe de Monte Carlo—to Tallchieva. But it was Agnes de Mille who really changed my name. My name was Betty Marie, after my two grandmothers. Miss de Mille said, "Why don't you put the 'A' on the end and be Maria Tallchief?" My relatives in Fairfax, Oklahoma, spell the name in two words: Tall Chief.

I have my grandchildren. One is seven and one is four—they just visited me this morning. I had bought some animals for the two children. They love stuffed animals.

In 1965, I founded the Chicago City Ballet. I'm still Director of Ballet for the Lyric Opera.

I wake up in the morning and I do my pilates exercises. I still do my splits at my bedside before I say my prayers.

> *"I still do my splits at my bedside before I say my prayers."*

Advice for the coming generations? Be sure you have a good teacher. That's a most important thing.

What was it that made me stand out from the other ballerinas of my generation? I was very lucky. I had Balanchine.

My mother wanted me to become a pianist. I said, "No." My sister was much more limber than I—she could put her leg over her head. But once I met Madame Nijinska, I knew I wanted to be a ballerina.

MARIA TALLCHIEF was born on January 23, 1925, in Fairfax, Oklahoma.

FRANKIE LAINE

For much of the twentieth century, Frankie Laine's firework phrasing and passionate musicianship kept him a favorite in America and England. He was the force behind twenty-one gold records, including classics like "That's My Desire," "Mule Train," and "That Lucky Old Sun," which is also the title of his recent memoir.

I WAS PERFORMING IN the *Palm Springs Follies*. One night, a guy mentioned that my voice was getting rough and that I ought to see the doctor. I went to see one and, unfortunately, he sent me to a nose and throat specialist, and she wanted to do a biopsy. But she wanted to learn how to do a throat operation, so she went to Germany for nine months. She came back and she still wanted to do the surgery. I said, "Okay." It was the worst decision I ever made. I had to have radiation. Apparently it saved my life, but who knows whether or not it will give me back my life, vocally? I'm still waiting.

They told me I had to wait two-and-a-half years before my voice would come back. My speaking voice came back right quick. But my singing voice is something else. I've had to lower keys. I'm afraid it's going to be a while before I can do everything I used to....

Fortunately, I love composing. So while I'm waiting for my voice to return, I'm composing.

I just live day by day, waiting to see what's going to happen to me vocally.

I'm ninety-two now. I have pretty good genes. My mother made it to ninety-one and my father made it to eighty. I've always loved what I do. I can't say that was true of my father. He was a barber, and I'm not sure he always enjoyed doing his work later in life when his hands began to shake....

What gets me out of bed each morning is usually composing and singing and trying to see if my voice is coming back.

> ***"I just live day by day, waiting to see what's going to happen."***

Herb Jeffries, a frequent weekend guest, had a good word to say for enjoying life. He says each morning he wakes up and thanks God for letting him wake up another day. Herb is ninety-four.

I can't say I see any advantages to being my age, rather than being a kid.

All I can say about that is I've been there already and the young still have to get there.

As far as advice to the young who are still facing the struggles and the hurdles, I'd say you have to handle it the best way you can at the time. Each individual has his or her own set of problems that are bound to come up and they've got to deal with as they happen.

As I lived my life, I did what most guys do. I relied on the past for experience and I used what I learned in the past to try to improve on the present. One of the problems I had involved a loan to my son-in-law for a winery up in the Napa Valley. He got out and left me hanging.

Life is full of surprises. When I recorded "Jezebel," I made "I Believe" and "Grenada" at the same time. I had high hopes for "Grenada" and thought "I Believe" was kind of a nothing song. It's become my Number 1 song of all time and it made me the top singer in England.

What's in the future?

I wish I could tell you. I really don't know what's ahead. If I did, I'd be president.

FRANKIE LAINE was born on March 30, 1913, in Chicago, Illinois.

HERBERT GOLD

A man of wit, charm, and literacy, Herb Gold is a resident of the City by the Bay.

As a young man, he read his poetry at coffeehouses, where he formed lifelong friendships with Allen Ginsberg and Jack Kerouac. He has published more than twenty novels, plus countless short stories, essays, and memoirs. Today he is a commentator on American culture. Herb Gold writes to master his world: "I need to make the world magic," he says. "I want life to be funny."

I THINK MY GOOD HEALTH at eighty-one is partly luck and partly that I've really enjoyed my life.

I hitchhiked all over America at one point in my life. In those days it was safe to hitchhike—or safer, I should say. I wrote a novel that came out of that called *The Man Who Was Not with It.* I got a sense of the adventure and the wildness of America then. I was fairly innocent about it. I'd get hired by an alcoholic to drive. I got hired as a busboy at a gambling joint off Key Largo. I got a job as a waiter in the Lower East Side of New York in a Hungarian-Jewish restaurant. I stole milk from doorways in the mornings.

There's a line in *Cat on a Hot Tin Roof* where one of the characters says, "You can be young without money but you can't be old without it." It's true. There was a line in one of Jack Kerouac's novels, *Big Sur*, where he complains he's too old to sleep on the floor.

I'm not rich now. I have plenty of money but in comparison with a lot of other people

I'm certainly not rich. I don't need a lot of money. In fact, my children live better than I do. They're going to inherit more of my estate than they would have if I really lived the way other people do.

The thing that makes me angry is when you meet people at a party and they say, "Hi, Herb. Still writing?" or "Have you retired yet?"

The idea of retirement is totally absurd to me. It would be ridiculous. I love what I'm doing. When you called just now, I was editing a chapter which I finished from a book I'm doing myself about aging.

I have fun, and I'm lucky to be really healthy at eighty-one. My doctor specializes in geriatrics. He says I'm the only patient he has who takes no medication whatsoever. We discussed taking one of the statin drugs and he kind of shrugged and said, "I don't know. You show no signs. Your blood pressure is low, your cholesterol is low." I did the treadmill stress test. They did an ultrasound. I have a friend who's a doctor. He said, "You should take it. Everybody takes it over fifty." He said, "Of course, sometimes there are side effects, but in your case, I don't see any need for it." So I'm not taking it.

Stress shortens a lot of lives. Stress and boredom. Boredom is a sort of stress. I think I deal with tension better today than when I was younger. I don't feel sexual jealousy now. I'm active both in my career and I'm a bachelor—I'm dating or looking for someone. I don't have that kind of anxiety. Actually, the chapter I've just written in my book on aging deals with the agony of divorce—separation from a wife. I dealt with it then by walking a great deal. I was somewhat of an insomniac. I'm not now. I exercise. If I have stress now, it's mainly because of something going on with my children. And that's somewhat manageable.

I have sexual interests. If a woman says no to me, I shrug my shoulders. "Okay, fine." I had a relationship for a while with a young woman. We were sitting in a cafe and I mentioned my grandchildren. When I said that, I saw a look on her face. It was as if the San Francisco fog was between us and she became invisible for a minute, and when it cleared I looked at her and I said, "Hey, it's over now. Isn't it?"

She said, "Yeah. It's over."

I just thought that was funny. I didn't blame her. It's biological. If it's a young woman, she wants a child and she wants a father who'll be around for a while. I've been a bachelor now for quite a while. In my experience it is easier for me to have a relationship with a woman in her twenties than in her thirties, because in her twenties she can say, "Okay, he's an interesting guy. He's fun. I can spend a year with him." If a woman is thirty-five and wants to have a child, she's getting desperate.

"Stress shortens a lot of lives. Stress and boredom."

Of course, there is some snobbery about, "I'm young and vigorous and you're older." I don't sense that. My kids' friends seem to like me and hang out. My son is a filmmaker and a musician. He's in a band which is now becoming a great success. His brother is playing in the band, too. I know a lot of their friends and I get along with them. Maybe because I'm the father of their friend.

Each person and each incident is different. I think if I talk about the stock market to my daughters and my sons, they absolutely listen because they think of me as an oracle. I had lunch today with one of my daughters who is divorced and she listens to me. There are obviously some people who say, "What does he know? He doesn't know who Britney Spears is." It varies. Maybe the same thing goes in reverse. A lot of times people of our age don't value the understanding of young people.

I have one bit of advice for young people. Don't play golf. I mean it. Don't play golf. It's boring. It goes with the clubhouse, the hat worn backwards. It's not real exercise.

That advice recalls what Kurt Vonnegut said in a commencement address, where he gave advice to the young. "Remember to wear sunblock." That translates to my "Don't play golf." Find something really interesting and energetic.

Occasionally I've done some teaching. In recent years, I've given a course in creative writing. Sometimes I'll have a student who says, "Well, I can't get my paper in on time because I've got a lot of work to do under my car. It has

mechanical problems. I've got to work on that." I say, "Hey! If your car is more important than doing your writing, then become a mechanic."

You can understand why people are insecure about their financial future when they see people suffering—not just the homeless, but people have sudden, dreadful medical expenses when they get older. So I can understand why people worry about those things. I don't have a TV. I don't own any property. I have a rented apartment. If their ambition is to have a tremendous amount of possessions, then they're always going to be on the treadmill.

Probably at this dinner tonight, people will start talking about wine and I'll insult everybody in the vicinity. I'll say, "Big people talk about ideas, medium people talk about things, and very tiny people talk about wine." Usually some people are insulted, as I want them to be.

William Saroyan wrote a very good book near the end of his life called *Obituaries*, in which he talked about aging and his own feelings about it. Saroyan was a friend of mine. I interviewed him. I wrote an introduction to an edition of *The Daring Young Man on the Flying Trapeze*.

My own book on aging is not technical. It's partly memoir. I'm dealing with the fact that so many of my friends, if they're still alive, have really faded drastically.

It's very sad. I don't have a single contemporary in San Francisco that I can call and say, "Hey, let's go to the movies." "Oh, I'm tired," they'll say. I have a close friend, who's the same age as I am, a writer, but he's got so many health problems and personal problems that he's really half dead. It's incredibly sad for me—he's someone I really love. He's a very good writer, but he's discouraged about everything. He has a wife who's twenty years younger than he is, who has Alzheimer's, and a daughter who's screwed up. He's got a lot of problems.

I suspect my own positive condition results from a combination of things. I think I'm lucky genetically. I've always taken care of myself. I've been something of an athlete and certainly exercised. I was never a drunk. I never smoked.

And I love what I'm doing. I enjoy. I think I'm probably metabolically optimistic. When I was most depressed after my divorces, I kind of enjoyed my misery. I'd say, "OK. I can't sleep. I'm not going to lie here and stew. I'm gonna get out and walk."

Sometimes I'd walk all night.

HERB GOLD was born on March 9, 1924, in Cleveland, Ohio.

JOE HYAMS

Joe Hyams is a protean writer whose wide-ranging oeuvre is as broad as his curiosity. His book Zen in the Martial Arts *sold two-and-a-half million hardback copies. He wrote quintessential biographies of James Dean and Humphrey Bogart; a book on Ronald Reagan that he co-authored with Michael Reagan; and books on tennis with Tony Trabert and Pancho Gonzales. Today Joe Hyams, in addition to his unflagging literary output, trains seeing-eye dogs.*

WHAT GETS ME UP in the morning these days is the thought that I've made it through to another day and whatever it is, it's going to be a nice day. What gets me up in the morning is the thought: Oh, I didn't finish what I was working on yesterday. I better finish it today if I can find out where I left off yesterday. That gets me up. The other thing that gets me up is hunger.

When stress and anxiety get a little heavy, I take a nap. I really do. I think to myself: To hell with this. I'm going to take a nap. Napping seems to get rid of it. The other thing about stress is that we always live with it and it gets to be kind of a steady companion. I've got to make a living, I'm getting older—old, I should say—and I've just got to see if I still have it. I sit at the computer and do the best I can.

I think about getting older all the time. When I get up in the morning I'm stiff and I have to exercise in the bathtub to get moving.

Actually, I never thought I would get past fifty-seven. Every male in my family—about six of them, including my father—died at the age of fifty-seven, and I was sure I was going to die around fifty-seven. I lived like a fool—I spent money unwisely but enjoyed my life. I did things I wish I hadn't done now. I bought lots and lots of very expensive old antique cars. I didn't invest in the properties that I should have invested in when they were available because I was always involved in trying to buy another car. Then, when I got to be about sixty-five or seventy—my mother was still alive, and she died, finally at ninety-four—I realized: Jesus Christ! I inherited her genes. I thought I'd inherited my *father's* genes. If I'd known I was going to live this long, I would have lived life a lot differently.

Today I'm a different person than I used to be. I'm much more compassionate than I ever was before; much more sympathetic to other people, particularly, as they get older. I'm a nicer person than I was—much, much nicer. I relied on wit, I don't want to say *good* looks but at least pleasant looks, and charm. Now, I realize that's not enough.

I'm not so critical. I think I've mellowed out to the point where I'm enjoying every day and I enjoy the people that I know, particularly the older ones. And I realize that we're not going to be together that much longer.

I've been having breakfast every Saturday with the same group of four people for almost thirty years now. One has died and now there's

three of us left. I just look forward to that. I realize that what really counts are the friends you've got in the end.

I'm always looking for something new to write that's interesting because I realize I don't have that much time left, and I want to write something that I'll be remembered for. One book out of the thirty-seven that I've written seems to be outlasting time, and that's a book on Zen that sold well over 2,500,000 hard copies. It still sells. That gives me great pleasure because I realize at least I'll be remembered for that one, if nothing else.

The study of Zen has taught me to take each day one at a time and not plan too much on tomorrow. Try to make the best of today, because it may be the last day. I do try to live each day to the fullest. I wrote a book about Humphrey Bogart, and Bogart's life taught me something, because he did rather badly for a year, but he died very, very bravely with great guts and great courage. He faced death with dignity. I realized, for me, if I become terribly sick and begin to realize the end is near, I'd like to die before I become a burden to myself and the people around me.

The only advantage I can see in being eighty is in retrospect you realize the things you should have done but didn't do and it's too late to do now, but there's no point in regretting it.

If I had any advice for the generations that are following us it would be to live life to the fullest and realize what's terribly important. And what *is* important, I think, is not so much the money that you make or the money that you leave, but the friends you have and the people you love whom you've had some impact on. That means a lot to me.

I was looking at the yearbook from my high school graduating class in Brookline High School about 1940, and the man ahead of me in class was Mike Wallace. I see him every Sunday and I think to myself, "My goodness, he's still going, and going strong!" I get the high school report every now and then and I read about Mike. So many of my graduating class went into the war—they died first in World War II and then later they died in Vietnam. When it was time to get discharged there were two signs on two doors. One said, "Immediate Discharge"; the other said, "For Those Who Want to Get in the Reserve." The reserve was a big deal. You got a hundred bucks a month, as I recall, if you stayed in the enlisted reserve. I had three years in the Army. I hated it. I went straight through the door that said, "Immediate Discharge." My friends who took the hundred bucks, the easy way, they stayed in the service and a lot of them died. It was just a trick of fate. I wonder why I've outlived so many of my contemporaries. I think it's just luck and genes. It has nothing to do with brains or anything else.

The thing I despair most about getting older is my memory fails. I see someone I knew, and I don't remember his name and I have to run through the alphabet in my mind. Last night, someone came up and shook my hand. I looked at him. I knew I knew him, but it's been about fifteen years since I saw him. This morning, I started going through the damn alphabet again and came up with it. Oh, Jesus! That was Rubin Carson.

There's one moment in my life that really stands out. My father and mother were both college graduates and in my high school class I was the last name read. They read the names off in order of academic achievement. I was the last name read! My father and mother were absolutely appalled. My father thought, "You have no future with anything, even the furniture business," so he put me in the business and I spent six months spraying furniture before it was shipped.

"If I'd known I was going to live this long, I would have lived life a lot differently."

I went in the Army after high school and got onto *Stars & Stripes* in the mid-Pacific as a writer. When I got out of the service, I got a job at the *New York Herald Tribune* thanks to people like Burt Bacharach, Sr., and a columnist named Hy Gardner. I started to get a byline and one day my father checked into a hotel—his name was the same as mine. I'm a junior. And the desk clerk said, "Are you Joe Hyams who writes for the *Herald Tribune?*" My father looked up and said, "No. I'm his father." My father told me that, and he cried. It was the first time he had ever looked at me with respect and pride that I was his son.

I think the reason I've outlived so many of my contemporaries is very simple. When I was in my fifties, I began running. I started out slowly walking, then jogging, then running, and then, finally, doing marathons. I kept running and I ran until about twenty years ago. My knees started to go out. I'd run every morning, no matter what town, what the weather was. I'd go out and jog.

I went to see a cardiologist. He did some x-rays and he said the running had apparently increased my heart capacity. He said I'd increased my longevity through just running. And I didn't do it because I thought I'd live longer, but I did. I think that's probably why I've lasted this long.

I had a friend named Ted Mann, the owner of the theater chain. I walked with Ted every morning for about twenty years until he died, recently. Ted got ill and he became blind and, at some point, I saw someone with a seeing-eye dog and I said to Ted, "Maybe you should get a seeing-eye dog." He said, "That sounds like a good idea." I went out to the Guide Dogs of America in Sylmar and I looked at what was going on and brought my wife out, and I brought Ted out, too. Ted couldn't see, of course, but we watched and were fascinated. I said to my wife, "We should raise a seeing-eye dog." We got one. We trained him. We did the things you're supposed to do for eighteen months. He went on to become a seeing-eye dog and we went to his graduation. He led a blind person.

It was a wonderful thing to see the dog that we had nurtured for so long was now doing something for someone else. I realized that was probably the best gift we could give. Since then, we've raised four seeing-eye dogs. Every year, we get a new pup and we keep him for eighteen months and we train him. We take him every place we go. Matter of fact, last summer we went to Canada with two dogs in the back of the SUV. We traveled about 3,000 miles, stayed in hotels, visited friends all over the country with these dogs. It's just the greatest joy.

I don't think anything has given me more pleasure than waking up in the morning with three or four dogs. They jump on the bed when it's time to wake up. I know they're going to go on and do something great for someone.

I've done so little in my life for anyone but my family and myself, and it's a nice, nice feeling to think, "Gee, we love these dogs. Our hearts break when we give them away. But that's the goal. You're giving someone the gift of sight."

It's wonderful. I'm finally doing something for someone else. That's a great joy.

JOE HYAMS was born on June 6, 1923, in Boston, Massachusetts.

GLORIA STUART

Age brought Gloria Stuart the fame and celebrity she deserved but never achieved during her Hollywood years in the 1930s and 1940s. In 1997 she was cast as the 101-year-old Rose DeWitt in the mega-hit Titanic. *She received an Academy Award nomination for the role but lost the Oscar to Kim Basinger. Ever since her titanic comeback, Gloria Stuart has found herself in demand and constantly employed, as much as age and health allow.*

I DON'T SEE ANY ADVANTAGE to being older. I think it's a pest. To be young—and by young I mean twenty-five or thirty-five—is utter bliss. At least it was for me. I was performing. I was doing what I wanted to do. It seemed life was important.

I don't think advice to the coming generations is helpful at all. It depends on what circumstances you're in. If you're in very advantageous circumstances, you just smile and keep working. If you're in hazardous situations, you can't smile and go ahead. So it's individual. I think it's helpful to keep hoping. There are many periods of despair and bereavement in life. I don't know how you get through them. Good things happen along the way. So I don't think there is any answer in this question of advice.

When my role as Rose DeWitt in *Titanic* brought me a lot of attention, I told the press that when I graduated high school I was voted Girl Most Likely to Succeed, but I never realized how long it would take. From 1927 to 1986? A long time!

People ask me how I'm enjoying my new career. Well, as a matter of fact, I just continued a career that I had started in 1932. I just took a long vacation of ten or twenty years. I'm still acting. I'm still doing what I started out to do.

I've always been interested in politics. I helped found the Screen Actors Guild. Now, of course, I can't walk a picket line, but I can give money and make telephone calls and support candidates.

My career in films has been eventful. I had proposals from both Universal and Paramount, so a fellow actor gave me an agent, because I didn't have one. The agent said, "Sign the Universal contract." And the reason she said that was because it was twice the money Paramount had offered. It was a terrible mistake, because Universal was a "B" studio and Paramount was an "A" studio. But a little girl from the sticks like me didn't know that. I signed with Universal. They had no stars in their contract division, except Lon Chaney. And no directors, except James Whale. Paramount had Marlene Dietrich, Maurice Chevalier, Claudette Colbert, and Ray Milland.

Most of the directors in the early 1930s were from silent movies, like John Ford. They were not directors from the theater. James Whale was a director from the English stage; he was also an actor in British theater. He knew what he was talking about when he directed actors. It was a great privilege to work for him. He was a man of great taste and great talent.

When I wrote my memoir a few years ago—*I Just Kept Hoping*—it was a very satisfying experience. There's still another book left that was cut out of it.

I belong to every organization that has to do with saving the environment. I'm fed up with venal and avaricious forestry people, mining people, oil people, gas people. I think the abuse of the environment is sinful.

I read about rivers that have been blocked or diverted and all the fish have died, and the animals that depended on the water have gone elsewhere. Or I read about letting ships dump their oil or their sewage into the water. And I read about the Great Plains that should have been left to the buffalo but are being mined for gold and oil. Unforgivable!

Unlike the heroine in *Titanic,* I never had any great dilemma about whether I should marry rich or not. My mother and father knew what I wanted to do and I must say they were very simpatico. I was very lucky.

Titanic is popular with young people. I know that during the first and second run of the film, the audiences were very young and the young people I spoke to after the performances were appreciative of the film. I think it's a Romeo and Juliet syndrome. The movie said

"How do I deal with stress? I go to sleep."

you can leave your parents and go on with your own life.

I learned about printing—hands-on printing—and book arts in 1983, and so I bought a hand press and type. I've been designing what they call "artist's books" ever since. That means that I design the book, I illustrate it, I write it, I set the type, I print it. The only thing I don't do is bind or make the paper, and that's because I started so late in life. I don't have the time, and it's too late for me to learn them. They are such elaborate and demanding arts.

The Library of Congress has all the books I've designed—and the Metropolitan Museum, the Getty, the Huntington Library, the Morgan, the Clark Library. I'm very busy now printing a book on the Butterfly Kite.

I don't have much time to "smell the flowers" these days. I don't play bridge anymore. I don't do luncheons anymore. I don't go shopping anymore. I just work at my press. I do travel, but that's all.

I haven't done any acting for about a year. The parts for women my age aren't very interesting.

I was in the Peter O'Toole comedy *My Favorite Year*. I played a woman who is having her twenty-fifth wedding anniversary, and her husband asks O'Toole, who was playing Errol Flynn, if he would say hello to his wife. When Peter O'Toole said, "I'll ask her to dance," it was the high point of my entire career. A non pareil!

Right now my focus is on finishing my book. I've been working on it since 1983. I've published eight other books, but this one is my favorite. When I finish it, I don't know what I'll do. Probably start another.

How do I deal with stress? I go to sleep.

When my husband died, I was a single person again. A lot of my friends who are non-professionals do lunch, they do shopping, they do charity work, but they're not driven by any ambition. I was always driven.

I would say the latter half of my life I was able to do exactly what I wanted to do.

Almost!

GLORIA STUART was born on July 4, 1910, in Santa Monica, California.

*"After age seventy
it's patch, patch, patch."*
—Jimmy Stewart

MONTY HALL

Monty Hall added the phrase "Let's make a deal" to the broadcast lexicon. The show's marathon run extended from 1963 to 1986. His wife Marilyn is the producer of an Emmy Award-winning film about Alzheimer's disease, and Monty's daughter Joanna Gleason is the Tony Award-winning star of the Broadway musical stage. In addition, Monty's charitable and philanthropic activities have brought him awards galore.

I'VE HAD A GREAT RIDE and lots of curve balls thrown at me in my life. I never believed I'd live to be eighty. I was a very sickly youth—double pneumonia, a scalding accident. The doctor said I'd never live past twenty. The ride has been one of... "Here I am again. And back on my feet."

My folks didn't treat me as an invalid. They told me to get out there and play ball and do everything I could. Even though I was a little weak and sickly as a youngster, when I was

about sixteen, seventeen, I sprouted and grew. I went to college and I played all the sports and I became an athlete. I think it restored my health.

I grew up in Canada and was working at a radio station nights and weekends to put myself through college. When I graduated, I went to work at the station full time. While I was there, the manager of the station called me in one day and said, "Listen, here's a map of Toronto"—I was living in Winnipeg at the time—"Here's a map of Toronto," he said. "And I marked off all the radio stations. Why don't you just go!" I said, "Go to what? I don't have a job waiting." He said, "I know. If you stay here any longer, you'll end up like all these old guys that you're working with. They're not going anywhere and you are, but you've got to go to Toronto. That's the big time."

So, I quit and said to my folks, "Well, I'm going to Toronto." They said, "Have you got a job?" I said, "No." They said, "Then why are you going?" I said, "I don't know. The boss told me to go," and I went. I got a couple of offers and I went on to Montreal and I got a couple of offers there and I said, "This is fantastic."

So I went to New York—I didn't get any offers there. They said, "You have radio in Canada?" They thought they only had hockey players and mounted police.

I went back to Toronto and took a job and met my wife, got married, and had two little kids and then television started, and I was in on the ground floor. Then, all of a sudden, one year, I had no shows. At the Canadian Broadcasting Corporation you couldn't get too big—

"Don't let the other guy talk you out of your future."

they would cut you off. That's why so many of the Canadians ran off to Hollywood. My wife said, "I'll stay here and be mother and father to the two babies, and you go to New York and try your luck."

It took me many months of commuting back and forth to Toronto and walking the streets, but I finally got a show! I sold my home in Toronto and I brought the wife and two babies down to New York. The day they arrived, my show was cancelled.

So, here we go again. You know what I did when the show was cancelled? I took my wife and two kids to Florida for a week's vacation. Everybody said, "How can you go now? You're unemployed." I said, "I'm thumbing my nose at fate." I've got off the floor so many times, I've got confidence in myself. We just went and told everyone we're sitting on top of the world. Take the week and come back and start over again. We had a few rough years, but I finally clicked.

My partner and I came up with the idea for a game show called *Let's Make a Deal*. We showed it to all three networks and they all turned it down. When they saw a run-through, they all said, "It looks terrific for a one shot. What do you do the second day?"

Finally, a guy at NBC took a chance. We made a pilot. But we didn't hear anything for six months. And then we get a call. They said, "We're having trouble with a certain time period. Can you be ready to go on in six weeks?" That's how *Let's Make a Deal* went on the air and never looked back.

It was on for twenty-three years.

I have a little advice for young people and it's embodied in a story that has nothing what-ever to do with *Let's Make a Deal*. It has to do with a young fellow I knew who was a second-string comic. I remember him coming to me and he started to cry. He told me he had just auditioned at some club and the guy had said, "Get out of the business. You're never going to make it."

I said to him, "You're never through until you say to yourself, 'I'm through,' not when somebody else says you're through. Don't let the other guy talk you out of your future."

My advice to young people is—if you think you have talent, you have to have the courage to keep going after that star until the day comes when luck intersects with your courage.

My wife coined a phrase back in the 1950s when I was unemployed in New York. She said, "Get on the train and go to New York with all the other people who are going to work, even though you haven't got any work." Then she added, "I married you for better or worse, but not for lunch."

I've been speaking around the country and that's all I do now. I do charity work. I raise an enormous amount of money for charity. I'm a raconteur. I've got a story about everything and about people that I've met. It's been a great life. Especially three things: My career, of course; but my marriage, my children, and my charity work.

I live life to the fullest. I enjoy my family tremendously. We're very close-knit. My wife and I have been married for fifty-eight years. She makes me laugh and I make her laugh. We've gone through such tough times together,

but she was always my anchor. We enjoy life. When things were the worst is when we spent the most.

I remember in Toronto when we had a little radio show and I sold my show to Colgate Palmolive. My wife and I, we were thrilled to pieces! This was on a Friday, and on Monday the guy called me up. He said, "Sorry, we changed our mind." We went out and had a steak dinner. You don't just go out and have chicken a la king; you go out and have the steak dinner. Show the world!

Every time somebody rejected me, it stiffened my spine. You live on failure. My whole family's in the business. My daughter is a Broadway musical star. My son is very successful producing television. And my other daughter's a senior vice president at Sony. These people are all very successful but when they started out, I said to them, "You're in a business called 'Rejection.' If you can live by it and surpass it and get over it, you'll make it." And with rejection comes another layer of steel."

Let me tell you what starts my engine in the morning these days. I get out of bed. I read two newspapers. I take over an hour to have breakfast—if I'm not out there playing tennis at 8:30, which I do a couple of times a week. I read the *L.A. Times* and the *New York Times* cover to cover and that gets me going intellectually and emotionally. It gets my blood boiling sometimes, but then I'm ready to face the world.

Frankly, I don't see a lot of huge advantages in being over eighty. I'd like to be thirty again.

I play golf and I'm hitting the ball thirty yards shorter than I used to. There's no advantage in that. When I play tennis and a guy lobs it behind me, back to the baseline, and I can't reach it, I'm not happy about that.

They say age gives you wisdom. Well, maybe that's so. I think experience gives you wisdom. I try to give my kids advice. Years ago, my son was married to a young lady who was a newscaster. She was up in San Francisco and an agent here in Los Angeles went up to try and represent her, and he came back and called me and said,

"She turned me down and went with somebody else," even though I had recommended him.

I said to him, "We offer our children three things: Love, money, and advice. The first two are always accepted, the third very rarely."

They have to make their own mistakes and their own investments. Kids are very independent and I love their independence. I have five hundred awards for my charity work—plaques and glassware in every room. I said to my kids, "Would you like to come and take some of this—divide some of them among yourselves?" And they said, "No, we'll get our own awards."

I never considered age to be more than a number. I live my life as if I were young. My tastes are young: my tennis, my golf, my charity work, my traveling around the country speaking, and so on. I did three events in Palm Springs last week all for non-paying jobs. I have enough of those.

People say, "When are you going to slow down?" Why should I slow down? I'm enjoying this. As long as I can do it, why shouldn't I do it? If I'm still acceptable to the people who want to hear me or see me, then why should I quit now? Why not quit at the age of fifty? If you're going to quit at the age of sixty, why didn't you quit at fifty? I'm past eighty and I'm having a hell of a time.

Nature will tell me when to slow down. Until then, I'm not ready for it. My wife, who is a few years younger than I am, is running a production company for motion pictures, and she's going all over the world. I look at her and she's still the young girl I married.

Do You Remember Love was a story about Alzheimer's. My wife was the co-executive producer. It was a great picture. It won everything. It won the Emmy and the Peabody. There's a marvelous speech at the end of the film where Joanne Woodward, who has Alzheimer's, wins a writing award and she goes up on stage to accept it—and she can't talk. She stands there frozen. Her husband, Richard Kiley, gets up and gives the speech for her.

MONTY HALL was born on August 25, 1921, in Winnipeg, Canada.

DICK MARTIN

In the early 1970s, exploiting the dwindling attention span of the TV audience, Dick Martin, with partner Dan Rowan and a band of gifted farceurs, concocted a show called Laugh-In. *Among other things, the show encouraged President Nixon to say, "Sock it to me" on camera, focused national attention on "the bippy," and spawned the careers of Lily Tomlin, Arte Johnson, and Goldie Hawn.*

I THINK *LAUGH-IN* WORKED so well because it was truly funny. I don't see anything funny today. And not much before that. Dick Van Dyke was funny. Bob Newhart was funny. Dean Martin was adorable, but that wasn't a funny show. The pace always bugged me about Carol Burnett's long sketches. Then once I saw Jerry Lewis do a six-minute sketch and he stretched it into seventeen minutes.

It's the pace—and *Laugh-In* had pace.

I had three marvelous and marvelously successful careers. I was a nightclub comedian for over twenty years. I played everywhere in the world with my partner, Dan Rowan. Then, we were successful on television, until Dan retired in 1973. I knew I couldn't compete with Rowan and Martin, so I became a television director. I did that for over two hundred shows.

I started off directing *The Bob Newhart Show.* Bob really put me in the directing business.

Then I directed *Archie Bunker's Place, In the Heat of the Night, Brothers*…

In recent years I've lost my wanderlust. I've been everywhere in the world and loved it, but I don't want to go back. I don't want to get in an airplane, even if it's mine. I don't want any of that.

It's gotten down to a marvelous life, a beautiful home in Malibu, and friends. It's gotten down to pretty much that. I'm not in the business anymore as such, because I don't go anywhere or do anything. But I think I'm involved. I stay abreast.

There was some stress in creating *Laugh-In*. Fortunately, when there are two of you, it's a little easier. When your partner arrives, you can talk over a problem with one another. With some problems, the solution is legal.

But the business has a way of telling you when to retire. It really does. In other words, we ran our course on *Laugh-In* and there was nowhere else to go. We couldn't top it. We didn't have the ambition.

I don't know that I have any advice for the kids who are just starting out, because the times are very different. I'd hate to have to make a decision in today's world of show business. I just know that what drove Dan and me was our mutual hatred of auditioning. I said, "Hell, let's do what Martin and Lewis are doing." Well, he'd never seen a nightclub. He said, "But neither of us looks funny. And I can't sing."

We went out and played clubs for almost two years. If you're willing to work for $400 a week, you can work almost anywhere. Well, we worked ourselves up the mountain. We went on and did well. It wasn't until *The Dean Martin Show* that we really kick-started our career. They came to us after that.

You've got to own a show. I hate to be dangling on a promise of, "We'll take care of you…."

If I didn't own a piece of *Laugh-In,* I would be living in Watts someday.

What gets me out of bed? Albeit a little later every year—I look forward to the day. I look forward to life. I look forward to reading my email. I look forward to a lot of things. I don't think I've ever been depressed in my life. I had an amazingly wonderful childhood.

I grew up in marvelous surroundings. There was adversity along the way. I was in a tuberculosis sanitarium for two years at age sixteen. When you're that age and you're thrown in with 150 guys walking around in their scuffs and bathrobes, you have a tendency to grow up pretty quick.

There have been a lot of turning points in my career. So many of them. I think it would be very difficult to narrow them down. Coming out of the sanitarium after being shut up for two years. I had a ball there, too. Incidentally. I ran the place. They had an inter-room communication

> *"In recent years I've lost my wanderlust. I've been everywhere in the world and loved it."*

system, and I said, "Why don't I play records?" I became the world's first tubercular disc jockey.

That was a turning point. I was sixteen.

I was a bartender for ten years. That's a marvelous education.

Then I met Dan. That was a turning point. When we first went to London and did well at the London Palladium it was another turning point.

I remember how the stage manager of the Palladium described our act. After we came off stage, he said, "It occurs to me, gentlemen, that you have a frightfully elastic script."

We *had* no script. We were just out there winging it and having a ball.

I'm told you can't do that.

DICK MARTIN was born on June 30, 1922, in Battle Creek, Michigan.

HERB KLEIN

Herb Klein lived a remarkable career, enjoying the various tensions and exhilarations of a journalist, a broadcast official, a media consultant, and, most challenging of all, communications chief in the Nixon White House. He participated in no less than five presidential campaigns at a senior level and helped make Nixon's famous "kitchen debate" with Nikita Khrushchev a political triumph for the then vice president.

WHEN YOU'RE A senior staffer in the White House, that's going to be the highlight of what you do in your life because you're serving your country at a high level. I created the Office of Communications, which is still an important part of the White House staff.

But I've been very fortunate in the occupations I've had since then. They've been interesting and keep me very active. I'm enjoying life.

The most satisfactory thing I've done was as a member of the team that won the presidency in 1968. I handled the communications part of the presidential campaign. I did that in five presidential campaigns. One of the most interesting times in my career was when I first joined Vice President Nixon's staff for the 1960 campaign, and I was assigned to organize the trip in 1959 to the Soviet Union. That turned out to be the "kitchen debate" with Nikita Khrushchev.

We were there ten days. It was one day of Nixon's debate and nine days of Herb Klein's debate with the Soviets. I did some things which were pretty bold. One time I threatened to pull the vice president out of the country and got the Soviets to back down. It was just an exciting moment I'll never forget. I learned from it.

I think White House reporters are still very aggressive today. I think the difference is—when you got to the time of Watergate, there was a very bitter battle going on. Some of the press thought that they had missed a story and they were trying to catch up. There were, of course, serious mistakes made in the White House. I think that was the most bitter time I've known with the press corps. It was much worse for Ron Ziegler, the press secretary. I think even if you go back to Jim Haggerty, who was Eisenhower's press secretary, and my role model for things I did with the press and the government, Haggerty had his opponents but he also had cooperation.

The best example I had of the media relating to the press secretary or communications director was when I threatened to have Nixon leave the Soviet Union in 1959 because they tried to prevent the full press corps from going with us to Siberia. I told the Soviets I'd give them four hours to change their policy. A couple of American reporters had heard rumors of what was going on and asked me about it. Scotty Reston was one of them. I said, "You just have to trust me that things will work out." They took me at my word and things did work out.

I've always told the presidents I've known that when things get tough, don't back away. It's my attitude toward presidents, and I still do some advisory things with President Bush. That's my advice in a nutshell. I think in life you've got to be willing to get down in the trough and work on it. Be aggressive. Be honest.

I enjoy working. I'm quite busy. I'm consulting for the White House. I'm consulting for three major corporations. I'm a National Fellow of the American Enterprise Institute and do some writing. I'm active in the community and with my university, which is USC. I'm very active and I think that's the best thing for my health.

"I think in life you've got to be willing to get down in the trough and work at it."

I think I've always been an optimist and that helps when you deal with stress. I always felt that I could find an answer, and I never give up. You lean on experience.

I'm concerned about the media today, in a couple of respects. One is we've had too many cases where we've had breaches of ethics in major newspapers and in television. The other is we've turned too much toward personal journalism. Instead of looking at the issues, we tend more to try to report it like a ball score on a campaign. Or else we tend to look for little things to be critical of, instead of looking at the big issues, which determines whether a candidate is going to be a good one or not.

Personal journalism means that you're looking for something to make a name for yourself by nit-picking or trying to find flaws. You've always got to be on guard if you're in the press. You also need to look at what are the big issues and how people understand them and how you portray them in what you write.

I enjoy the fact that I'm not editing anymore; I can do a lot more writing. I try to lean on the experience I've had to convey some thoughts today.

I smell the flowers by being really interested in sports. I find if I go to a ballgame I'm relaxed. Sports is a great relaxation.

I'm not looking for more things to do. I don't have time. I look ahead because I think there's a lot to be done in the press and media. I think there's a lot to be done in every community and I'm very active as a civic leader.

I was Mr. San Diego a few years ago. I'm past president of the Holiday Bowl. I'm a chairman for committees in the Chamber of Commerce and the Economic Development Corporation. There are a variety of things I think are important.

I think what saved me in times that could have been pretty perilous was my determination to be honest. I think whether in journalism or in government or in business, that's the key thing; you've got to have credibility. Today, credibility is a problem in all forms of public office and all the public media.

I think the "Eureka moment" for me came when I accepted the opportunity to be White House director of communications and to really modernize the whole administration, the whole government media approach, in 1969. If you look at what's being done in that office today, a lot of it is based on things we did—dealing with the press directly and with the facts.

Politically there's too much spin today and not enough facts.

The key word is credibility.

HERB KLEIN was born on April 1, 1918, in Los Angeles, California.

AHMET ERTEGUN

Ahmet Ertegun is one of the giants of the music business. When he founded Atlantic Records in 1947, it was mainly a jazz and R&B label. In the 1960s it became a major player in the music business, with famous pop singers like Sonny & Cher. In a commencement address Ertegun once said, "There are advantages to being old, but I can't remember what they are." We think he remembers.

I CERTAINLY SEE ADVANTAGES to aging. Experience is not everything, but it counts for a lot. Experience is gained through years of work and the more years one puts in, the more experience one has. However, creativity comes at a younger age, and what we try to do is keep as much creativity in what we do as we can.

Unfortunately, in the world today such a large proportion of people have to spend their day working at something that they're not in love with. Often they actually dislike something that they have to do in order to put food on the table and take care of their family. To support themselves, people have taken on all kinds of work that is unpleasant to them. The greatest thing in life is to be able to make a living at something which you love to do. If you're able to do that, then work is not like work. The great people who win Nobel Prizes didn't win those prizes by working at what they do from nine to five. They, obviously, did whatever they did with such great love that however many hours a day they spent on it, that was their greatest pleasure. That's the most wonderful thing if you can find the thing you have a passion for in life and work at that thing. It will be a great pleasure to do whatever you're doing and not seem like work at all.

I'm very fortunate to have a wonderful marriage, and I enjoy living my life with my wife. I'm also blessed with having good friends who make my life very pleasant. My curiosity hasn't waned. I love travel. I love to go to places I haven't been to. I love spending my summers in the country of my birth, which is Turkey, such a beautiful place. I have a house in Budrow on the Mediterranean where I can actually continue to do a lot of work.

I have thought about getting older in recent years, because I've had physical setbacks. I've had a triple bypass heart operation. I had a couple of minor strokes and thank God I'm able to get around and do everything the way I had been doing all my life. I do look forward to my night's sleep, these days. I try to get at least eight hours each night.

First thing in the morning, the phone rings, and it's Europe calling. I have other interests as well as the music business. I have investments in real estate in a couple of countries. I'm interested in contemporary art. I have a lot of other hobbies. My days are very full. As a matter of fact, I can't find time to play bridge anymore. I wonder how I could do that many years ago. I used to love to play bridge and I even took time off to play golf, but now I don't have the time.

We go to South Hampton almost every weekend and I love to walk out in the garden and up on the beach. In Turkey, I swim all day long, and we have one of the old-fashioned, wooden Turkish boats that we go out on. We have a great lunch out there. The vegetables and fruit are so good there, and the fishermen bring the fish right to the boat. It's just a great life.

Stress has never been a really great problem to me. I understand that people have stress and sometimes are overworked and so on, but I haven't had a problem with that. If I have to work sixteen hours a day for three or four days—maybe I take two days off and sleep for two days straight. I don't really have psychological stress problems.

I first became involved with American music through my love of jazz blues. Through that I developed a great taste for the rock 'n' rollers, the rhythm and blues musicians, and I think that keeping up with that music has kept me younger. We have today the biggest debut record we've had in the history of Atlantic Records by a young singer named T.I. It does certainly keep you aware of the trends and new

"What is important is to lead a good life, one which is ethical, morally correct."

tastes. It does tend to make you aware more than other people your age of what's going on with young people. Until a certain age, I was able to very much feel the sentiments of young record buyers because I needed to do that in order to produce records. I'm not producing records today for young kids, but we are, of course, as a company—and I have a lot of young people in the company who do that beautifully. One keeps abreast of the feelings of the generations, if you're involved in music, actually. I still am. I'm enjoying being part of what is a great renaissance in our company with great, young new people at the helm.

Achievement or getting rich are really secondary to being a good person. What is important, I think, for the world and for each person is to lead a good life. By a good life, I mean one which is ethical, morally correct. Whether you're religious or not is not important. How you act, behave, and how you are to yourself is what's important. As long as you can be a good person, it doesn't matter if you don't achieve the material wealth or the fame or the power that other people reach. By just being good you're doing the most that any person can do, and that should bring you true happiness, which is what everybody wants.

AHMET ERTEGUN was born on July 31, 1923, in Istanbul, Turkey.

"Few enjoy the consideration enjoyed by the oldest inhabitant."
—*Ralph Waldo Emerson*

JUDITH CRIST

Judith Crist has had a remarkable career in movie criticism. She went directly from journalism school to one of America's most prestigious newspapers, the New York Herald Tribune, *where she became a reporter, an arts editor, and a motion picture critic. She concurrently served on the* Today *show as their film and theater critic. And after the demise of the* Trib, *she went on to become the cinema critic for* New York *magazine, originally launched by the* Trib *as its Sunday supplement.*

THERE ARE DEFINITE advantages to being my age. Prime among them is that I have such vivid cultural and political memories. I find myself empathizing with young people. I love astounding them by saying, "Oh yes, I covered Ed Murrow. I knew him…." They all saw *Good Night and Good Luck*.

I've never really thought about my age. I remember at one point, my older brother saying to me when I turned fifty, "I hope you know that after you're fifty, it's all downhill." Well, in my case, it was all uphill.

When I was forty my lifelong dream came true when I was made the movie critic for the *New York Herald Tribune*. Then I hit television through my newspaper work. And I became, as you say, rich, famous, and beautiful. When I became the *Trib*'s movie critic, I also began a ten-year stint as film and theater critic for NBC's *Today* show, and a twenty-three-year stand as *TV Guide*'s movie reviewer. After the

Trib died, I became the founding film critic for *New York* magazine. I also did a lot of lecturing.

Ben Bradlee once asked me, "Are there any glories to the movie reviewer's business?" I was among the blessed because I was a critic in the 1960s and 1970s when all the great foreign directors and all the great stars were in flower. It was a fantastic time.

This continued into my fifties and sixties. My seventies and eighties became my best years. I really don't think I had time to think about being eighty until recently when I got an attack of hepatitis and lost about forty pounds. Doctors told me, "You've got to put on some weight." I weighed what I had last weighed when I was ten years old. Bring on the Häagen Dazs!

Today I'm engaged in my teaching at Columbia's Graduate School of Journalism. I teach two seminars a semester. Dealing with graduate studies puts me in contact with twenty- and thirty-year-olds, the generation that my son has now grown beyond. It tells me what young adults are thinking. I have to be prepared and alert for the course—and I call the students "my adrenaline."

Their passion is going to the theater and the movies. Of course, I've seen far more movies than I want to see at this point in my life. I support activities in the film, the theater, and the dance. I indulge myself.

"My older brother [said], 'I hope you know that after you're fifty, it's all downhill.' Well, in my case, it was all uphill."

Believe me, the kids today with few exceptions are "kids." I get them when they've already been exposed to high school and college. They are all born yesterday! Though I hate to be one of those naysayers about the younger generations, their cultural background is God-awful. Here's an example. Out of twenty students in my two seminars, only three had heard or knew anything about the *Rubaiyat of Omar Khayyam.* And their ignorance of even twentieth century history is abysmal, let alone of what happened before that. Only those who had attended European universities knew what "*O tempora, O mores!*" or "*sui generis*" meant.

Here's another. In the course of one of my classes, the students had to attend some cultural event and write an essay on it. One student wrote a review of *La Traviata* by simply detailing the plot. It was like writing about *Hamlet* by just telling the story. I said that's ludicrous. He said to me, "Well, you didn't know who Kurt Cobain was." Cobain had been on the cover of *Time,* and I had walked into class and said, "Who the hell is Kurt Cobain?" So now I carefully follow the rock scene and pop music. But I assured them that a hundred years from now, people would still be listening to *La Traviata* and Kurt Cobain would not even be a pimple on the face of our culture.

I can recall the major turning point of my life. I was the arts editor of the *New York Herald*

Tribune. There had been a long newspaper strike, which I had survived by reviewing theater and film on TV. I was called back after the four-month strike and there were Jock Whitney, our publisher, and Jim Bellows, our editor, and they said, "You may have guessed that we're planning on resuming publication. And we wanted to tell you about the changes we're anticipating. We're going to make Herb Kupferburg the editor for the arts." I looked at them in a state of shock, and then they said, "We're going to make you our movie critic." And my immediate reaction was, "What's the matter? Wasn't I a good arts editor?" It took about five seconds for me to realize—*at last*—what I had longed for since I was ten was going to happen. A dream come true!

JUDITH CRIST was born on May 22, 1922, in New York City.

FRANK PIERSON

"What we have here is a failure to communicate," says a character in Cool Hand Luke. *There has been no such failure in the screenplays of writer/director Frank Pierson. Through films like* Cat Ballou, Dog Day Afternoon, Cool Hand Luke, *and the Barbra Streisand version of* A Star Is Born, *Pierson has earned Academy Awards and the acclaim of critics and the public. He also served as president of the Motion Picture Academy for four consecutive terms.*

A YOUNGSTER CAME UP TO Oliver Wendell Holmes on his eightieth birthday and said, "How does it feel to be old?"

And Holmes said, "Old? I don't feel old. I feel like a young man with something wrong with him."

The main thing is interest in life and appetite for it. I don't know if that's something that you can will or make a decision to do. It's something that you either have or you haven't.

The real secret of a happy old age is to be interested and have an appetite for life, even though you're pissed off every morning when you read the goddamn newspaper.

I think that, in the span of my lifetime and my parents' lifetime, we may be at the high-water mark of human civilization. I look around and I worry terribly about the future for my grandchildren and what their lives are going to be like. So many bad decisions are being made at every level in the governance of our planet.

That doesn't discourage me. It's a stressful challenge. I think stress is good for people. It forces you to stretch and cope.

I don't know any worse prescription for living a happy life, especially in old age, than just having no stress at all—nothing that is challenging; nothing that you have to overcome and deal with.

It was always interesting to me in the combat infantry in World War II to see the farm boys from the Midwest who really hadn't had much happen to them in their youth. They were the ones that tended to crack up when things got rough. It was the neurotics, little guys from the cities who survived—because they were used to anxiety and fear and uncertainty. It was nothing new for them to deal with those feelings when they got in combat.

As a screenwriter, the writer from whom I learned the most is Paddy Chayevsky. He distilled into writing for the cinema everything that had been learned by all the people who had struggled through the 1930s and 1940s to write for the screen. Because nobody really knew. It was all being invented as they went along.

At first, the New York dramatists brought to Hollywood the habits of writing for the stage. Everything was in three acts and discreet scenes. It wasn't until Paddy Chayefsky came along that not only the political and social voices of the country were brought to the screen, but also the screenwriting techniques.

I find that the most difficult part of screenwriting is the puzzle of how to move the characters around so they seem to meet naturally and not by coincidence or forcing them into situations. The "cute meet." It's solving that logistical problem.

At the same time, it's letting your characters develop the story, live in the story in their own way, rather than imposing your will on them. I think it's flipping from the level of construction back to the issue of character. Because the characters are always tearing up the goddamn construction just when you've got the screenplay written so it seems to work in terms of believability—this is the way life is, two characters meet in this way, and then this has happened, and that happened, and it all seems very natural.

"The real secret of a happy old age is to be interested and have an appetite for life."

Then the characters suddenly take off in their own direction, and all that hard work that you put into solving the puzzle has just been thrown to the wind. You have to start all over again. Stress—very stressful.

Take the main character in *Dog Day Afternoon*. Until I understood who he was and what his principal need in life was, I couldn't write a thing. Once I understood him, it made everything very simple. But he kept tearing up the script that I had written.

There was a long time between *Cool Hand Luke* and *Dog Day Afternoon*. During that time there were an awful lot of screenplays that I wrote that never got made for one reason or another—they couldn't be cast, or I would start writing them for one studio head and by the time I finished, he was replaced by another, and the new guy comes in and cleans house.

Some of the screenplays I've done that I personally think would make great pictures have not been made. They're just gathering dust in studio archives and, of course, they're owned. If you work for hire, they're copyrighted by the studios. I've had a studio head say to me about one script I wrote, "Listen. Listen to me hard. We don't want to make this picture and we don't want anybody *else* to make it either."

Sometimes when a film appears that has lasting value, it just happened that all the right people were in the right place, in the right frame of mind to do that picture at the right time. That's something that has very little to do with the quality of the screenplay, or even the character of the screenwriter. It has to do with just sheer luck of getting everybody together at the right time. It's a collaborative business.

Screenwriters don't get the respect they deserve. The difficulty is that we do most of our work before anybody else comes on. You even have trouble getting paid while you're doing the first draft, because the project doesn't even have a charge number on it with the studio accounting office. Nobody knows what you're doing. Everybody hates writers. This is something that

Bob Towne once said, "The reason everybody hates writers is because nobody can go to work until the writer's done."

I think there are two big mistakes that writers make. The biggest mistake is trying to imitate what they see as being a success. *Chicago* is a big success, so they try to write *Chicago*, or *Spider-Man*.

Those of us who have been around for a long time know how to do these things. It's dumb of a neophyte to try to compete with that. The thing to do is to write something straight from the heart, something that you really know and feel with a passion. Even if you know that nobody in the current marketplace is going to make the damn thing. The point is that you will write the best you possibly can. What will happen is, people will pass the screenplay around and say, "You know something? Nobody's ever going to make this picture, but this guy can *write*." If you start out by trying to compete with the "A" players, it's a tough row to hoe.

I have always taken time to smell the flowers. I have known so many people who were terrible workaholics. They worked all the time. The issue of working twenty-four hours a day, seven days a week, just eats you alive and I would never let that happen. Even when I was producing television shows, I took the time to go out to dinner and be with friends and take vacations.

I'm a former *Time* magazine correspondent, but I never miss that life. I really found those articles hard to write, though I do write prose pieces from time to time. My mind just happens to work entirely in terms of fiction. I guess that's why I gravitated to motion pictures. Journalism was an absolutely wonderful thing to do for a short period of time.

When I was working for *Time* and *Life* magazines, it opened doors. When I look back on it these days, I kick my ass for not taking the opportunities that were offered to me—to spend a day with Aldous Huxley, or a day with Marilyn Monroe or Marlene Dietrich, to witness the first atom bomb explosion, to see airplanes tested and blown up on the launching pad, to have long conversations with truly important people of the age. It was a very special time in journalism. It was before everything was being spun, before public relations experts were in charge.

I do see certain advantages to age. That I never have to live through junior high school again. There's another advantage to the advance of old age. If you keep on living, short skirts come around every seven years.

I guess the turning point in my life was service in combat in World War II. When I came back from that, I was determined to find something that *meant* something. The experience went a long way toward explaining to me why we're here, what it is we're doing to each other, and why it's all worthwhile. Until then, I really hadn't known that. I was just moving fast, trying to make the most difficult target.

My only wish as I get older is that the manufacturers and designers of electronic equipment will make the goddamn print larger.

FRANK PIERSON was born on May 12, 1925, in Chappaqua, New York.

ART MODELL

Art Modell changed the face of professional football. He was the legendary NFL owner of the Cleveland Browns from 1961 to 1995 before moving the team to Baltimore, where he owned the Ravens from 1996 to 2004. He transformed pro football by negotiating the league's lucrative television contracts and the equal sharing of network revenue among all the teams.

AFTER I SOLD the Baltimore Ravens, it was tough to fill the vacuum. I spent forty-five years in the NFL, and I miss the competition. But I've taken up a new line of work. I'm very involved with the Johns Hopkins Heart Institute. They've elected me chairman of the Board of Governors. And we're building a new Heart Institute and that's very exciting. That fills part of the void, not all of it. There still is a lot of time to fill. But we have a good life. We've built a beautiful home on the ocean in Orchid Island, Florida.

It was a glorious run in the NFL, very successful, and I enjoyed every second of it. The games on Sunday were great. But the years went by very quickly. And I'm very grateful to God for sparing my life on a number of occasions. I've had two heart attacks and a stroke. But here I am. I told somebody on a conference call this morning that I get up every day. I pick up the *Baltimore Sun,* I turn to the obituary page. If I don't see my picture, I get up and have breakfast.

I fought to divide the TV income equally among the NFL teams, whether large or small markets. I told the media, "We're twenty-five Republicans and one Socialist." There was opposition, of course, from the major markets. But that step turned the whole league around. The equal sharing of the proceeds made the league. That was a big step for us—it made the league fiscally sound and viable. And it's been a rollercoaster since then.

I started out in the television business (before pro football) developing TV shows. When I became the owner of the Cleveland Browns, I stayed in the television business, because I chaired the committee that negotiated all the contracts for TV broadcasting rights for the league. I never lost my touch. Never lost my contacts in the television industry.

How I bought the Cleveland Browns: I got a call from a theatrical agent who knew of my love for the game of pro football. And he asked me if I wanted to buy a football team. I thought it was the New York Titans.

"Which team is it?"

"I don't know."

"What league is it?"

"I don't know."

"Find out and call me back."

He called me back and said, "It's the NFL." He didn't tell me the team.

I had a date with a lovely actress that night. I called and cancelled it. I said "Something big has come up." And the rest is history. I borrowed every nickel I could lay my hands on to buy the damn thing.

Today I'm very engaged in healthcare services. Having had illnesses galore, I know what it is to be well and not to be well, so I want to help other people if I can from a position of some strength, so I'm working with Johns Hopkins.

I still have a very small piece of the Baltimore Ravens which gives me rooting privileges. I go to every home game. I have a box inside the loge suite. I invite some close friends to go every Sunday and I still love it. I gave up the road trips at a certain point.

"If you have good health, age is a chronological thing."

Politics is an important part of my life. I'm an active, staunch, conservative Republican. And I enjoy the game of politics, because it somewhat resembles the game of professional football—the contest, the meetings—I like politics. I like the ruthlessness of it. I'm involved enough to make me happy. They wanted me to run for lieutenant governor in Ohio, but I passed that up.

How did I handle stress? I was hospitalized fifteen times. I was named the surgical patient of the year by Johns Hopkins. You don't handle stress, you just have to deal with it. You try your best to stay well, be examined, go to doctors routinely. And try to keep the pressure down.

My wife Pat kicks me out of bed in the morning. Now I'm taking a lot of physical therapy—I work out three times a week. I'm involved with Johns Hopkins, and with some investments I've made that are very promising, and with my boys, John and David. John made a contract with IMAX, went down to South America, and signed the U2 group. He films all their South American shows in 3-D.

If you have good health, age is just a chronological thing. If you don't have good health, you can be a miserable bastard at age forty. I celebrated my eightieth a few months ago, and now I'm getting closer to eighty-one.

My advice for the kids who are just starting out is work hard at it, make your hours count. And hopefully things will come your way. But there's no blueprint for success. You've got to work at it. Everyone in this book is a success because he worked at it.

I've had a great run. I'm very grateful for coming out of my illnesses and sustaining myself in business. I sold my team and I didn't know there was that much money in the world.

Turning point? For me it was when I sold my idea to ABC and to the Grand Union Company to allow me to put TV sets in their stores. We had a point-of-sale captive audience for advertisers. That got me on the air, and I stayed on the air for years.

My son John was at a meeting last week in California, and a guy brought him an idea—the guy thought he had a big idea and would make a bundle—it was to put sets in supermarkets. And John said, "Are you crazy? My father did that sixty years ago."

ART MODELL was born on June 23, 1925, in Brooklyn, New York.

STANLEY SHEINBAUM

A recent documentary about Stanley Sheinbaum, called Citizen Stan the Action Man, *is well named. Its subject is a former college economics professor who never shrinks from an argument, and never hesitates to embrace an unpopular cause. Stanley Sheinbaum helped Norman Lear found People for the American Way; engaged in the defense of Daniel Ellsberg in the Pentagon Papers trial; and has thrown open his home to fundraisers for countless political and humanitarian causes.*

FOR THE PAST TEN YEARS I've been the publisher of *New Perspectives Quarterly*. I publish it to reach an intellectual readership. There are two geniuses at work here. One is my good friend Nathan Gardels, who is the editor. The other is myself, a genius because I recognized his genius.

I had been active in the politics of Greece, helping free Andreas Papandreou from jail. Nathan and I were sitting on a wharf in Athens when we got the idea to develop *New Perspectives Quarterly,* and it has turned out to be very rich—I don't mean in money, but in quality.

I had a better view (because I'm older than Nathan) of the intellectual world and I had better contacts. So I was able to generate an interest in *NPQ,* which I turned over to Nathan and *he* is now the operating star of the magazine.

I taught at Stanford and at Michigan State University in the late 1950s, and then I met

Robert Maynard Hutchins, who had a view of academic work that fit my own thinking. I was anxious to leave university life, and when I met Hutchins, it led to a new attitude on my part toward academia.

The problem is that the education system is failing us. It is too oriented toward how to make a living. It ought to be about what is right and what is wrong with society.

I had become very opposed to the Vietnam War. America had taken over from France in 1954, and I had been made the head of a project by Michigan State University to develop an economic system, an agricultural system, and even a police system in Vietnam. I was already dubious about the U.S. role, and here I was running a project under contract to the U.S. government. The project had four components and fifty-two staff, all of whom I had recruited.

When I finally went to Saigon to see what I had accomplished—how my projects were going—I found that one quarter of the staff were CIA operatives. Nobody was supposed to know. *I* was not supposed to know. I was appalled and thus resigned from the project. I felt that a university should not be used by a clandestine organization for political purposes. I began to speak out more and more against these projects and also against the policy.

> *"I've got a pile of things on my mind I want to get involved in. That keeps me going."*

Think about knowledge. I didn't use the word "knowledge" before. There is a difference between the social sciences and the normative approach. The social sciences describe what is. The normative approach describes what *ought to be.* When you become convinced of that approach, you think in those terms—what *ought to be.* Today institutions are not giving us insights into what *ought to be,* so you can become very critical.

As I get older, I find there are more aspects of life, of society, that interest me. I've got a pile of things on my mind I want to get involved in. That keeps me going.

One thing leads to another. When I was focused on the social sciences doing mechanistic research, that is, the collection of infinities of facts, that stuff was not that intellectually interesting. But when I got into the normative question of "What ought to be?" and what questions ought to be asked, I found myself attracted to the next thing.

To the younger generations I would say: Find out what is intellectually interesting. Intellectual interest requires depth and substance—depth of approach to various problems.

Today, education doesn't give young people the ability to understand our society. I think that's a major problem. Most of our educational system today is geared toward how to live in this technological world. One should focus on understanding society and the world, to get the feel of what is important and what is not.

STANLEY SHEINBAUM was born on June 12, 1920, in New York City.

"My doctors have forbidden me to chase women unless they are going downhill."
—Duc de Richilieu

RAY EVANS

Ray Evans wrote the hit song "Que Sera Sera," but during his long-time collaboration with composer Jay Livingston, Ray Evans never practiced that bland philosophy. Evans and Livingston wrote countless hits (e.g., "Mona Lisa," "Buttons and Bows," "Silver Bells"), won three Academy Awards, and brought two musicals to Broadway.

THE YEAR I HIT NINETY, I had a big birthday party. A friend of mine took over the Hillcrest Country Club and had 250 people there. There were lots of stars. Now, I'm talking about having a ninety-fifth birthday party with the same folks.

About a month ago, I was in an auto crash. A woman went through a stoplight on Roxbury Drive. She totaled my car and almost totaled me. Now I'm doing chiropractics every morning.

Also every morning, I wake up and I say, "Wow! Okay, what a wonderful life I've had and I'm heading toward my ninety-fifth birthday."

I'm doing new things all the time.

I'm successful enough to be able to have nurses around the clock. They take care of my needs twenty-four hours a day. And I don't have to drive a car if I don't want to. That's one of the advantages of age for me.

Most of my songs with Jay Livingston were written for movies and for television. We had won three Oscars and were kind of the glamour boys on the block in Hollywood. We had done three movies with Rosemary Clooney, and she suggested us to Jose Ferrer, who was producing *Oh Captain* for Broadway with Tony Randall. It was a musical version of Alec Guinness's classic film *The Captain's Paradise.* Ferrer called us to his home. He said, "Write a couple of songs." We did, he liked them, and we were given the job.

It was a wonderful experience. There were a lot of things that went wrong with the show. The producer had sold over 100 percent of the stock, and he was a compulsive gambler. He had been in a lot of high-stakes poker games with Walter Matthau and Jule Styne. When we got to the dog days of July and audiences fell off, there was no money in the bank. It had been lost at the poker table. The show closed.

Broadway was a completely new experience in all kinds of ways, good and bad. It was one of my dreams. That's one of the things I wanted most of my life—to be on Broadway, and we did it twice.

Our second show on Broadway was called *Let It Ride,* a musical version of the George Abbott comedy of the 1930s, *Three Men on a Horse.*

I come from a little town sixty miles south of Buffalo. Before I became a lyricist, I worked as a musician. I played sax and clarinet. I wasn't very good. But my partner, Jay Livingston, was a very good musician and a really talented man.

I was just an average musician. I had a bad sense of rhythm. We spent a lot of time on cruise ships. The Holland American Line liked us and we could have any cruise we wanted. We went on trips to the Caribbean, the West Indies, a sixty-day cruise to Russia, a sixty-day cruise to South America.

Coming up the Hudson River on our last journey, I said to Jay, very naïve and ignorant of what was involved: "Let's go to New York and write songs."

A lot of years later, with a lot of incredibly lucky breaks, we got to the point where I can talk about my career in Hollywood and on Broadway.

I went to the Wharton School of Finance. I was a Phi Betta Kappa, and I couldn't get a job. It was during the Depression and I was also very bad in an interview. I had no confidence in myself. Thank God, I never got a job. Otherwise, I wouldn't have had the wonderful life I've had.

"I'm proud that I'm ninety-one. I'll take every year."

The list of people who have given us a lift on our course is unbelievable. It started with Olsen and Johnson on Broadway in *Hellzapoppin'.* Ole Olsen brought us to Hollywood. That's how we got our first song on the Hit Parade in 1941. But a little accident interrupted our career. It was called World War II.

Jay was drafted. I wasn't because I played football in college and a couple of varsity guys fell on my knee and I never walked right after that. Jay had an interesting time in the Army. In the middle of the winter he was in Long Island Sound in an Army overcoat with a shotgun, looking for Russian submarines. He was an asthmatic and he couldn't keep going. When he got out of the Army, we started over again.

We finally got a job on a "B" movie. It was going to be an epic. The picture wasn't important enough to impel anyone to record our song, but we met Johnny Mercer, who was running Capitol Records. He heard the songs we had written for the movie and he liked them. And a week later a call comes in from Capitol. "Mr. Mercer heard a song you wrote called 'The Highway Polka' and he'd like to perform it." He had a radio show in those days. He did our song three times and always mentioned our names.

Since then, a lot of stars have sung our songs. Jane Russell sang "Buttons and Bows" to Bob Hope, Doris Day sang "Que Sera Sera." Both tunes won Academy Awards. And Nat King Cole sang "Mona Lisa."

But there were some songs that didn't win the Oscar—"To Each His Own." The studio that produced the film asked us to write a song with that title that could be played on the air and publicize the film. But when they heard the song, every record company turned it down. So *Billboard* magazine had a review that said "A new band has just recorded 'To Each His Own,' and we predict it will be a hit." They were right, and it led us to write songs for thirteen Bob Hope movies, and to many awards and other successes.

But there were frustrations. We did a song called "Tammy" for the Debbie Reynolds film. The picture opened, and after three days, the distributors are pulling it out of the theaters because nobody is coming to see it. Then the song was released and became an overnight hit. So the same theaters that had pulled the movie out put it back in. It ran forever. It was Universal's biggest grossing movie up 'til then.

As a young man, I had very little confidence in myself. I had feelings of inferiority. I tried to fight it, but I couldn't. Today, I try to forget about it, and go through life thinking about the good times.

When I wake up every morning, I say, "I'm the luckiest guy in the world." And I've had a fantastic career. People are giving me great compliments. I can't believe what's happening. Life is so beautiful.

RAY EVANS was born on February 14, 1915, in Salamanca, New York.

RISE STEVENS

Rise Stevens played a major role in developing and assuring the future of opera in the United States. She brought opera to hundreds of American cities where it had never been available. And then millions more fell in love with her in movies like Going My Way *and* The Chocolate Soldier, *as well as her frequent radio appearances.*

I AM NOT EIGHTY-SOMETHING. I'm ninety-three.

I had a fabulous career. A beautiful career. I don't even think of problems with it. There were some, naturally, but you handle them at the moment, whatever way is possible.

Though I retired from singing opera, I have never left the Met. I am busy there as a member of the Board. I'm very much involved with the Metropolitan Opera. As a matter of fact, we have engaged another general manager. Peter Gelb is coming in and Joseph Volpe is leaving.

I haven't sung for years. I don't really miss it, but once in a while when I hear something that I'm very familiar with, then I start getting pangs. Otherwise, no. It was an enormous amount of work. If you love it, it's the most beautiful thing in the world. And I loved it. I loved my whole career. I had a wonderful husband who was really very involved with my career. God love him. I wish to God he were around today to see everything that's happening. There was no man like him.

What starts my engine in the morning? I have to get out of bed. Period. It's a question of energy. That's the whole thing. Energy and determination.

You say to yourself, "Now you have to get up!" and that's it.

They say that with the passage of years, we turn into new people. You're not aware of it, but I think as life goes on, you do change in very strange ways. In retrospect, I think about that. There were changes; that's bound to happen. As age comes on, you start changing.

I don't teach today. You have to have enormous patience for that. Unless you pick up exactly what I say, immediately, I get impatient. I know it's wrong, but that's the way I am.

I knew when I went into opera as a career that it was going to be very, very difficult. It took enormous concentration. It was a total involvement. I put years into studying before I even went out and sang professionally. Today, young people don't have the patience. They want to make a career. They come in, they have a lesson, and the next thing they know they're singing *Tristan and Isolde*. That to me is absolutely crazy.

With your own career, you've got to be very careful and very patient. You have to know exactly where you're going, and don't deviate.

I love being older. I get a great thrill out of listening to something that's very successful and very exciting that goes on at the Met, because that's where I am most of the time. That to me is very exhilarating and very beautiful.

I think the turning point in my career came when I went into film. I was debating whether I should do that. My husband was a great manager and he helped persuade me to take that step.

I made a couple of Hollywood movies—one with Bing Crosby and one with Nelson Eddy. Nelson and I were very good friends. We starred in *The Chocolate Soldier* together. That was my first experience in movies, and he knew that. He was very helpful, very collegial.

Then came *Going My Way* with Bing Crosby. I loved Bing. He and I got along very well. I understand that with many people he had a kind of stand-offish attitude. He didn't with me. We had a nice feeling with one another. I think it had to do with the fact that I didn't make movies most of the time. I had a different career outside of film and he recognized that.

There was a time when I thought of noth-

"*It's a question of energy. That's the whole thing. Energy and determination.*"

ing but *my* career, *my* singing, *my* life, and then suddenly, after retiring, I started thinking of other people, young people, and how they should build their lives. I give advice whenever I'm asked.

RISE STEVENS was born on June 11, 1913, in the Bronx, New York.

GRANT TINKER

It is said that the public will accept anything, even quality. Grant Tinker evidently subscribes to this view. He took NBC, the last-placed network at the time, and revitalized it by permitting series with poor initial ratings to survive long enough to find their audiences. Hence, quality shows like Family Ties, Cheers, *and* Hill Street Blues *carried NBC to dominance. And as head of MTM, he allowed television's most creative voices to be heard.*

I'VE NEVER BEEN much of an embracer of life, a celebrator. People have always thought of me as sort of a downer. It's just that I'm always worried about what I haven't done, or what I should be doing, or what I'm going to have to do next. It's not that I don't appreciate my life or what I've accomplished. It's just that I hurry by it in a rush to get to the next thing.

I don't remember ever having a really bad day in the fifty years that I worked. There are some jobs that are harder than others, some task where I may have stumbled a bit. But I was very lucky to have fallen into the business I did, because I enjoyed it. I enjoyed the people. All of that was to be celebrated, but I don't know how to celebrate things. It's very internal with me.

When I was younger, within the first ten years of my working life, I got very anxious. I couldn't tell you why exactly. This was a time when shrinks were not, at least among my friends, something that anyone either talked about or did. But my anxiety was such that I sought one out and spent quite a bit of time—up to four times a week at one point—just trying to figure out what the hell I was worried about. I never did get anywhere.

But I did come out on the other side, and it obviously did me some good, because the severe anxiety went away. Then I just felt anxious to the extent that everybody is anxious. Today, having touched all the bases and having done it for fifty years, I guess I would celebrate it by going back and doing it again. I would enjoy it. But I'm getting to the point where old age is clearly the writing on the wall.

I'm eighty. I think it would be odd if one didn't think about getting older. Things happen to your body. Parts begin to go as well as your memory. And all the things happen that people talk about so frequently and humorously, or that they *pretend* to be humorous about. But you do realize that you're not that far from taking a major walk. I'm just hoping I do it well.

What starts my engine in the morning? It's that New England Jonathan Edwards kind of thing my dad drummed into me. You've got to get up and do something. My father was a very hard worker and he came from a line of hard workers, so it's kind of natural. I don't mean that I could never sleep in if I had the opportunity on a Sunday.

> *"I regret now that I didn't work another eight to ten years."*

I think you've got to have some specific activity or goal or job, to have that feeling of urgency. Now, urgency to me is—have I tipped all the people at the golf course?

I regret having retired too early. My dad worked for about fifty-five years and gave it up at around seventy. I gave it up earlier than that. I became involved in some do-good things in the community. I thought I could make a day out of that. I regret now that I didn't work another eight to ten years.

I have only the most pedestrian advice to offer the coming generation. I took everything very seriously and urgently and I worked my ass off, and there were years in the beginning when I didn't take vacations. I used to kid people and say, "If I go away, they're going to find out somebody else can do my job better than I can."

Actually, there was some truth to that. I was not quite as confident as I might have been. I run into young people and they've got it knocked. They know they should enjoy it as they go—not just the work but the downtime, the away time. I was not good at that. If you're not good at it, you should *learn* to be good at it. No one ever said to me, "Don't work a hundred percent of the time." I made the mistake of doing it that way. You could say, "That's okay, you succeeded." I think I could have succeeded just as well, maybe better, if I had balanced my life a little more. You should start smelling the roses almost immediately in your working life, and I didn't know how to do that. I thought it was wrong to even think about it.

That would be one bit of advice. The other—don't pack it in too early. We live longer these days. My wife reminds me of this sometimes. She says, "You still have some pretty good ideas and you could be useful." Once you've retired, it's very hard to go back.

I was always embarrassed when I found myself involved in a television show that wasn't quality. I was reminded of one last night. *60 Minutes* did a piece on Howard Stern. I fired Howard Stern because I didn't want his stuff on NBC. He was doing very well on the NBC radio station in New York. I heard it and I said to Bob Walsh, "Get rid of this guy." Walsh said, "He's going to do awfully well somewhere else." I said, "Fine. Let him do that."

No one ever told me to seek quality. I guess it was a matter of what I enjoyed—my personal taste.

I was crazy about good writers. There used to be so many fine writers. There aren't now. I don't know where the hell they've gone. There's much less demand for them. With all the reality shows, there's not that much of an apple to grab.

I wasn't a writer. I could write if I sat down and tried. With a lot of sweat and tears I could turn out something decent. But not like these guys I'm talking about that I truly admire. I wanted to work with them. I respected them so much that I wouldn't dare alter their work—I would sometimes make a suggestion, but mostly I was just thrilled to be associated with them.

When I went to NBC in the 1980s, I thought the public was awfully slow in coming around to some quality shows. But they finally did.

GRANT TINKER was born on January 17, 1926, in Stanford, Connecticut.

LIZ CARPENTER

From a fledgling reporter covering the press conferences of Franklin and Eleanor Roosevelt, to the press secretary for Lady Bird Johnson, to writer of spontaneous humor for President Lyndon Johnson, Liz Carpenter has been wired to the White House and the world of the Washington press corp. An award-winning journalist, Liz is the author of the best-selling Ruffles and Flourishes.

I'VE HAD A GOOD TIME for my eighty-five years. I've seen a lot of action as a reporter and then working at the White House. I've always lived in the world of words, and they've served me well. I've written four books and all of them are lighthearted. I still earn a living making speeches and writing of life's experiences.

There are certain advantages to being my age. I've seen so much of history being made. That happens if you've been a reporter or have been associated with people in public life. Following a story on television is still a big habit of mine—watching what's happening each day.

When you're older, it's important to feel needed. I live in my own home and I keep a steady stream of people of all ages coming through. I entertain quite a lot. I think to be set aside in a retirement home with everybody of the same age would be desolate. I do think laughter helps a lot. It embodies your own view of yourself. I remember from my childhood on, my mother saying, "Try to see humor in the situation."

In today's world, there's a grand turmoil being stirred up by President Bush. I'm working on a book called *From George the First to George the Worst*. It's a collection of humor of the forty-three presidents and nearly every one of them had something he called humor, even though presidential humor didn't really come out of the closet until Lincoln's time.

I first went to Washington back in the early 1940s as a reporter, and I called on my Congressman, whose name was Lyndon Johnson. Franklin and Eleanor Roosevelt were in the White House. I was in love with being a reporter. I got a job for twenty-five dollars a week at a small news bureau headed by a woman we called "The Duchess." She helped me get a press pass to cover the president as well as Eleanor. It wasn't hard to get passes for Capitol Hill. The people running the country were much more accessible then.

The glory days for me were when Lyndon Johnson became Majority Leader of the U.S. Senate and Sam Rayburn was Speaker of the House of Representatives. At that time I'd married Les Carpenter. He was also a reporter. We represented eighteen papers, most of them in the Southwest.

When LBJ became president, I worked for Lady Bird as her press secretary. LBJ would send Jack Valenti to see me. "Tell Liz to get me some jokes," he'd say. He wanted some topical humor for his speeches. So I put together a handful of people I considered the funniest in the White House, and we met every Thursday in my office in the East Wing. One of them was Ernie Cuneo, who had worked in the Roosevelt days. He would appear with a bottle of good Scotch and we'd all sit around my office and sip Scotch and think about what was topical that we could make funny. It was a great time. I loved every minute of it.

LBJ used a lot of Johnson City stories of rural life in the Texas hill country. The best humor for a president is when it has shaped him, from his own roots. Some of the speech writers who were left over from the Kennedy days would try to give Johnson Martha's Vineyard jokes, but they didn't play with this Texan.

I traveled with LBJ and Lady Bird during the 1960 campaign when he was running for vice president. Then we did a Lady Bird Johnson special in 1964 when Johnson was running for president. In both campaigns, we made whistle stops, which is my favorite form of politicking. If you stop at a small town, everybody turns out. In 1964 we made forty-seven stops in four days through the South. We held four of the eight states for the Democrats, even in the wake of Johnson's civil rights legislation.

"When you're older, you realize and appreciate all you've seen in the history of our world."

Today I still feel propelled by my intense interest in politics. I'm still campaigning for Democrats, of course. I'm dismayed at the high cost of electing people, which I think creates corruption.

Young people today don't have much sense of history. I don't know why that is, because they have more information than ever. Maybe they are so overridden with information that they don't have time to enjoy the past.

I think they are all such creatures of television. In fact, the worst audience in the world today is high school or college students because they don't respond. They don't *have* to respond to a TV set. I grew up in the Depression—we didn't call it "The Great Depression" at that time. People who went through it didn't think it was so great. But I grew up in a time when you had an appreciation for your fellow man.

The death of my husband was the big turning point in my life. We were very much a reporting team in Washington—Liz and Les Carpenter were often a joint byline. After his death when I was fifty-three, I came back to Texas. The Republicans were in, and it wasn't much fun for me anymore. Today I have a whole different world down here, and I'm still very interested in what's happening on the national scene.

LIZ CARPENTER was born on September 21, 1920, in Salado, Texas.

*"I believe we live
two lives—the lives we learn
with and the lives
we live after that."*
—The Natural

RALPH YOUNG

Feuer and Martin produced five smash musicals in a row, including Guys and Dolls, The Boy Friend, *and* How to Succeed. *Therefore, when they chose Ralph Young to star in their newest musical,* Whoop-up, *Ralph celebrated. But the show opened during a long newspaper strike, went unreviewed, and promptly died. Ralph Young soon joined French singer Tony Sandler and fashioned a bilingual act. If you've ever seen Sandler and Young onstage, you know how well the story turned out.*

SOMETHING HAPPENED to me when my daughter was in a coma and I had to rush to her side in a San Francisco hospital. The first thing I see is the doctor coming toward me. He was a little man. I can still see his face.

I said, "How's my daughter?" And these are the words that are indelibly imprinted in my head. He said, "You've got to let me know when to pull the plug, so we can donate her organs."

From there, I went to my daughter's little apartment where she was living at the time. There was a sign on the refrigerator. I didn't pay any attention to what it said. Then, little by little, this doctor was proved to be wrong, and my daughter today is doing great. You know what the sign read?

"Question authority!"

That's what I tell people. Everybody I listened to in my early years in show business said, "You're going to be this, you can't do that." All the naysayers and the prophets of gloom, they don't know. Only *you* know. I don't know the secret of success, but I know the secret of failure. It's trying to please other people.

"Question authority!"

Some doctors are better than others. I heard one doctor on television talking about a medical group that went into a retirement home. They did all sorts of tests on the folks. They took their pulse, they took their blood pressure, they took their heart rate—everything you would take before an operation. They got the numbers. Then they talked to these people about their lives. Then they took the same tests again. And now these folks had the blood pressure of youngsters! All the readings were like a young kid and all because they were talking about their lives, and the pitfalls and what they had been through.

I think of that a lot. Whenever I got to take my blood pressure, I think about that. And son of a bitch—the reading is like a young guy. I know I'm going to go off one of these days, but I'm always making jokes about it. I'm not sitting here with my hands on my cheeks, waiting.

Things are never as bad as you think they are, and they're never as good as you think they are. I remember something Walter Winchell wrote about me in his column in the *New York Daily Mirror*: "For a dozen years, Ralph Young, a handsome man who can sing, went nowhere

"I'm not sitting here with my hands on my cheeks, waiting."

along the Broadway carousel. Last year, it looked as though he finally had it made. He teamed up with a comic for television at night spots, but the bookings were scarce. They slid and Ralph Young was reduced to handling the production girl numbers in a Broadway bistro, but that folded too and he was broke. Two weeks ago, he had lost it all, had told everyone he had had it and would take a job as a pitchman in a five-and-dime store. But that was two weeks ago. He's the happiest man in New York right now. He has the season's big plum—the lead in the new musical *Whoop-up*. Moral: Broadway is the toughest street in the world to lick but look how many have licked it."

The punch line is—six weeks later, *Whoop-up* had folded. It opened during a newspaper strike, did not get reviewed, and passed out of existence.

The show had been produced by Cy Feuer and Ernie Martin, the kings of the Broadway musical. They had had five hits in a row—*Guys and Dolls, The Boyfriend, How to Succeed, Where's Charlie,* and *Silk Stockings*. But my show died. It was like a stab in the heart.

At that point, I thought they were right about my having failed all through the years. I must be under a cloud, I thought. Then I found Tony Sandler and we formed a singing act. The voices of gloom emerged. Friends called Tony, "You're going to work with Ralph? A failure for thirty-five years?" But Sandler and Young was the biggest thing that ever happened to me. Tony and I had a long glittering career together. The climax was at the Plaza Hotel in New York. They gave us twenty-two minutes on the *Today* show.

Now, forty-five years later, Tony and I have an Internet site where we sell albums of our songs. Every one of the orders comes in with a message: "Christmas won't be Christmas unless we can hear Sandler and Young." To this day, the songs must move people and that's what keeps me going. People stop me on the street and tell me, "Whenever we were in Las Vegas we had to go see you guys." I've been in a hospital when some woman in a hospital room saw me pass in the corridor and came out and said, "My father just recognized you. Could you come in and say hello?" I went in, and when I left, she said, "You did more for my dad than all the doctors."

They wanted me to star in the *Palm Springs Follies*. That's a stage review in which they offer a picture of an era sadly past, in which singers, dancers, jugglers, and octogenarian showgirls offer a look at a bygone era. And they feature a star from Memory Lane. They've had Frankie Laine and Howard Keel and Kaye Ballard. They wanted me.

I thought I would give it a crack. But my friends said, "Ralph, you're making a big mistake. Why do you want everyone to know you're an old man?" But I had not appeared alone for decades. I wanted to see if I had anything to offer at my age. Well, I had never gotten a reaction like I did at the *Follies*, unless it was with Tony. And here I was alone, and people loved it. The accolades as I was leaving the theater were like an adrenaline shot. From then on, the people who told me not to do the show were telling me, "It's adding ten years to your life!"

RALPH YOUNG was born on July 1, 1918, in the Bronx, New York.

NINA FOCH

Nina Foch was generally cast as cool, aloof, and sophisticated. In An American in Paris *she subsidized Gene Kelly in his artistic efforts. In* The Ten Commandments *she served the Biblical vision of Cecil B. DeMille. In* Executive Suite *she lent elegance to the work of director Robert Wise. Today she teaches a class in acting at USC and the American Film Institute, where her talent and insight guide a new generation.*

I HAVEN'T ENJOYED getting old. It's very uncomfortable. Physically, it's not good. If I didn't have a very strong will, I wouldn't be able to do it, because my body is not behaving as well as my mind. That's the way it is. I don't spend much time with many people my own age who are not doing anything. They bore me.

There are many advantages to being old. You're smarter about an awful lot of things and your insights are much better. I'm having trouble learning new computer programs, because you simply can't do that kind of thing when you get old. As for the things I know—and I'm always delighting myself by knowing the answer to things—I say, "Where'd I get that?" I just have these answers. That, of course, is the accumulation of a lifetime of reading and thinking and doing things.

I'm a professor at USC and have been, off and on, with a stint at the American Film Institute, since 1965. I teach Film Directing in the Graduate Film School.

I have been for many years a consultant with directors and actors. I prepare films with directors because most directors don't know how to prepare. They can do a certain amount of preparation—the technical part—but they're not capable of doing the really in-depth human preparation of the material. I teach them how to do that.

For a while, I had an acting studio but I stopped it because people didn't work hard enough for me. Now, I only work with actors on particular roles. I charge so much money that nobody comes to me except people who mean to work!

Of course, all along I've been acting, too. Last year, I did *NCIS* and Hallmark. I'm still doing that, but not very often (because there are not many parts for eighty-one-year-olds). This year, I did *NCIS* again with an age makeup in the same part.

I've been directed by a good many directors. Some were good in one way and some in others. The ones I enjoyed the most were Sidney Lumet and Mark Rydell.

I have many regrets. I didn't make right decisions about my career. Over and over I made mistakes. A big mistake, for instance, was the year I was nominated for the Academy Award. I foolishly did *The Ten Commandments*. It tied me up for a terribly long while at a time when I was getting many, many offers to do really interesting things. The reason I did *The Ten Commandments* was that I felt I should work with Cecil B. DeMille because he was a part of the history of filmmaking. I learned many things from him and I really liked him. He was an interesting man, his politics aside.

> *"It would be a pity if I went to my death without giving back all this great stuff that I've learned."*

Luckily for me, I'm doing something now that makes me feel useful. People do come to me for wisdom and that gives me great pleasure. Anyone who feels obsolete in their eighties hasn't put themselves in a position where they're teaching the young. It would be a pity if I went to my death without giving back all this great stuff that I've learned. It's not that I'm so golly whiz. It's just that I've studied with the greatest teachers and I've worked with very interesting people, and I know a hell of a lot. I just know it. I enjoy giving back these techniques because they're so exciting.

I have never taken a vacation in my life. Every time I tried to, I got another job, so I never could. I've always lived in a very pretty environment and I like that. I've always enjoyed cooking, although now I can't do it. My health is such that I mostly eat out or I have people cook for me.

I've one bit of advice for the younger generation: Stop indulging yourself. Demand the most from yourself. Don't pay attention to the present day habit of accepting your failings.

Be tough on yourself. Demand the best of yourself. Nobody loves you as much as you do. Others may be indulgent with you. Don't you do that. You be as tough as you can on yourself. And then life will be wonderful and well worth living.

NINA FOCH was born on April 20, 1924, in Leiden, the Netherlands.

BUD YORKIN

Back in the 1970s, Bud Yorkin and Norman Lear turned the television business on its ear. They became the most influential people in the history of the TV medium. All in the Family, Maude, Good Times, *and* The Jeffersons *were pioneering comedy shows that were acerbic, literate, witty, and explored mature subjects after years of TV shows featuring hillbillies and talking horses.*

ONE OF THE THINGS you have to look at is: What are your choices as you arrive in your eighties? Many of the things that used to be an open door, those things aren't open to you anymore. Billy Wilder never got another job from the time he was about sixty-nine. He never got another picture made.

This unique entertainment industry that we're in really does go for youth. I don't necessarily find anything wrong with that. I would say it's similar to a kid graduating from Harvard and going into a law firm and they stick him in the library and he moves up. I think that's true with show business. They always want to find a young genius. The young people are now in the executive suites, and they are hiring young people.

I feel, in a way, that I'm outside that ring today. I'm not in the area where I can do the things that I did in the past. I do work to raise money for certain things that are important to me, which I guess takes some creativity. Anyone that sends me a script, I read it. I give them my opinion and if I have any thoughts that are helpful, I offer them. I get pleasure out of that, but it's not as though I'm trying to come up with something for myself.

I still have a good deal of intellectual curiosity. I read the *New York Times* every day. I was deeply involved with Bill Clinton. I was the first one to open up California show business for him. His first dinner was at my home.

Politics is an area that occupies a great deal of my time. I write letters complaining about issues that trouble me. And I express my point of view to other people. I read a lot. I find I'm reading books that I never had time to read before. This is a wonderful country, but where's it going? I have concerns about it for my family and for the nation. Where are my kids heading? Why is this country taking a turn? I don't remember it ever being as bad as it is right now.

Somebody once said, "Life can only be understood backwards but it must be lived forward." We can look at it backwards, but we've got to live it forward. That's very true.

Do I believe that I'm as creative as I was? No, I don't think so. I think the reason I'm not is that I've reached a point in my life where I enjoy not having the pressure of having to make a living. So I spend more time with my family.

I'm fortunate enough to have had a second family. I've gotten a second bite at the apple. I now have children who are eleven and thirteen. I know that I missed a great deal with my older children because I was working all the time. I don't want to do that this time around.

There's a filter on what I allow to upset me today. When I was younger and doing radio and television—most of it was "live" during the so-called Golden Age of Television—I felt an enormous amount of pressure on me. I was able to handle it but, I must say, it took something out of me. I don't let things get to me that much anymore. It would have to be something significant. I put a lid on how upset I'm going to get.

To be honest, I think a lot of my success was luck. Being in the right place at the right time. I got into the television industry when it was just beginning. That certainly boded well for me. The other thing was that, for whatever reason, I seemed to be able to get somebody's confidence and they went with me. Even the first movie I ever did—with Frank Sinatra and Lee J. Cobb—for some reason, I wasn't terrified directing those people. I felt they got along with me and trusted me. I worked with a lot of people that folks said were difficult. I didn't find them difficult. When I did the Fred Astaire show, everyone said, "Well, you know Fred is so meticulous. He'll drive you crazy." I loved his calm and precision. We got along famously."

I had a pretty firm idea of what I wanted to do and Astaire bought most of it. The reason I

"How many more summers have I got left? I want to enjoy every one."

got that job was interesting. He was interviewing people. I came in and his first line to me was, "What would you do with me?" And I said, "I don't know what I'd do, but I'll tell you what I wouldn't do. Astaire said, "What's that?" And I said, "I wouldn't open the show with you coming out with top hat and tails and singing a song you're famous for. I would open with a Count Basie vamp, where you were by yourself doing something that was very cool...."

Three days later I got the call that Astaire wanted me to create his show.

I can tell you about how meticulous he was. I was in the control room and we were going on the air in thirty seconds, and I said to the stage manager, "Tell Fred, thirty seconds." The show was being done live. It was a huge undertaking. We had four studios and four different crews. We fed the music in from David Rose and his orchestra in another studio.

When I said, "Tell Fred, thirty seconds," I had a close-up on Astaire's feet. The camera was going to pull back. I suddenly see his hand come into the shot and he calmly started to straighten his shoelaces. And I thought to myself: "So composed—so devoted to perfection—to make sure his shoelaces were aligned."

We were up for nine Emmys with the Fred Astaire Special, and we won all nine. Fred and I walked over to a party at the Beverly Hills Hotel and President Eisenhower was waiting to talk to him on the phone.

I don't exactly stop and smell the roses. I can't afford to at this moment. I get up every morning and look forward to the day. I say, "How many more summers have I got left?" I want to enjoy every one.

What gets me out of bed in the morning? Getting my kids to school. I'm up at six. I wake them at 6:30. We go down and have breakfast together and they get dressed and I car-pool. That's my daily routine. There's something wonderful about that because I never had time to eat breakfast with my kids. And if I did have time, I would run to the phone because it was either a meeting or a script that had to be rewritten.

There are some advantages to aging. Number one, I think I'm wiser. Number two, I can see a finite time for my life. When you're younger, you don't think about that. Now I do have those kinds of thoughts.

Every day I reflect what was good about that day and what I can take out of it. I try to do that on a daily basis.

I ask myself: What can I look forward to today? I put down some things that I'll do. Maybe I'll hit some golf balls. I want to finish a script I'm writing. I can sit down and spend a couple of hours on it. I look forward to the kids coming out of school at three. I want to take them someplace and we'll have some fun. I think about the day in terms of just enjoying life, which I didn't have time to do when I was young.

BUD YORKIN was born on February 22, 1926, in Washington, Pennsylvania.

"If I were running in the stadium, ought I to slacken my pace when approaching the goal? Ought I not rather to put on speed?"
—Diogenes

JUNE HAVOC

Her mother Rose became the prototype of every ambitious stage mother. Her sister Gypsy became an "intellectual" stripper and the subject of a groundbreaking musical starring Ethel Merman. June Havoc's own life has been a fascinating and tempestuous journey—Vaudeville, Broadway debut in Pal Joey, *Hollywood stardom in films like* Gentlemen's Agreement, *and two cosmic memoirs. Actress-dancer June Havoc, in her nineties, is as fiery and passionate as ever.*

I WROTE A COUPLE of memoirs—*Early Havoc* and *More Havoc*. I love writing. Right now I'm in the middle of a book with Hilary Knight. I'm doing the text and he's doing the illustrations. It's funny and it's wise, like the famous *Eloise* books that Hilary illustrated for Kay Thompson. His drawings are magnificent!

I'm surrounded with beauty. My animals give me an enormous insight into the world. I'm a member of Wildlife and Best Friends and all sorts of animal associations.

I don't know how I handled some of the stress and anxieties in my life. They've been so terrible. I just try to keep my head above water and be proud of myself, no matter what. I try not to let them get to me.

The stress is worse today because of the political scene. The world seems so horrible now. There's so much more to worry about.

I've been at it professionally since I was three. That's a long time. That's ninety years.

You can't help but think about age. Everything starts to fall off. You can't do anything you used to do. You can't drive or swim or do things physically. I used to be a very active person. Now, I'm arthritis bound. I don't get out of bed. But I've been "smelling the flowers" for the last ten years. My farm is wonderful. I have animals, zoo animals, wild animals. They give me great pleasure. I love

"I try to keep my head above water and I try to be proud of myself."

the growing and the seasons. The green and the autumn and the spring and the snow. Oh nature! That's my greatest joy!

I have only one thing to say to the young. If you want to do something, nothing in the world should keep you from doing it. If you want to do something bad enough, if it's your life, you'll do it. I don't know anything else.

JUNE HAVOC was born on November 8, 1916, in Vancouver, BC, Canada.

PETER MARSHALL

Peter Marshall was a twenty-five-year-old show business veteran when he was chosen to emcee a game show called Hollywood Squares. *Fifteen years, four Emmys, and five thousand episodes later, Peter Marshall and* Hollywood Squares *had outlasted five presidents to become one of the longest running game shows in television history.*

I LAUGH AT MY AGE. Eighty is really old? I'll be eighty next week. Give me a break. When I was a kid, *fifty* was old.

My father died at thirty-eight, my grandfather at forty-five. I had four uncles; just one lived to be sixty. When I was a youngster I said, "Hell, let's have some fun!"

I've never thought about age.

What engages me today? You would think it would be golf or that kind of thing. But what engages me today is my work. My family is the most important thing to me—my wife Laurie, my four kids, my eleven grandkids—but I wouldn't be quite as happy with my family if I didn't have my work. Work is so important to me. Right now I'm producing and starring in a show devoted to the great female songwriters.

When I was sixty they found I had cancer. I was doing *La Cage aux Folles,* the great Jerry Herman musical. It had just opened in Philadelphia. They found this tumor in my left kidney and one in my right kidney. If you can believe it, I wasn't panicked at all. I knew it was going to be okay. The surgeon removed my left kidney and part of my right. He said I'd be out of *Le Cage* for six months. I was back in six weeks.

I don't see any advantages to age. Not really. My golf game was much better when I was younger. I'm singing just as well, but I can't do a lot of things I could do. If they asked me to do *Le Cage* today, I don't think I could do it. The only advantage to age is you might be a little smarter and you don't take things as seriously. I enjoyed my youth and I miss a lot of things about it.

My advice to the young—Don't take yourself too seriously. Enjoy what you're doing and remember, as famous as you may become, they won't know who the hell you are in thirty years. Ask a youngster about Bing Crosby or Al Jolson or Maurice Chevalier. They won't know. The guy who helped me and was my idol was Dick Haymes. Nobody remembers Dick Haymes.

The turning point in my life came when I was offered the chance to host a new TV game show called *Hollywood Squares*. That was a thirteen-week job that turned into sixteen years. I wasn't thrilled with the show. I didn't want to do it, yet it was a huge turning point. People still remember that show; not the young kids, but

> *"The only advantages to age is you might be a little smarter and you don't take things as seriously."*

my peers. *Hollywood Squares* made me independent and gave me a name of sorts.

Paul Lynde was hilarious. He tried his best to dislike me. Paul didn't like many people. He liked me 'til he learned how much money I was making. Then he *hated* me. Except for me, all the stars on the show received the same money. It was a "favored nation" arrangement. Everyone received $750 for the day we taped. I told the producers, "You should pay Paul more. He's a great addition to the show. Just tell the others it's a favored nation except for Paul." And they did.

I remember the first joke Paul Lynde did on the show. I asked him, "Why do motorcyclists wear leather?"

And Paul said, "Because chiffon wrinkles."

What I've enjoyed the most was starring in stage musicals. Besides *Le Cage*, I've done *The Music Man, Bye Bye Birdie, Anything Goes, High Button Shoes*, etc.

I've had a great life. I sang with big bands in my teens, starred on Broadway with Julie Harris, Chita Rivera in London, played a short Jew in the Neil Simon farce *Rumors*, and made a CD called *Boy Singer*. I've written a memoir called *Backstage with the Original Hollywood Square*, was half the comedy team of Noonan and Marshall, produced reviews at the

McCallum Theater in Palm Desert, and hosted *Hollywood Squares.* But what I've really enjoyed the most is getting up in front of an eighteen-piece band and singing those great standards. What could be better than that?

PETER MARSHALL was born March 30, 1926, in Huntington, West Virginia.

MARSHA HUNT

Marsha Hunt had a thriving film career, acting in fifty movies before the dark shadow of "scoundrel time" settled on Hollywood. Since then she's been in eight. Though never associated with left-wing causes, Marsha Hunt became a leader of the campaign against the Hollywood blacklist, and thus became one of its victims. She has been involved in many charitable activities and worked for numerous UN projects. She is also a woman of immense charm.

THOUGH I'M IN SPLENDID health, partially diminishing sight and sound have slowed me down. This has taken me off all the committee boards of trustees I was on. I have trouble understanding people when they mumble, and people do mumble a lot. Because of macular degeneration, I can read, but only see two or three letters at a time. It takes forever just to get the basic news of the day. My mailbox is crammed every day and it's an effort just to work through the mail, which is largely pleas for worthy causes. The trouble with me is I'm interested in what they're doing and I really want to read all that material. There goes the day! I have to be ruthless to try to get any writing done, which is great fun for me—a treat after all that mail.

The advantages of upper age are enormous. I don't know how typical this is for people my age, but I wake up in the morning and it isn't, "What do I have to do today? Where do I have to be? What time am I due?" It's, "What do I feel like doing today?" Because to be widowed, for all the loss and the pain and poignancy of that, there *are* compensations about being entirely on your own for the first time in your life. There isn't someone else whose nervous system has to be considered, whose preferences or needs or temperament have to be blended with one's own. To just have the absolute choice of how to spend the day, how to fill it, or let it just go wandering on by contemplating the sky, the butterflies, the hummingbirds, the rose garden, whatever. Even that is okay. I find lots of compensations. There are bargain days for seniors at certain stores. I guess you can go to the movies at bargain rates. As an Academy member, I'm spoiled. I get sent the output of the year in the hope of nomination and then an Oscar.

Any advice for the younger generation? There are too many that come to mind, like what's the mad rush? One thing that is rarely mentioned is something that I think adds pleasure to life. Both my parents had it. I think the name for it is *appreciation*. To savor what you're eating. To savor the melody you're hearing. To savor the look of a sunset. Enjoy it, get into it, notice it, pay attention to it. If you can add to your own awareness, your enjoyment and appreciation of it, the whole thing is a lot more worth living.

At seventeen, I broke into movies at Paramount playing romantic leads—always ingénues—sweet, young things. I was burning to act then. Between the Paramount and MGM contracts there were a lot of freelance movies, some that were "Poverty Row" quickies. *Winter Carnival,* which Budd Schulberg wrote with Scott Fitzgerald, was among the more costly budget films I did.

Nothing was happening of real interest in my career until MGM let me commit my first and second screen suicides, and I was ecstatic to be at a major studio again and given a chance to play a wide variety of roles.

Pride and Prejudice was my first crack at comedy. I had the most wonderful time playing the bookworm of the five Bennett sisters. I relished singing off-key, wearing steel-rimmed glasses, squinting and being nearsighted, and emphasizing an already long neck.

It was total delight making *Pride and Prejudice,* with Laurence Olivier as Mr. Darcy. I had discovered Olivier on my own before *Rebecca* or *Wuthering Heights,* before all of that sudden stardom. I saw him in a small film he made in England, and was just overwhelmed. I memorized his name and kept looking for it. So to be in the same film with him was exciting. We never had any scenes together, but it was a delight to watch him work. I met him a few times afterward and found him immensely charming. And Greer Garson was a memorable Lizzie Bennett.

The House Un-American Activities Committee's investigation into Communist influence in the movie industry is a painful topic, but I think it's a very important one to make known to today's public. We need to be on guard against that kind of hysterical political virus sweeping the nation again.

I came to know of Dalton Trumbo as one of the Hollywood Ten. I knew that he was probably the preeminent screenwriter at the time that the bubble burst. Later, I knew him just slightly, because my husband "fronted" for him. With great courage, Robert allowed his name to go on a script that Dalton wrote so that Dalton could pay his bills and feed his family. Robert never accepted any payment for it. It was a very risky thing for any writer to do because if it had come out that Dalton had in fact written that screenplay, it would have been the end of Robert's career. Then in 1971 Dalton cast me in his anti-war masterpiece, *Johnny Got His Gun.*

I knew Ronald Reagan in those days socially, and then on the board of the Screen Actors Guild. Ronnie was very active and involved in Guild matters, as was George Murphy. I could have told you then that these two were destined for political futures, i.e., California Governor and then President Reagan, and U.S. Senator Murphy. They had great charm, they had an aptitude for getting things done. It was fascinating to watch how they got what they wanted passed. It was like clockwork. We liberals sat there with our heads spinning because it happened with such wonderful efficiency. They had a splendid appetite for things political.

"I wake up in the morning and it isn't, 'What do I have to do today?'… It's, 'What do I feel like doing today?'"

How am I engaged in life today? I guess the easiest answer is that I need a forty-eight-hour day. There is just never time enough to get anything done or to catch up with the things I want to know about. The one thing that can be praised about the 1950s' blacklist is that, for the first time in my life, it gave me free time, in which I was able to discover the outside world.

There hadn't been time for that before. I had lived on soundstages and had gone from one movie to another. Then, after a 1955 trip around the world, I became enamored of this planet and all its inhabitants. I fell in love with the United Nations. It became my mission to work in any way I could to further its goals of global peace and progress. It made more sense to me than anything I'd ever heard about. For twenty-five years, that was my life—studying, writing, producing, directing, speaking about the UN, trying to further public interest and understanding of it. I wasn't interested in the politics of it, but in all those specialized agencies that are out there improving the human condition in myriad ways. Americans hadn't even heard about them. This became a dedication for me and it remains that, although I have to be far less active. Now my happiest pursuit is writing songs—words and music. Almost fifty so far, melodic with crafted lyrics, like our standards.

Along around 1980, I started writing a book—*The Way We Wore*—a coffee-table book about the styles and customs of the 1930s and 1940s. That has taken over my life. There's a lot of fascination and nostalgia for the subject. It's largely a picture book but it also deals with the mood of the country in that era—the way things like the Depression and World War II affected the way women dressed. It was fun doing the book. It's having a lovely reception.

Then around the early 1980s, they made me honorary mayor of Sherman Oaks. It wasn't a full-time job and it's an ideal title, because there are no powers and no duties. You just carry the title around and show up at community events when you can. I became aware of the homeless existing in the San Fernando Valley of all places, which has come to be regarded as the bedroom of Los Angeles, where most people lived, but indoors, not in the streets. To learn there were thousands of people living outdoors here appalled me. So I sought out Tom Bradley, who was then the fine mayor of all Los Angeles, which includes the Valley, then the elected mayors of Burbank and San Fernando, and we started the Valley Mayors Fund for the Homeless. For eighteen years, I turned my life over to that. We had dozens of volunteers, were never paid a salary, and never paid office rent. We just worked as volunteer citizens. And we worked hard. It was an engrossing, badly needed thing to do.

I'm working on a book now—I hate to say "memoir" because they've now become an epidemic. It won't be the story of my life. It's going to be moments and episodes, just little fragments of time that I recall, that were poignant or funny or suspenseful, rewarding or awful— moments or episodes that strike me as perhaps interesting to someone else. Funny, you pull the cork and those memories start bubbling out.

MARSHA HUNT was born on October 17, 1917, in Chicago, Illinois.

MARV LEVY

Coach Marv Levy led the Buffalo Bills to four straight Super Bowls. After forty-seven years of coaching , he retired in 1997. In 2001 he was inducted into the Pro Football Hall of Fame. And in 2006, at the age of eighty, he was made the Bills' general manager. His hero is Winston Churchill and his motto is Churchill's words, "Never, never, never surrender."

I EMBRACE LIFE VIGOROUSLY. I'm the general manager of the Buffalo Bills and I returned this year after retiring as head coach some years ago.

I don't encounter any stress in my work, only adrenaline and excitement. I deal with problems the same way I always have. And it's as much fun as it ever was.

I've always been passionately committed to my work. I've put in long hours, but I've never "worked" a day in my life.

I've never thought about getting older. I'm old enough to know my limitations and young enough to exceed them.

What starts my engine in the morning? My alarm clock.

I'm afraid I don't spend much time "smelling the flowers." That sounds too lethargic to me. Rather than smell the flowers, I'd rather taste the delicacies.

My habits have changed through the years. I don't run five miles a day anymore. Three miles is enough.

I'm not looking for the next challenge. I don't have to look for it. It finds me.

Do I see any advantages in getting older? Oh, yeah! A *lot* older.

My advice to the youngsters just starting out? Know when to be serious. And know when to have fun.

And remember—ability without character will lose.

The "Eureka moment" in my life? The big turning point?

The day I was born.

> *"Do I see certain advantages in getting older? Oh, yeah! A lot older."*

MARV LEVY was born on August 3, 1925, in Chicago, Illinois.

DORIS LESSING

Doris Lessing's novels are often autobiographical and emerge from her life in Africa where she grew up in the British colony of southern Rhodesia. She was nominated for the Nobel Prize for Literature and her novel The Golden Notebook *is viewed by many—herself excluded—as a feminist classic.*

I SEEM TO DO NOTHING BUT write, speak, hold forth about being so old, what I think can be summed up by George Bernard Shaw's dictum, that we should be careful to choose our forefathers well. How he has been justified by our new knowledge about genes.

"Choose your forefathers well."

Of course it is important not to get involved in wars, epidemics, bird flu, mud slides, or famine, let alone find yourself living anywhere near an ocean, with the sea levels rising.

And there is always the imminent Ice Age to look out for.

DORIS LESSING was born on October 22, 1919, in Kermanshaw, Iran.

"I am long on ideas,
but short on time.
I expect to live to be only
about a hundred."
—Thomas A. Edison

A. C. LYLES

They call him "Mr. Paramount" or "Mr. Hollywood." In either case, A. C. Lyles is a legend. He had an office in the Reagan White House, and several other presidents—Ford, Carter, the senior Bush—have welcomed him to the Oval Office. His seven-decades career at Paramount stretches from office boy to movie producer to goodwill ambassador.

IN MAY I WILL BE eighty-eight years old and will have been associated with Paramount Pictures for seventy-eight years. You have to be active physically and you have to remain active vocally. I go out and speak a lot about Hollywood at colleges and dinners. They say "exercise your body." I think you have to exercise your brain as well. You can do that by talking constantly. My two closest friends in life have been Ronald Reagan and James Cagney. They were always active. Someone once said, "If you ask A. C. Lyles or Ronald Reagan the time of day they'll tell you how to make a watch." I talk a lot and reminisce a lot—I exercise my brain by talking.

Every week, I do a couple of appearances talking about my career at Paramount, talking about *Deadwood*, the series on which I am one of the producers, that appears on HBO. Last year, Governor Fletcher of Kentucky called me. A friend told him about me and [he] invited me to be his guest at the Kentucky Derby.

Then he came out to Paramount and had lunch with us.

Right now I'm writing a book of anecdotes about things that have happened to me in the seventy-eight years I've been at Paramount. I've told 3,100 stories and anecdotes, encompassing 750-some names. I talked to Arnold Schwarzenegger this morning, who's a dear friend. Last week I spent a day at his office with him, and that night we went to a screening. He was called to the stage and he started talking about our many years of friendship and how I had an office in the White House with Ronald Reagan. President Reagan had appointed Arnold physical fitness coordinator for the country and Arnold would come to the White House and I'd have lunch with them. In Arnold's remarks at the theater, he talked about me and my longevity at Paramount. "I have a message for A. C.," he said. "A weed never dies." He called just a while ago and said, "How's the weed?"

I've been blessed. On my tenth birthday in 1928, I saw a movie called *Wings*—the first picture to win the Academy Award. It was a silent movie with Clara Bow, Richard Arlen, Charles Buddy Rogers, and a new actor. He had about three minutes in the picture and he walked away with it. It got him a Paramount contract and he became the biggest star in Hollywood. His name was Gary Cooper.

"I have a very short resume—1928 to 2006, Paramount Pictures."

When I saw that movie, I said, "I want to work for Paramount. That's what I want to do—make movies." I got a job at Paramount and have been with them ever since. I have a very short resume—1928 to 2006, Paramount Pictures.

My first job was as an errand boy at a theater Paramount owned in Jacksonville, Florida. It was the Florida Theater. One day Mr. Zukor, the head of Paramount, came to town. I managed to meet him and asked him to take me to Hollywood and teach me to make movies. He said, "You go to school and keep in touch." I wrote him a letter every Sunday to keep in touch. I knew he was just waiting for me to come to the studio for my job, and I was saving my money to get to Hollywood. One day Gary Cooper came to the Florida Theater. I arranged to meet him and I said, "Mr. Cooper, I'm going to be at the studio with you." He said, "How do you know that?" And I said, "Well, Mr. Zukor is waiting for me. He has a job for me. I write him a letter every Sunday." He laughed and asked, "He ever answer you?" I said, "No. But he's aware of me and he's waiting for me to come out." He said, "Give me a piece of paper," and he wrote on it, "Dear Mr. Zukor, I'm looking forward....What's your name, kid?" I said, "A. C. Lyles." "...I'm looking forward to A. C. Lyles being with us at the studio. Respectfully, Gary Cooper." I put that in my next Sunday letter to Mr. Zukor. For the first time I heard from him. Not exactly him…I heard from his secretary—Sydney Becker. She wrote "Mr. Zukor feels you don't have to write every Sunday, write every three or four months…enough for him to keep you in mind." I kept writing Mr. Zukor every Sunday plus a letter for *her* every Sunday, too.

I bought a one-way train ticket, day coach, on the train. I had two big jars of peanut butter, three loaves of bread, and a sack of apples, and I got on the train with twenty-eight dollars that I had saved. When I got to Hollywood, I went to the Paramount gate. I said, "My name is A. C. Lyles and Mr. Zukor is waiting for me."

The guard was dubious, but I said, "Mr. Zukor is expecting me. You can call Miss Becker." Mr. Zukor remembered me and gave me a job as his office boy. I became like his second son. Cecil B. DeMille was a daily visitor to his office. Frank Capra would be there. Howard Hawks, Billy Wilder, William Wyler, and Preston Sturges would all be there and they all taught me how to make movies. I was in "school" every day and my professors were the greats of Hollywood.

I was getting fifteen dollars a week and Mr. Zukor would give me incentives and I would take notes. He once said to me, "I want you to buy a Cadillac. I want you to buy a lot in Bel Air—build a home there. I want you to live in Bel Air. Now, this is very important. I want you to dress British, but think Yiddish."

When I came to Paramount the pictures were silent. When television and sound came in,

Mr. Zukor took some of the pictures we had made and reshot scenes with sound, so they were silent with a talking sequence. I saw talkies come in, I saw color come in, I saw the big screen come in. I saw all the technology that is there now.

In the thirties, I remember some young stock actors were getting one hundred dollars a week, and they included William Holden, Susan Hayward, Robert Preston, the Gabor Sisters, and Anthony Quinn. We were producing fifty-five to sixty features a year—releasing more than one a week. There were 125 to 150 term or multiple contract actors and actresses, and fifty producers and directors. At the time, most women on the lot were typing, and there were very few minorities. Now they're writers, directors, producers, actors—even heads of studios like Sherry Lansing.

I've produced many westerns at Paramount. I love westerns. John Wayne was at the studio and we became close friends. HBO owns the domestic rights to the *Deadwood* series, and Paramount owns the foreign rights. David Milch, who co-created *NYPD Blue* and *L.A. Law,* came over to Paramount to create *Deadwood*. He said he grew up on my westerns and asked me to be a consulting producer on the show. It was an honor to say yes. David is a genius.

Ronald Reagan and James Cagney taught me many things in our long friendship. Ronnie said, "The bottle is always half full and if it's stormy, the sun's going to be out tomorrow," and I did find out that everything works its way out. I produced all those westerns on my own. I was pretty much a one-man studio within Paramount. I accepted the problems, and things always seemed to work out in the end.

In real estate there are three words—location, location, location. In my work, I have three words—obsession, obsession, obsession. When I was ten years old and saw that picture *Wings,* I said, "That's what I want to do. Work at Paramount and learn to make movies." I was ten years old, but I was obsessed. And today, every morning when I wake up, I am obsessed to get to the studio. I feel the same enthusiasm when I arrive at Paramount each morning as I did the first day I walked on the lot. I've been blessed that way. I think that helps my endurance and my longevity—being absolutely obsessed with what I do.

A. C. LYLES was born on May 17, 1918, in Jacksonville, Florida.

DEBORAH SZEKELY

Deborah Szekely is dedicated, energetic, and determined. She is also quite a remarkable woman. She founded the world class health spas, the Golden Door, and Rancho La Puerta. Volunteerism is the catalyst for her growth. Her efforts as a volunteer have brought her awards as Woman of the Year, the President's Council of Women's Service Award, and Benefactor of the Year. She is a lecturer, educator, fitness expert—a truly Renaissance woman.

HOW DID I GET HERE? There cannot be one answer, for I have led a charmed life—not one but many—each one distinct and each one building upon the preceding. Through all of them, the single thread—and my north star—has been how can I make a difference? From the beginning, this has been paramount. My husband long ago said, "When we began Rancho La Puerta in 1940, we wanted to 'make healthy people healthier so that they may change the world.'"

My many lives, career upon career, were not planned. Each one emerged spontaneously and the fact that they were successful surprised me as much as it did the onlooker. Today I am still a person in the process of becoming. My life makes no sense when I look at pictures and press clippings of fifty-plus years ago. I feel as though I am looking at a different person.

Of course, I was young and shy and very insecure—worried equally about the inconsequential things and the important ones—I didn't know one from the other. Even then, I was stubborn and determined, and trusted my gut instincts. By the time I had my first child in 1956, I was a tigress, vis-à-vis protecting her and assuring her future well-being. There was no challenge too great. I was determined to provide for both my daughter and son everything I lacked growing up—especially a stable, secure, respectable childhood.

My unusual mother—the old fashioned term "seeker of the truth" best describes her—led us from a prosperous Brooklyn home life (two children, two nannies, maid, and chauffeur) to a plaited coconut palm home on a lagoon in Tahiti, where my future was laid. Life as a child in Tahiti (1930 through 1934) and in Mexico (1935 and1939) not only prepared me for the pioneer life of early Rancho La Puerta, but Tahiti [was] where my family first met "the Professor": Edmund Szekely. When I was seventeen, he asked me to marry him.

When the two of us set off for Mexico to found the Ranch, I had already spent years working in a vegetable garden and doing without electricity, running water, and plumbing I knew how to cook on a wood stove, so preparing food for Rancho La Puerta's first guests in 1940 was hardly daunting. During those early days, when we charged $17.50 and asked guests to bring their own tent, the physical labor and

"I truly see aging as an opportunity— choices upon choices, rather than frustration."

long hours were a lark. I was housekeeper, chef, and chief correspondent, spending many nights by the kerosene lamp with an old Remington typewriter, sending letters to the professor's and my friends, explaining the virtues of our beautiful valley: the pure air, pure water, pure sunlight, garden-fresh organically grown food, goat milk and cheese—all this, plus a great mountain for hiking. Another lure was my husband's promise to lecture several times a week on the philosophy of the simple life. He spoke of "sustainability" long before it became a popular term for the eco-conscious life.

As the Ranch grew and prospered, I began to ascend a ladder, one rung at a time, through seven distinct careers. Each one utilized the same tools (my experiences) but in different ways. Another one of my husband's mottos was *Siempre Mejor* (always better). It was a greeting he used as he walked around the Ranch. In my mind I added the words "and always changing," and I lived it as if it were my personal creed.

Founding the Golden Door was inevitable. By the 1950s, numerous Ranch guests had begun asking me for a smaller, more private retreat for women only. I needed the challenge as well: I used to joke that I wanted myself and my two children to become accustomed to a life I never had, and so the Golden Door was a perfect entry into a world of intellectuals, sophisticates, and the glamorous—for I took care of them all. At first we accepted only twelve guests at $250 per week each. Today the Golden Door has metamorphosed into a Japanese inn at $7,500 per week—if you can get in.

From there I ventured on to found COMBO (San Diego Combined Arts and Education Council), an organization that served as a clearing house for arts and education fundraising. It became so successful that at one time we had a prime time Saturday night benefit auction that aired simultaneously on ABC, CBS, and NBC. You might say I became a *fundraiser par excellence*.

I ran for Congress in 1982, but was defeated in the primary—I was pro-choice much too soon.

I soon went to Washington, D.C. anyway, a la Mr. Smith, to try and make Congress more efficient. I conceived a Congressional management manual. *Setting Course* is now in its ninth edition and used by all the chiefs of staff in both Congress and Senate offices, especially the ones who are setting up the offices of incoming lawmakers.

Soon I was heading the Inter-American Foundation, where I served six years as president and CEO. It was an independent agency of the U.S. government, with a mission of grassroots development in every country of Latin America and the Caribbean except Cuba. Later, I would receive several appointments representing other choice and beneficial areas of U.S. foreign policy.

I learned a great deal in the process of giving away almost $100 million. I decided to "bring it home," and the result was Eureka Communities, a nonprofit I founded to work with, and connect, the CEOs of community-based nonprofit organizations throughout the United States so they could learn from each other.

I'm not sure where my path and the nation's Capitol would have led, because after seventeen years in Washington, I was suddenly called back to my home base of San Diego by my son's illness and his subsequent death from melanoma. All my best laid plans fell into disarray. I soon found, however (to my surprise), that taking back the baton and managing Rancho La Puerta was once again exhilarating.

I am enjoying the challenge today. It is a 24/7 task, but I am supported by a fine staff and many friends. My knowledge today makes it much easier. There is so much I have learned over the years that I find the well of energy refilled as quickly as it empties.

I truly see aging as an opportunity—choices upon choices, rather than frustration. The later years are a time when you are more experienced, with greater self-knowledge and expanded dreams—all ringed by possibilities. So many elders today think they have nothing to do but get old and sick. How wrong!

My guests and friends see me as a guru, a mentor—a heavy responsibility I take seriously and I try to set a good example. In the evening I speak to the guests and point out what aging represents today versus years go. Without fail, I observe that normal people today act and feel ten years younger than their parents—and people with high energy (the abnormal ones like me) seem twenty years younger. I am really not eighty-four, it is just a date on the calendar. In every way, shape, and form, I am the equivalent of sixty-four. It is my perception and my expectation for myself, and this, as far as I am concerned, can be a self-fulfilling prophecy.

I am very frugal—I hate waste and my deepest frustration now is the wasting of the lives of our elders, because our society "twins" the words "old" and "sick." If you're one, you must be the other. I rail against this stupidity. Our elders need to find a role other than simply waiting. Heaven knows it's not easy. The ads today are either about food or fast cars, and when they're not, they're selling drugs. Our reliance on drugs refutes Hippocrates's faith in the body's ability to regenerate itself as well as his admonishment to "do no harm."

My friends, all in their sixties—the peers I spend my spare hours with—share my passionate dream of building a better future. We love talking about politics and justice and what to do about them. There is so much we can do if we all put our shoulders to the wheel.

Today I find my greatest joy once again in service—in affecting the lives of my guests at the Ranch and Golden Door, two hundred people each and every week, hundreds of thousands over these many years. Yet I'm nagged by the thought that there's so much still to do…and lots of it I hope to do. It will be fun to live to a hundred!

DEBORAH SZEKLEY was born on May 3, 1922, in Brooklyn, New York.

RABBI LEONARD BEERMAN

Throughout a career involved in issues of peace and justice, Rabbi Leonard Beerman, a child of the Depression, has built a national reputation with his simple profundities and humanitarian instincts. His personal goal is to diminish the agony in the world and help his followers define themselves as human beings.

THE QUESTION THAT'S ALWAYS put before us is the very question put to Adam in the Garden: Where are you? Where are you in your life? Of those years allotted to you, what are you doing with yourself?

My answer is that I'm still searching for the answer. Maybe the searching is what gives me whatever vitality I have. That question that first came to me when I was very young still clings to me now that I'm old; maybe something of the young person is still very much alive in me.

I am filled with the yearning to live in a more humane world—a world with a greater measure of decency and compassion. And I want to do whatever I can to help bring that about.

One of the formative events of my life was being a child of the Depression, growing up in a small Michigan town in those dreadful years, and seeing ordinary people being cut down by a force greater than any of them—a force they couldn't understand—and by seeing my father cut down, too. He lost his job and was no longer able to support our family. We had to leave Owsso, Michigan, and move back to Pennsylvania to live with my grandmother, where we wouldn't have to pay rent.

That event seared itself into my memory and left a stain on my conscience. It created in me what some might feel is an exaggerated sensitivity to injustice, and an almost irrational passion for the plight of the poor. I think that those feelings, joined with the values that I learned from my parents, became more developed as I matured and became a more educated human being, and a serious student of the Jewish heritage. And those concerns became my song. They came out of my youth and I carried them with me everywhere, including into my work as a rabbi, and they are with me still.

American Jews of my generation experienced exclusion and discrimination, but nothing comparable to what was experienced by the blacks. Nonetheless, it limited some of the possibilities that would have been possible for us as Jews. We didn't see that our Judaism set us apart from the rest of the world. We were eager to preserve our distinctive identity as Jews without separating ourselves from the rest of society.

A cardinal principle of the Jewish faith is to have responsibility for "the other."

"The other" is not limited to just a Jewish other; "the other" is another human being. And concern for "the other" is always placing a demand on me. "The other" is always present in my life, even when I am alone. There's a dimension of obligation. Something is being asked of me: Nothing human can be foreign to me.

It's generally true that as one rises on the economic ladder, one tends to hold more conservative economic and political views. We Jews have risen and now occupy a position relative to the rest of the populations of considerable comfort. We are, indeed, one of the most successful groups in this country—politically, culturally, educationally, economically.

And yet we've still tended to hold onto basically liberal political views.

I think it has to do with some sense of our own history; some sense of the discrimination and persecution we've suffered in the past—some recognition of our connection to anyone whose human potential has been limited and narrowed. So that, regardless of how we have risen, some sense of history and connection lingers on, and helps us put compassion before our own welfare.

I retired in 1986 but I'm still involved in many of the issues that have always engaged me—war and peace, poverty, affordable housing, capital punishment, and more. I serve on several boards, including one that deals with issues of medical ethics, the Institutional Board of Cedars

"You look in the mirror and you see the sagging cheeks, and you're still searching for the boy behind them."

240

Sinai Hospital, which is concerned with protecting the rights of human subjects. I'm also a rabbi in residence at All Saints Episcopal Church in Pasadena. The retired rector there, George Regas, is my oldest and dearest friend. We met almost forty years ago at a demonstration against the war in Vietnam. We formed a friendship that brought us into many anti-war activities and eventually to the issue of the nuclear arms race, and more recently to opposing the first war in the Persian Gulf, and now the present war in Iraq. Our friendship has brought me courage, inspiration, and comfort in the times I felt very lonely as rabbi, estranged from many colleagues because of certain positions I had taken. These are things that engage me.

But what lies at the very center of my life is a great love. My first wife, to whom I was married for forty-one years, died suddenly a month after I retired. A year and a half later, I married again. Everything else in my life revolves around our love. She came to me and flooded the darkness of my life with the light of her love. We both hold the same basic values. And together we are deeply connected to our five wonderful children and six wonderful grandchildren.

My life is very full. I love the theater, art, music, and literature. I lecture at churches, synagogues, and mosques. And I'm a member of the Los Angeles Institute of Humanities, where I meet with scholars, artists, and writers to discuss significant issues. Throughout my life I have felt called to do what I could to diminish the store of agony in the world. While I haven't always fulfilled the ideals I held up for myself, I haven't given them up, nor have I given up the will to do something about them—even now that I am an old man.

What are the advantages of being my age? I would say having the wisdom that comes with sorrow and with having experienced the joy and agony of being a human being, and having few illusions about what life really is. To see all the contradictions, and yet not give up the hope that love and joy are still beckoning.

Being my age is sobering. You look in the mirror and you see the sagging cheeks, and yet you're still searching for the boy behind them. And something of the boy is always there. And you know you want to go along with him wherever he will take you. But that is merely an expression of my response to the first question—Where am I in my life? What does it mean to be a Jew, a human being?

RABBI LEONARD BEERMAN was born on May 4, 1921, in Altoona, Pennsylvania.

BETTY WARNER SHEINBAUM

Betty Warner Sheinbaum grew up as a child of Hollywood in its glory days. She breathed in the politics, pop culture, and atmosphere of Hollywood during the Second World War. Today she is an artist and activist who thrives on the polemics of the day. Her home is a crossroads of the worlds of entertainment, industry, and society.

I AM A FIRST generation American—my family came to this country in the early 1900s to seek freedom and opportunity to make a living.

My father became the patriarch of a large family—worked as a cobbler and a salesman before starting Warner Brothers' Studio. His morals were strong, and we were brought up to consider others, especially those in need. He believed in equality and justice for all—regardless of race, gender, or religion.

My family discussed politics at the dinner table. Thanks to those discussions—and to FDR's election—I became politically aware by the time I was a teenager. I eventually joined groups to fight McCarthyism. Throughout the years, I have been involved in community and grassroots politics. I have traveled a great deal and stayed involved in national and international politics.

I became interested in art in my twenties and thirties—while bringing up four children.

In my forties, I learned to weld. I bought cars in junkyards, took them apart, and created sculptures from the pieces.

For many years I have taken classes to improve my skills as an artist, and this has made art more and more exciting for me. I also opened two galleries—one in Santa Barbara and one in New York City—these were among the first to promote contemporary American crafts. I am currently preparing for an art exhibit of my paintings of downtown Los Angeles.

When I wake up each morning, I love everything around me. I like to look at things—to know more. I read newspapers, magazines, and books. I talk to people with strong opinions.

One thing that worries me is our education system. There is not enough awareness of history. Politicians get away with so much by exploiting our ignorance and apathy.

I have many younger friends who are politically savvy, but too many people are not involved in their communities. When you start talking about taking responsibility for others, people think you are a dinosaur.

"When you start talking about taking responsibility for others, people think you are a dinosaur."

If you talk to some young people about the Second World War, their eyes start to glaze over. Fascism? Socialism? Communism? They aren't even clear on what it is to be a liberal.

I don't know if it's my age or the times, but I am not as optimistic as I used to be. People have always been corrupt. People have always gone to war. But, in a "global world" there seems to be more divisiveness than ever.

Politics has been muddled with no separation between church and state. As a child I heard, "What's good for General Motors is good for my country." This is a concept that is now popular in Washington, D.C. in the extreme. People do not respect each other's differences and debate is discouraged—political activism is considered unpatriotic. I worry about the direction our country is going. People are anxious, even despairing, and do not know what to do, where to go, or how to make things happen.

There are few answers out there at this time. Democracy, freedom, justice, and economic security—things my family came here for—seem to be eroding.

BETTY WARNER SHEINBAUM was born on May 4, 1920, in New York City.

LEONARD STERN

Leonard Stern was the publisher of Mad-Libs, *the producer of* Get Smart!, *the writer of* The Honeymooners, *and the alter ego of Steve Allen and his zany band. According to Don Rickles, he had a messianic streak. "I said 'Beautiful day, Leonard,' and he said, 'Thank you.'" He has certainly made it a beautiful day for anyone in search of laughter.*

AS I'VE GROWN OLDER, my enthusiasm for what I do has never changed or diminished. I might get out of bed a little slower than I did in the past, but the effort is always there, to rise and shine, and be funny, I guess.

But there is a change. I find that I have a more philosophical approach to failure. It isn't a surprise any longer. I've learned from it. And I still try to write with subtext in everything I do.

I've worked with a lot of humorous performers—Jackie Gleason and Phil Silvers and Don Adams—and the one thing they seem to have in common is a general disinclination to enjoy themselves.

I think this was caused by a fear of acknowledging success because it might go away. They were always in constant pursuit of it, even if they had it. Actors seem to live more stressful lives than writers, or perhaps we're more aware of their stress. The writers keep it as a private enterprise.

If you were to ask me how I deal with stress, I would answer in one word: inadequately.

The stress in my work has always been an acceptable part of the package, because writing also provided joy. The theft of joy from the business has made the stress unduly harsh. As the cost of everything goes up, so does the anxiety about every project. I think younger writers are suffering inordinate pressure.

My feeling has always been that no matter how stressful the work, you were amply rewarded by the atmosphere in which you worked. You must remember I worked at a time when the executives were knowledgeable and recognized the importance of writing. Today, young writers are subject to the opinions of the uninformed, who report to the unimaginative, who are supervised by the unknowing. At my age, I handle stress differently. I assign it.

I have always enjoyed my work tremendously. The playing field is no longer level, but that doesn't stop me from attempting to be innovative and different if at all possible. My instincts, honed by experience, have helped me be a survivor.

I'm not sure that young people today are in search of fun in their work.

They're working in a highly pressurized atmosphere. The cost of everything is five times what it should be, so the risk is far greater. It demands repetition instead of experimentation.

"Today, young writers are subject to the opinions of the uninformed, who report to the unimaginative, who are supervised by the unknowing."

When I was very young, I decided it was prudent to go west. Two of my peers were in the same situation. They decided to stay in New York and each wrote a play. They were Neil Simon and Woody Allen. They took the chance and took the risk. They succeeded phenomenally.

I'm still very much engaged in life and my antenna are always seeking a new idea. I'm involved in book publishing. I'm also on the board of a little theater called Theater Forty, here in Beverly Hills, and I encourage experimental work. I'm always in tenacious pursuit of what has yet to be done.

I do see a significant advantage to age. People open doors for you. That's important if it's the right door. In the opening moments of *Get Smart!*, there were quite a few doors opening. So I'm a great proponent of opening doors.

Advice to the young? The only thing I know and firmly believe is to do what you do as well as possible. If it's writing that you do, write the best possible. Don't compromise. Don't be victimized by bromidic responses. Develop what you believe in and do it with a passion.

I was unique among writers in one respect. My parents got along extremely well and presented me with no problems.

I wasn't preoccupied with investigating my own life. Almost everyone I know got into writing to compensate for some problem. My parents left me without a problem. And I can't even thank them.

LEONARD STERN was born on December 23, 1922, in New York City.

*"Old age lacks
the heavy banquet,
the loaded table, and
the oft-filled cup.
Therefore it also lacks
drunkenness, indigestion,
and a loss of sleep."*
—Cicero

MARJORIE FASMAN

Daughter of cinema icon Sol Lesser, Marge Fasman grew up inhaling the air of the Golden Age of Hollywood. She wrote a book about Pride and Prejudice's *Mr. Darcy, with whom she felt an affinity. She also wrote one of her father's numerous Tarzan movies. But as Oscar Wilde wrote of* Dorian Gray, *her days are her sonnets. Marge Fasman devotes herself to serving humanitarian causes and creating breathtaking flower box works of art.*

I WAS THE DAUGHTER of a motion picture executive and children were not meant to be seen or heard.

I wrote one of dad's Tarzan pictures and rewrote a lot of them, but on *Tarzan and the Amazons* I got a screen credit.

I remember being with Douglas Fairbanks frequently. His studio and my dad's were next door to one another, and I used to play on the movie sets.

I also remember meeting Walt Disney. Dad sent upstairs for us and said there was a man he wanted us to meet. The man had these lovely drawings of Mickey Mouse. He was a very callow and shy young man, sitting sort of trembling and holding his knees together. Then he asked for his first loan, which he got from my dad to build his first studio in Burbank.

There's something a little sad about my father. He was the most creative, the most generous, caring person of them all. He would come up with these great ideas—like the Hollywood Motion Relief Fund and the Motion Picture Home. Louis B. Mayer would throw him out of his office. But dad couldn't stop spouting when he had a good idea. Then someone else would take the idea and run with it and not acknowledge him. The Hollywood Museum was his idea, but Universal ran away with the main idea and created Universal City.

The influence of the motion picture business was kept out of our home pretty much. My mother had no use for movie actors and actresses or movie producers. They weren't refined like my parents, who had very elegant manners. Mother was shy and scorned all displays of wealth.

If you're in your eighties, diet, exercise, and being engaged in community needs are all important. Also, you've got to keep doing things physically. I played tennis into my eighties and then, when I started writing a book, I didn't want to play anymore, so I just quit.

You need good genes, too. Longevity genes. My mother was eighty-six when she died. She didn't have a wrinkle on her face. And dad was over ninety.

I was a totally different person until I met my second husband. I was used to not being acceptable, to being wrong. I was always being scolded by my mother. Whenever anything went wrong it was my fault.

I tried to be the perfect lady my mom wanted, but I wasn't. So, I was basically very unsure of myself. I married the most beautiful man in Los Angeles. He left me for a famous judge. The entire time I was married to him, he was not nice to me, and I accepted that because mother had never been nice, either. I was scared to death of doing anything wrong. I didn't get over that until I married Michael Fasman, who taught me what love was all about.

Also, *Pride and Prejudice* propelled me back into writing. I saw the BBC version of *Pride and Prejudice* with Colin Firth. I went out and bought what I call a "six pack"—there were six tapes in it. Millions of women around the world were in love with Colin Firth. I had a kind of crush on him, too. I was fascinated by the relationship between Mr. Darcy and Elizabeth. And I was intrigued by Mr. Darcy's character and what had produced it. It impacted me so that I sat down and wrote his diary.

"Old age doesn't have to be old. You can have a lot of fun."

After being married to Michael Fasman, I now knew how it felt to be loved. What I saw in Darcy was his impeccability, his gorgeous manners, his coolness. I liked that he was not demonstrative. Also, what I think I related to in Darcy was the fact that somehow he must have been tarnished or stricken in his youth, so that he behaved the way he did. I understood how it felt. So in my book, I gave him the same kind of fear of his parents that I had.

My second marriage—and Mr. Darcy—changed me totally. I became an entirely different person. I became the person I always should have been.

I think that elegance is important and I don't think there's much left. People are behaving very badly. I think they're rather crude and vulgar. I don't like the humor. I don't like open sexuality and the way it's being expressed. It isn't that I don't like sexuality. I love it. But I don't like it when it's just crass, which it frequently is. I think people are inconsiderate. Get into an elevator, does anybody talk to anybody?

Advice to the young? Learn what's beautiful. Learn to look at a sunset. Be sensitive to the world around you.

Michael Fasman was very much the opposite of who most of my friends wanted me to marry, because he didn't come from the right corner of society. I remember one night when we were with a bunch of movie people—Julie Epstein, Maurice Rapp, Budd Schulberg—they were at one end of the table, Michael and I were at the other. The gang was cracking their usual Hollywood jokes and Michael was trying to get into the conversation and they weren't letting him in.

When we came home, I was very quiet and he said, "Marj, what's the matter?"

I said, "Well…you have to learn how Hollywood people are…how they don't want you breaking into their joshing. What will they think?" I added.

"Marge, who are *they?*" he said.

It just turned me upside down. And I thought: who the hell *are* they?

I have huge energy. Apparently, I still look very good. Nobody can believe I'm this age. Great genes. I have a lot of talent. I'm a good writer and I am a good artist. I'm a genius with flowers. Modest? Not anymore.

I love to go in and help people. I was president of the Women's Division of the United Jewish Welfare Fund. And I introduced Hollywood people into Jewish community affairs. But I was not a good chairman, because frankly I don't like working with women.

Old age doesn't have to be old. You can have a lot of fun. You really can.

One more thing. After Michael died six years ago, I said to myself, "What am I going to do to keep myself going?" Michael was a good social dancer. One thing I always wanted to do was dance with people like Gene Kelly or Fred Astaire. So I went to the top. I've been dancing with the top dancers three nights a week. I'm really pretty good. At my eightieth birthday party, I hardly saw my own guests. The minute I'd leave the dance floor, one of these gorgeous men would grab me and I'd be dancing again.

I can still tap dance, but I don't. What I love to do is ballroom dance. When I'm ballroom dancing, I feel like I'm twenty and I don't have a care in the world. I really miss Michael, desperately. But when I'm dancing, I don't.

MARJORIE FASMAN was born on December 1, 1916, in San Francisco, California.

MORT LACHMAN

American comedians always keep their wits about them. That's why Bob Hope always kept Mort Lachman nearby. Mort had the ability to create jokes on whatever the needed topic for one of Hope's ubiquitous Paramount movies, his Pepsodent-sponsored radio shows, or his trips to entertain troops or presidents. Today, Mort Lachman is a bibliophile who owns more books than Hope owned punch lines.

WHEN I WAS WITH Bob Hope, there were some exciting times and I miss that life.

I loved it. I have no way to replace it. Bob made me play golf, and we played every day. We played all over the world. He had great patience with my lack of ability.

I was at home working anywhere in the world. And at the studio, when a Hope picture was in trouble, I would just sit down and start writing. I learned how to work anyplace—on a plane, on a submarine, on a boat, in a cave or on a mountain, in a trench hiding from gunfire. I could sit there and do his monologues and do his next act. I could write anywhere, any time, but only on demand—only when it was needed.

We both loved travel. We both knew how to make a home and be comfortable anywhere, how to live anywhere, under any circumstances.

I inherited from Bob Hope the love of golf. I still play. I'm eighty-eight. I still play every day.

I think that that has kept me moving: the movement and the insatiable desire to be better. That's part of the game of golf—you just try and try.

I didn't know how to deal with stress because my whole working life was spent under stress, and it was very difficult. I was used to it. But the pleasure of being able to deliver when it was needed was my reward. There's something about having the whole studio depending on you and watching every page as it comes out of your typewriter so they can go to work. It's very satisfying. But I'm not subject to that kind of stress today. I miss the excitement. I miss being needed. That was very important to me.

I could be very productive, but only when they had to have it that minute. Bob Hope once said, "If Mort Lachman could write one day ahead of time he would own the world." I never could do that. I never could write one day ahead of time.

I see no advantage in aging. I loved working and I miss it. I loved being involved and I loved when I didn't have to think about my body aching. I loved when I didn't have to think about death being next door. I loved it when I didn't have to worry about what books I was going to put in the box with me.

The only thing I would advise anyone is to try and make your living by doing something

"I see no advantage in aging. I loved working and I miss it."

you get a kick out of. Then life is a pleasure instead of a bore.

You have to find something you really would like to do and work at that. Then if it hits, you're home and you lead a wonderful life. I was lucky that I never had to do nine-to-five.

I've had a successful, productive career. And I put the good fortune down to being involved where I belong, and finding something that challenged and excited me. I loved Bob Hope and I loved his family and I loved the people at the studio and the stars I got to meet who became my friends.

I loved the same thing for seven years on *All in the Family*. I had a fabulous crew on that show and we had a ball together. It was the greatest cast in history, four perfect people who were perfect for the show. And a fabulous group of writers.

I remember how it all started. My agent was a famous, wonderful writers' agent, George Rosenberg. He was one of the greatest agents in the world. And he couldn't get me any work. I spent almost a year out of work and I said, "George, I read in *Variety* that Bob Hope's agent is desperate. If I wrote a few jokes, would you give them to him?" He said, "Mort, they'll never be able to read all the submissions they've got. They'll never get to yours. You're just wasting time." I said, "George, what else have I got to do tonight? I'll waste the time."

So I wrote twelve jokes. The most boring jokes you've ever read. I picked a subject: back to school. I can't believe it was such a dull subject.

Back to school. Of course, kids were going back to school. I wrote twelve jokes. It was so dumb. I gave Hope as many jokes as he did on the air. I didn't realize the guys were writing ninety jokes to get three on the air.

I just wrote these twelve jokes and turned them in. I gave them to George and he put them on the desk of Bob Hope's agent. The next day, I got a message: "Your agent called." That was a good sign. George had never *been* my agent before. I'd been one of his rejects.

"They want you to come to work," said George. "They liked your jokes and they'd like you to start. They want a seven-year contract, which is illegal, and they're paying you seventy-five dollars a week, which is also illegal. So, I think you should turn it down." I said, "I'll take it. It sounds wonderful."

That's how I started writing for Bob Hope. Back to school.

Imagine what I could have done with a really good subject. I could have gotten eighty-five dollars a week.

MORT LACHMAN was born on March 20, 1918 in Seattle, Washington.

ESTELLE REINER

Estelle Reiner, Carl's wife and a remarkable ninety-two-year-old grandmother, has, in recent years, been singing up a storm at a Hollywood club and various other crowded venues on both coasts. During these seismic events, Carl can be found hovering in the back, tapping his toe and smiling with affection and awe.

WHEN I WAS ABOUT SIXTY, Anne Bancroft asked me if I would participate in a project she was doing as a student at the American Film Institute. She was directing two thirty-minute TV shows and asked if I wanted to be in one. I was never an actress and I hesitated. Finally I said okay.

After that, Anne wrote a movie called *Fatso* and she gave me a part in that. It was a pretty good part for somebody who'd never acted before. She loved what I did. It was a pleasure for me, because I was getting out of the house for the first time. Up until then, I had been an artist, exhibiting, working at home while raising three children. Working in Anne's movie, it took me ten minutes to get to the 20th Century Fox Studios. I was mingling with adults and doing something new, and getting paid for it.

It was a delight. I said to myself, "I ought to learn how to do this." I started taking acting lessons with Lee Strasberg at the Actor's Studio. After studying with him for six months, he passed away, and then I shifted to Viola Spolin. However, once I was on my feet on a stage, I said, "Rather than pursue an acting career, what I really love and know how to do is sing." So I studied performance. At the age of sixty-five, I had my first professional singing job. My opening night was traumatic. I had laryngitis on the day I was supposed to open, and I had my celebrity friends coming to the show. I didn't know what to do. I went to a doctor who specialized in throat and voice. He said, "What time do you have to sing?" I said, "Eight o'clock." He said, "Come in here at five. I'll give you a shot. It should work before eight." I went in at five. Eight o'clock came and I got up on the stage and I sang a couple of songs. Then I said to the audience, "I'm sure you didn't come here to hear this voice," but they applauded. Somehow they were interested in what was coming through, and luckily, halfway through, my voice came back and I ended strong.

My repertoire consists of some standards, and songs by Fats Waller, Duke Ellington, very early jazz. Among them are seldom performed songs like "Million Dollar Secret," "T'ain't Nobody's Bizness," "The Joint Is Jumpin,'" "Wild Women Don't Worry," "Aggravatin' Papa," "Gee Baby," "Ain't I Good to You," "Go Back Where You Stayed Last Night," "I Know How to Do It," "I Want a Two-Fisted, Double-Jointed, Rough and Ready Man."

"Life is full of surprises."

When I began singing professionally, it was exciting to perform in some of New York's jazz venues, like Michael's Pub, Greene Street, and Danny's Skylight Room. My first gig in Los Angeles was at Le Café, and places like the Vine Street Bar and Grill, Cinegrill, Jazz Bakery, and Catalina. Now, at ninety-two, I'm happy to be singing in one place—The Gardenia Restaurant and Lounge. And happier that people come to hear me and say they enjoy my performances. My goal is to keep singing.

Right now, I'm experiencing some ailments, which are a pain. But I've always had a good feeling about my body. Perhaps it's because I was an avid athlete when I was young, and felt able to depend on my body. I try to forget about the physical things I can no longer do. I will be ninety-two years old when I perform my next gig—I'm lucky and very grateful to have a supportive and helpful husband who tells me that I'm his favorite singer.

Life is full of surprises. I never thought that I'd become a recognized personality when I delivered that famous line in *When Harry Met Sally:* "I'll have what she's having."

ESTELLE REINER was born on December 14, 1914, in New York City.

ED GUTHMAN

Editor of the Philadelphia Inquirer, *national news editor of the* Los Angeles Times, *winner of the Pulitzer Prize, press secretary for Attorney General and then U.S. Senator Robert Kennedy, author and historian, Ed Guthman is a man for all media and political seasons. He presently teaches a class in investigative journalism at USC as a way of giving something back.*

I LEARNED DURING WORLD WAR II that whatever happened, it was essential to keep functioning, and that's how I've coped with the big blows of life. I think my experience in combat during the war taught me to never lose my bearings. I have a lot of faith that things are going to work out, so I hang in there.

I was raised that way. My father was a grocer. I was the youngest child and there were three older sisters. I always wanted to be a journalist. I think my dad had a lot to do with my outlook on life. That was sort of the way he was. He would say, "Never lie. Just never lie."

You're unlikely not to mellow somewhat while aging into your eighties.

I would say only that I think of old age health-wise. My health is okay, but I don't have the energy that I had. I don't have any big clues on aging. But here I am. And one of the interesting things is I'm finishing my seventeenth year teaching at USC. That's the longest I've worked anywhere.

It's great to have the opportunity to teach, and one of the things you see now is the students are kids who have had computers all their lives and they use them. I say to my students, "But you can't use them unless you confirm that what you saw on the database was right."

I had a girl come up to me after class and she said, "I just can't find anything about this assignment on the Internet." I said, "Why don't you come with me?" We're walking out of the building and she says, "Where are we going?" I said, "To the library."

I don't think it ever occurred to her to go to the library. The idea of checking public records is a serious thing. You've got to go to the original and make damn sure that it's there, that it hasn't been changed. All those things were just sort of basic for us. I keep bringing it up in my Investigative Reporting class and they kind of laugh at me.

The advantages of age are having seen and done a lot and had a lifetime of experiences, ups and downs that give a perspective on life.

We all have to go through it. There's no way to avoid it. As you're growing up, you have different experiences. If you don't learn or profit by these experiences, I don't know what to say about it. I was very fortunate to get the opportunities that I did get. When I go back and look at my career, I was very lucky to work for the people that I worked for as a young reporter. They were wonderful people at the *Seattle Times.*

I wouldn't have won a Pulitzer Prize on my own. I did what I was told. One of the things about my generation, the World War II generation: We did what we were told. When the managing editor said, "You do this," I did it. There were no ands, ifs, or buts about it. This involved a University of Washington professor, Melvin Rader, who had been accused by the State Un-American Activities Committee of attending a secret Communist training school in upstate New York in the summer of 1938. He gets on the witness stand and he testifies under oath that he had never been a member of the Communist Party and never attended a secret Communist training school. This became the *cause celebre* of a very contentious hearing. The committee said it would settle it, and the prosecuting attorney accused the witness of perjury. Three or four months go by and there's an extradition hearing in New York and the judge refused to send the witness, George Hewitt, back to Seattle to stand trial. Said the judge, "I'd be sending him to his slaughter. The courts in Seattle are controlled by the Communist Party."

That was ridiculous. But, the next day when I came to work—and I covered the hearings—

"The advantages of age are having seen and done a lot and had a lifetime of experiences, ups and downs that give a perspective on life."

the managing editor, Russell McGrath, said to me, "Okay, the committee's not going to settle this, the courts aren't going to settle it, it's time for a *newspaper*. You find out what happened." I checked everything out and it all checked out. There was no possible way the professor could have been in upstate New York in the summer of 1938. Great. I've done it.

"No, Guthman. Now, you find out where he was in the summer of 1939 and the summer of 1937," McGrath said. The McCarthy era had started and here was this little paper out in the corner of the country standing up. That's why I got the Pulitzer Prize. I didn't even know they had submitted it!

So here I am, I'm eighty-six years old and doing a full teaching schedule. It's not like I'm straining myself. I'm not the oldest member of the faculty. Norman Corwin is ninety-five. He's wonderful. One of my students last spring had taken Norman once, and he just took the course again because it was so good.

Bob Kennedy once asked me to climb a mountain with him. I said, "Look, Bob, I've climbed mountains and I know what it takes and I'm not up to it now. When I was young it was a different proposition."

Things would have been very different in America if Bob Kennedy had not been killed. I think that there was no question, having won the California primary, he would have got New York and he would have won the Democratic nomination. Whether he would have been elected president, of course, we have no way of knowing. But the point that is just so clear in my mind—if he gets elected president, two things happen that are very important to this country. First place, the Vietnam War ends in 1969. That's four years sooner and I don't know how many thousand lives would be saved. The second thing that wouldn't have happened was Watergate.

I was the national news editor at the *L.A. Times* in 1968. We attended the GOP presidential convention that nominated Nixon in 1968. We saw this incredible, unusual security around Haldeman and Ehrlichman and all of Nixon's staff and we couldn't figure out why. It was just crazy. We talked about it. Finally, we decided the only thing it could be was the Watergate burglary which had taken place a few months before. So we decided that when the convention was over, we'd go in and we'd investigate it and we did. We never got any credit for it because the *Washington Post* used everything we wrote plus everything that Woodward and Bernstein did, and they did a great job.

Today, besides my USC course, a lot of other things engage me. I'm on the Board of LA's Best, which is an after-school program for children. I have four grandchildren and I see them a lot. I have a lot of friends. I belong to the Council on Foreign Relations and the Pacific Council. There's plenty to do. It's not like I'm sitting here waiting for something to happen. The best thing, I have good health.

But look, I'm eighty-six—you don't go on forever. I just go as long as I can do it. Why not?

There's no reason not to. I have a lot of experience to impart to the kids.

I don't see any advantage to being my age and I don't think you can even decide what's better. To be young? To be old? Look at my generation, born after World War I and growing up and then being in the Depression.

We lived within walking distance of the University of Washington and it cost thirty dollars a quarter to go to the state university. You think that's pretty good? Half of my high school class couldn't afford to go to the university. That was in the depths of the Depression. I could go because I was living at home and I walked to the school and it was thirty bucks and I could get thirty bucks. Then World War II.

I don't think that you can look ahead and say this is good, this is bad. I'm concerned about the future. I think that the political thing now all turns on polls and ideology. They don't tell the people what they really believe. They tell them what their pollsters and their campaign consultants have told them—"This is what works. This is what goes."

That worries the hell out of me. You see the press changing. And if the press doesn't do its job of reporting information that the people in power don't want people to know, our republic's not going to last. That concerns me. It's a constant fight that we're in, and I just hope that sanity prevails.

ED GUTHMAN was born on August 11, 1919, in Seattle, Washington.

ANNETTE KAUFMAN

Annette Kaufman was married to the most famous concert-master in Hollywood. When he died with his memoir A Fiddler's Tale *unfinished, she completed the book. She embraces many of the good things in life—theater, opera, chamber music, history, and science. She is active in city planning and architecture and lays claim to the ultimate sign of curiosity: she has never succeeded in walking past a bookstore.*

I'VE ALWAYS HAD a compelling interest in other people. I think that's one of the secrets of the good life. If you are only concerned with yourself, you get off balance. You imagine you aren't feeling well. If you're truly interested in other people you can have a very interesting life. It's a wonderful thing if you keep opening doors for yourself.

I'm always interested in what others are doing. My husband, Louis Kaufman, was very much like that, too. We were both interested in reading and we could never walk past a bookstore.

Titian was still painting in Venice when he was in his nineties. Stradivari was making instruments in Cremona when he was ninety-six. I think that if you are doing what you like, you're apt to be a happy person.

Musicians and composers usually are doing work they like; conductors, especially. Sometimes, orchestra musicians are unhappy. They don't like conductors. Actually, conductors are interested in the bigger field of great symphonic music, so they have a vision of what they want to achieve. And I think that promotes longevity. They're doing work they're fascinated by.

Hollywood composers like Alfred Newman, Franz Waxman, [and] Victor Young were passionately interested in music. Hollywood sort of chewed up people. When you did work for music departments, they usually gave you the movie after the picture was finished, so they wanted it done the day before yesterday. They had to do a lot of work hastily.

Everybody died of heart trouble in their early fifties or sixties. Bruno Walter lived a long time. So did Sir Thomas Beecham. It depends on your personal habits. Leonard Bernstein burned the candles at both ends. He was always smoking and drinking heavily, and that tears you down.

A musician has to live a life of discipline. If he doesn't have good habits of eating, or a good frame of mind, he won't last long.

I think you need to have a friendly attitude toward life. I've always felt that politeness helps a lot. If you are polite to people and if you smile at them, you can turn away their wrath if you got into a bad situation.

I can't think of just relaxing. I like to be places where I can see things and do things.

"It's wonderful to have the accumulated knowledge of what not to do."

I never think about my age, except when people talk about it.

I think the best thing about age is, going through life, you have experiences and you learn how to cope with bad news as well as good news. You learn not to make the same mistakes. It's wonderful to have the accumulated knowledge of what not to do.

I have lots of friends who concentrate too much on themselves. They start thinking, "I'm old. I can't do this. I can't do that." Well, I think you can do it. If someone says, "Get up and move," you can do it. Don't just expect people to do things for you.

I don't think young people ever want advice or ever listen to it. I'm a little upset about the education system. They worry about whether the teachers appeal to the students, not that students need an education. It's hard for me to be so pessimistic, but I do think this is a terrible tragedy for young people. They don't really want to know about history, about the world, about the arts.

I think we should have people who are conversant with Arab languages—they just discharged nineteen people from the Army because they were gay who were studying Arab languages, that's stupid!

Youngsters have expectations of material benefits, rather than knowledge. I've met young people in Europe with a much stronger feeling that they have to *do* something. They have to know about the things that make a life possible on this planet. I don't think a lot of our young people are interested in education. We have a war going on in a lot of our schools where people don't know how to be polite to a teacher.

I think if you work to contribute to society, you'll be much happier when you get older.

It's a privilege to be on this earth. It's quite a remarkable place. All the universe, the vastness of it, we can't be so arrogant as to think we don't have life in some other places. We're a very small speck—a tiny place in the universe. We should contribute to it. Make it a better place when we leave it. If you do that, you'll be a happier person.

ANNETTE KAUFMAN was born on November 29, 1914, in Chicago, Illinois.

*"We grow old of a sort
of creeping common sense,
and discover too late that the
only things we never regret
are our mistakes."*
—*Oscar Wilde*

LENNIE GREEN

Lennie Green owned a fabled midtown Manhattan nightclub called Basin Street East where he spotlighted Benny Goodman, Peggy Lee, and a then-unknown named Barbra Streisand. He sent America's greatest musicals, including Fiddler on the Roof, Cabaret, *and* Man of La Mancha *abroad to Hamburg, Vienna, and Tel Aviv. Today he is the Sol Hurok of Palm Desert, California, where he has brought more action to the desert than anyone since Lawrence of Arabia.*

I'M ALWAYS CURIOUS to see a new idea, a new concept—a way to take existing things and rearrange them in a different pattern. If you came to me and said you had an idea, let's invest some money, I'd say let's try it, provided it offered the promise of fun. I'm always ready to step into the batter's box. I may strike out, but I go down swinging.

God knows, I make mistakes. When I was still very young, I turned down Tony Bennett. I felt he was too homely for a career on the stage.

And I thought rock 'n' roll wouldn't last. But my average is pretty good. And I've always felt it isn't the destination that counts, it's the journey. And my journey has been full of fun and adventure. It keeps me young.

At this stage, I can get up in the morning whenever I want. But what gets me out of bed and gets me running is my desire to bring talented people together, to get involved, to work on the projects on my desk. I'm lucky. People are always bringing me into interesting projects.

They know my reputation and they know my appetite for making things happen.

My goal is to find interesting things to do, things that will keep me laughing and busy. Frankly, after a while, I find almost anything becomes mundane and boring. So I enjoy moving on to a fresh challenge.

My personality was described very well in this old newspaper clipping that I found in the garage. It's from an astrology column. I'm an Aries. It said, "You are positive." Yes. "Energetic and independent." Yes. "Hates monotony and routine." Definitely. "Generous and stimulating but can become hasty and impatient." That's me in a nutshell.

I have a birthday coming up. I stopped counting them. I don't like birthdays and I pay no attention to them. I don't want to know about birthdays and I don't celebrate them. I celebrate life.

I love people. When I first heard Barbra Streisand sing that song, "People who need people are the luckiest people in the world," I said that's absolutely true. Life *is* people. If I don't have people, I have nothing. What do you fundamentally need to live? A roof, some food, a television set. But that's not the way I want to live. I want to be *with* people—talking to them and laughing with them.

"I'm always ready to step into the batter's box."

I don't spend a lot of time thinking about my health. I've been lucky. I've had good health all my life. Until recently, I never put a pill in my mouth. Then ten years ago, I was taking a brisk walk and had a sudden shortness of breath. I visited a doctor and he put me on a treadmill. His nurse was taking my blood pressure. When the doctor saw how high it was, he pulled me off the treadmill. He told me my heartbeat was irregular and I needed a pacemaker. So I got a pacemaker. So what else is new? I don't think about it. I take a thirty-minute walk each morning and I watch my diet. I have a suspicion that attitude is as important as exercise.

I had worries in my youth, but I dealt with them head on. Today I have less to worry about. I'm secure, both financially and in self-awareness. As a young man, I had some insecurities, because of my lack of education and breeding. But today, there's no one who can condescend to me. I love my life today. I have a wonderful wife, fine friends, a lovely home, a dog, two cars, and everything is paid for.

What have I to worry about? The only problem is that I'm closer to the abyss. As I said to my friend Peter Marshall, "Next year, you know what we should do if we're still alive?"

LENNIE GREEN was born on April 8, 1920, in New York City.

MARIAN McPARTLAND

Jazz legend Marian McPartland highlights the world's great musicians on her National Public Radio show. It is the longest-running, most widely enjoyed jazz program in the world. Marian formed her own trio for a two-week gig at New York's Hickory House that turned into a ten-year stay. It became a gathering place for jazz greats like Benny Goodman, Oscar Peterson, and Duke Ellington.

I FIND THERE'S MORE STRESS in my life today, not less. Things that used to be easier to do—like catching a plane—were a lot less stressful than they are now. You go to the airport and find the flight is cancelled, or the plane just sits on the tarmac for two hours—things like that. But I just go with the flow.

I thought about getting older more when I was younger. I remember this write-up I had in *Time* magazine, and the article said, "Forty-year-old Marian McPartland...." I remember being

so chagrined. I didn't want the world to know I was forty. Now I've got to the point where—who gives a damn? I'll be eighty-eight in March and it would be pretty hard to tell everybody I was fifty or sixty. And I really don't care. Being in good health and working at any age is just great.

I think people in their eighties are all very proud survivors, proud of being the age we are and still working. That's the thing I like—to be busy, to be involved and doing things that are not exactly run-of-the-mill, but having something new and different to do every week, every time I record my radio show.

I've been hosting a musical program on National Public Radio for twenty-eight years. I have a guest and we talk and play their music. I'll have Tony Bennett, George Shearing, Oscar Peterson, Billy Taylor, people like that. I make the introductions and I get the guest to play and then we talk. We'll do a duet, then perhaps I'll play the piano. I do three or four radio shows a month. And in between, I do various concerts. We recently had a big bash at the Kennedy Center which we recorded on the Concord label.

What gets me up and going each morning? A cup of tea. Every English person must have a cup of tea. My husband used to bring me tea in bed. He died about ten years ago, so now I have to get my own tea. I make a thermos bottle full at night and then I drink it in the morning.

I'm always looking for new ideas. You don't want to look back at things you've done. They're done. I always want to look for something new.

The advantages of age? I don't think about things like that. I'm glad I'm the age I am. I'm glad that I'm alive and well. That's all I can say. I'm glad I have things to do that keep me busy.

The coming generations? I just hope there's something for them. So many bad things keep

"That's the thing I like— to be busy, to be involved and doing things."

happening, and I'm afraid there are probably more in store for them.

I'm terribly concerned about the state of our environment. People just don't seem to care. They want to have the biggest car and use gasoline to go down to the corner for cigarettes. I don't think people are giving too much thought to what's happening. I was watching a TV show on how the icebergs are breaking up. That's not a bright picture for kids in the future. The young people I'm really involved with are musicians. One young man from the Eastman School was a guest on my show. He's nineteen! I love having somebody that age on the show. There are more fine young musicians in the offing, and that makes me very happy.

Today in the average school, the arts are the first thing to go when the budget gets cut. The flaws in our educational system are troubling. But the average person doesn't seem too interested. They watch a lot of television and eat popcorn and snacks and get overweight.

When I look back over my life, I see a lot of turning points. One of them was World War II when I met my husband Jimmy, who was a foot soldier while I was on a USO tour. A friend of Jimmy's pulled some strings and he got to play his cornet on our show. That's how we met and later we got married in Germany. That certainly was a turning point!

When we came to America, a lot of won-derful things just kept happening—working with Jimmy, and then having my own group, and through it all, being able to play and com-pose and be involved in music, and I still am.

MARIAN MCPARTLAND was born on March 20, 1918, in Windsor, England.

GEORGE McGOVERN

George McGovern wore many hats in his illustrious career, among them history teacher, bomber pilot, congressman, senator, and 1972 presidential nominee. During his presidential bid the former war hero found his valor under attack. His support of America's withdrawal from the Vietnam War may have cost him the presidency. In his earlier years McGovern campaigned for Adlai Stevenson during his presidential bid and served as John F. Kennedy's Director of the Food for Peace Program.

I USED TO SAY when the subject of aging came up that it doesn't matter how long you live—it's what you do with the time you have. But now that I'm about to turn eighty-four, I don't say that anymore, because I want to live a long time. And I think that enthusiasm for constructive change is the driving force in my life that keeps me going.

I'm supposed to be retired, but retirement for me means going from working fourteen hours a day down to twelve. I think an appetite for life promotes longevity. Of course, we all know wonderful people with a great zest for life who died young—Mozart, John and Robert Kennedy, and Martin Luther King—so that's no guarantee.

I have never quit caring about what's happening in the world. I try to keep learning, to keep digging, and when the opportunities arise, I keep speaking and writing. I just finished a book that's now in the hands of Simon & Schuster. The title is *Out of Iraq*, and the subtitle is

A Practical Plan for Withdrawal Now. It's going to come out in September of 2006. I wrote the book with William Polk, one of our leading authorities on the Middle East and Iraq. I'm enthusiastic about the book.

I've always thought that a sense of history was one of the indispensable qualities that make a good citizen. In the first Kennedy–Nixon debate, one of the reporters asked each of them to say in one minute the most important quality that commended him to be president. Nixon talked about his experience, and it was a persuasive answer. And then Jack [Kennedy] said, "I think if I have any one quality for the presidency, it's my sense of history." And the substance of what he said was this—he had the capacity to know what the historical forces were that made America a great country. And he knew the forces in our own time that were most admirable and the ones we had to improve. When he said that, as an old history teacher, he had me hooked.

I mourn the absence of historical knowledge in many of our young people today. As I travel around the country, I see that history is badly neglected. Many kids think it's dull. You've heard the questions that Jay Leno asks young folks and their incredible answers. Some don't know who was president during the Civil War, or what the New Deal was. Perhaps the "No Child Left Behind" agenda has given history too low a priority. Worse yet, even our leaders seem to be ignorant of history. How is it possible that those who took us into Iraq have forgotten so soon the lessons of Vietnam? And why are the leaders puzzled over the Iraqi insurgency when even an alert high school student knows that the American insurgency of 1776 was created because our forefathers did not want British troops occupying the American colonies?

(Are there) any advantages to age? Absolutely. First of all, you have the corrected wisdom and memory of the long years. You have a little more time, you don't have to work quite so hard to make a living, you have the time to read more, to think more, and even to modify some of your earlier opinions in view of more wisdom and tolerance and less fanaticism. Will Rogers warned us long ago: "It ain't what people don't know that's dangerous; it's what they know that just ain't so."

I think older people, with obvious exceptions, should be consulted more on national and international questions. For example, I wish that George Bush the Younger had paid more attention to advice from his father, from Jim Baker, from Brent Scowcroft, or to such veteran senators as Robert Byrd, Edward Kennedy, and Bob Graham. He would have been better off had he listened to some of those

> *"Older people… should be consulted more on national and international questions."*

older heads. We might not now be floundering around in the Arabian desert and alienating a billion Muslims and Arabs.

During the Kennedy years, there was the Bay of Pigs and the intervention in Vietnam. I was opposed to those things then and (have been) ever since. But there was an excitement, an enthusiasm, an innovativeness: The Peace Corps, Food for Peace, the Nuclear Test Ban Treaty, Civil Rights, etc. I think we're missing that today. My colleagues in the Senate tell me that politics isn't much fun anymore. No one ever said that about the Kennedy era. It was exciting, it was intelligent, and for the most part (it was) well directed. I've always thought it would have been better in a second Kennedy term of four years. The Kennedys were quick learners. They were very educable. Jack grew every day he was in the White House. Assassination deprived us of his growing experience and wisdom.

I admired Adlai Stevenson's high intelligence. I admired his eloquence, his humor, his capacity to laugh at the ridiculous aspects of the human condition. He had a sensitivity about issues that was more than just words. Those were the things that drew me to him. I still think he would have made a great president. Of course, ego commands me to say that America would be better off if I had been elected in 1972 instead of Nixon.

The press today, with notable exceptions, has let the Bush people get away with a lot that is not in the national interest. I'm not anti-Republican—my mother and dad lived and died Republicans—but what we have under the Bush-Cheney team is quite fraudulent: too many things held in secret, too much sham and not enough substance. And when they do offer substance, it's usually wrong-headed. Witness their war in Iraq, the big tax giveaway, and a mind-boggling national debt, to say nothing of such folly as their opposition to stem cell research in the interest of saving lives.

My faith in the American voter is shaken at times. I still have faith in the common sense of the American people, but they've been misled by our leadership, complicated by too timid a response from the Democrats and the press. I understand why many people are off the track. I think they're inclined to trust the country's leaders, and with bad leadership, you're usually going to get bad results. Voters don't always see beyond the demagoguery and the sham.

With huge issues such as global warming now threatening the world, it is ridiculous to see our leaders playing politics with abortion, marriage by gays, and flag-burning. Does anyone believe that some nut burning a piece of cloth or paper with a flag on it is going to threaten our constitutional freedom? And should a bunch of old men and women decide how a desperate young woman handles an unwanted and perhaps dangerous pregnancy? Do genuine conservatives really want the long arm of Washington invading our bedrooms and marital relations?

But I'm hopeful. I think this country has the

capacity and the resources for a promising future. So I don't give up on us yet. I've always thought I lived in the greatest country on earth. And we must be great, because we've made such horrendous mistakes and we still survive. It must be our Constitution, our Bill of Rights, and the decency of our people.

Come October 31, 2006, I will have been married to Eleanor for sixty-three years. That's another reason why we are still young—both of us now eighty-four. We were both twenty-one when we married during my days as a B-24 combat bomber pilot in WW II. I was awarded the Distinguished Flying Cross after completing a full tour of thirty-five bombing missions over Hitler's most heavily defended target. In 2000 I won the Presidential Medal of Freedom— the nation's highest civilian honor. I hold a PhD in History from Northwestern University. I take pride and zest for life from these three honors—from Eleanor and our five children, a dozen grandchildren, and three great-grandchildren—plus my marvelous New Foundland dog Ursa—an inseparable companion.

GEORGE MCGOVERN was born on July 19, 1922, in Avon, South Dakota.

LILA GARRETT

For her work as a political activist, Senator Barbara Boxer presented Lila Garrett with the Women Making History Award, and she also received the Eleanor Roosevelt Lifetime Achievement Award. Not bad for a woman who won a couple of Emmys for writing situation comedy. She also helmed the Dennis Kucinich California campaign when he sought the presidential nomination.

DO I SEE ADVANTAGES IN AGE? None! Are you kidding? My friends and family tell me I'm ageless. I assume I am expected to keep on toting that barge and lifting that bale. This places me in the position of being extremely independent, which fortunately I like. But I'm human. There are times when I feel like leaning a little. I have yet to find a pillar.

My advice to the coming generation is to think less about its own little world and more about the real world. What's out there is as personal as anything around your table or in your room…from the price of gas to the pressure your kids are under in school.

People think it's strange that I'm so active at my age. I don't agree. Engagement is part of my generation. My mother died at sixty-one, my father at eighty. They both worked until the last day. If you're born with a work ethic, there's no other way. You feel as though you're living in a world where everyone is part of you. Edna St.

Vincent Millay said it, "A man was starving in Capri. He raised his eyes and looked at me. I felt his stare, I heard his moan, and I knew his hunger as my own." Good rhyme, although a starving man in a rich-man's paradise like Capri is a reach. Still, nothing rhymes with "skid row."

I lived in New York and in the 1960s moved to California. In New York I read more, I had more esoteric conversations. I went to more operas, more symphonies. In L.A. my writing career in TV took off. That was competitive. But a woman producing and directing? That was impossible.

In the 1960s the world and I were in a state of emergency. My work, my tumultuous marriage, my children, that starving man in Capri, there was a lot of pressure. All the parts of my life kept bumping into each other.

In a funny way, New York life was much more laid back. There were more theoretical discussions. The work was not as intense, because I didn't work as much. But in Hollywood, I was the first woman to write, direct, and produce her own material on television. I put a lot of pressure on myself to do it. I was famous in my fifties. (Well, let's say I was known.) I won two Emmys during that period. Then I decided to try to do it all. They wanted me to write and let them produce my material.

"'Oh wait! Let me stop!' Never said it. Age was never a factor. Years would go by and I would forget my birthday."

I refused. Mike Ovitz, my agent, told me to "stoop to conquer." The thought of it gave me a rash.

I just got a letter from the Museum of Television and Radio: "We are pleased to inform you that in recognition of your considerable achievements in the industry, you are among the fifty accomplished women who will be saluted and inducted into the Museum's 'She Made It' collection in 2006." It makes me laugh to think what it took to "make it." On the first pilot I produced, I had an all-male crew who deliberately lost a can of film, forcing me to turn an hour show into a half hour. On my first directing job, *All in the Family,* two cameramen deliberately missed shots, forcing us to go overtime, always the director's fault. Women have moved forward by a light year since those early years, and I'm proud of that. But I can still feel the pain of breaking through. Believe me, pioneering is overrated.

At first I wrote because I needed to feed my family. But then it became second nature. Don't misunderstand me, it wasn't as though I was a bricklayer who hated bricks. Ultimately, I was doing the work I liked, even loved at times. I never said, "Oh wait! Let me stop! I'm fifty!" Never said it. Age was never a factor. Years would go by and I would forget my birthday.

For a long time I wrote, produced, and ultimately directed situation comedies and movies for television. Then I became passionate about politics and the state of the country. You might say, for twenty-five years I went for the joke. Now I go for the truth.

Truth is hard to find and even harder to take. But I think it's essential, especially now. The press lies constantly, and the Bush-Cheney gang bases its actions on lies. People are drowning in them. I do a weekly radio show on KPFK in Los Angeles interviewing Senators, Congresspeople, disenchanted CIA officials, experts in many fields. I don't have time to smell the flowers. I think there are fewer flowers to smell, anyway. The world is more needy now and much more dangerous. I feel compelled to keep working, preserve what I can for my grandchildren. I owe them that.

I don't enjoy raging against the government. It raises my blood pressure. I'd be thrilled if we had an administration that knew the only thing preemptive war preempts is peace. But that is not to be…not with this gang. So the work goes on…and on and on….

But sometimes I relax. Most of my friends are political junkies like me so I escape with my grandchildren. I have four. I collect art. I play bridge…well. I enjoy relatively good health. I think that's major. I'm not wealthy, but I don't have a lot of economic pressure. I'm one of the privileged people who don't have the everyday money problems that make life very difficult to enjoy.

I deal with pressure poorly. I get rid of it quickly, sometimes with too little thought. Pressure of bad marriages I dealt with in the most obvious way—divorce. I had money pressures and I dealt with them head on. I worked harder. The pressure of bringing up my two daughters while being a working mother and often single was intense. I felt guilty when I was at work because I wasn't in the sand box. I felt guilty in the sand box because I wasn't at work. I would have liked to pass the guilt off to my kids, but they would have none of it! They were and are way ahead of me.

I've always looked at my work as a refuge. I love the total concentration it requires. I look at my political life as a calling. (I never realized that before this interview.) I almost never go on vacation. Hot beaches and sky blue water are for postcards. They always tempt me, but once I'm there, I can't wait to leave. My idea of a holiday is six shows in five days in New York. I never linger in bed, not now, not ever. I'm actually uncomfortable at the thought. I know some people enjoy it, and I envy them. But I can't relate.

I note that the baby boomers have started to turn sixty. They're new to being old. You know what I would say if I were advising them in how to prepare to be "old"? I would say, "You're grown up enough now to stop being so self-involved."

LILA GARRETT was born on November 21, 1925, in New York City.

"Nietzsche said that the life we live we're going to live over and over again the exact same way for eternity. Great. That means I'll have to sit through the Ice Capades again."
—Woody Allen

BOB SCHILLER

Premier comedy writer Bob Schiller was once walking alone across the Warner Brothers lot, without his long-time partner Bob Weiskopf. Jack Warner passed Schiller and automatically said, "Hello, boys." The Bobs, as they were known, were among the most gifted comedy writing teams of radio and TV. They helped make I Love Lucy *an epochal success. Schiller also wrote for Jack Benny, Carol Burnett, Fred Allen, Eddie Cantor, Red Buttons, and Ed Wynn.*

I THINK YOU'VE GOT TO have a sense of humor about aging. Longevity and life is a joke. We all know we're going to die and we laugh it off.

I said at my eightieth birthday party, "One of the advantages of turning eighty is that you eliminate the possibility of dying prematurely."

I've worked for a lot of stars with outsized egos in my career. There was a certain amount of tension. But I accepted it. It happens when you're writing against a deadline. It can be very stressful.

The alternative is not to work. Working and eating is better than not working and starving.

I've always loved my work. Actually, it's a love-hate relationship because it's awfully damn hard.

How did I learn to look at life from a humorous angle? I had two parents who were very funny. My father was a salesman who had a great sense of humor; no education, but a great sense of humor. My mother once asked my father, "Do you want to be buried or cremated?" He replied, "Surprise me!" My mother was funny, too. So, I inherited that quality. When I came down to Los Angeles from San Francisco in the seventh grade I was a stranger and an outsider. I found out that if I wrote amusing things in the school paper, I would no longer be the outsider. "Hey! He's the guy that writes that funny stuff!" That's how I began writing.

But today I have more time to enjoy life. You work on a weekly show, you don't have time for anything but work. So my attitudes have changed. Today I have the leisure time to smell the roses. It's nice. I didn't know there *were* roses.

I'm content with my life today. I married a woman half my age. We have two beautiful daughters, two beautiful granddaughters. And I have time to enjoy them. I had two sons with my first wife, and I really had very little time to spend with my family. But now I'm enjoying my family. It's wonderful.

Of course there are real advantages to being older. People open the door for you.

But the most important thing about living into your eighties—without a doubt the most important thing—is don't die! That's good advice, but not everybody takes it.

Ed Gardner, the bartender in the radio show *Duffy's Tavern,* was always looking for writers and I once asked him, "What do you

"My short-term memory is very poor. Long-term memory is good. I'm not sure if it's the other way around."

look for in a writer?" And he said, "I look for people who think crooked." That's my email address: thinkcrook@aol.com.

I have good genes. My father died at ninety-four. My mother was eighty-nine. I'll tell you a story about my mother. I once said, "Mom, I just completed five years of psychoanalysis." "And what did you learn?" she asked me. I had to make it important enough so it sounded worthwhile, but not so important that she's going to keel over. I said, "Well, I found out that I don't particularly like my sister." My mother said, "Schmuck! Nobody likes your sister. I could have saved you all that money."

I worked on some pretty good shows: *I Love Lucy, All in the Family, Maude.* I started out on *Duffy's Tavern* where I learned to write jokes.

I don't know if I mentioned it or not—my short-term memory is very poor.

Long-term memory is good. I'm not sure if it's the other way around. (I'm not sure if I told you that before.)

I see that the baby boomer generation is turning sixty. Millions of them are turning sixty every day. And I have something to say to them to prepare them for old age.

Just two words: Grow up.

I'm always looking for new information. I guess you'd say I'm intellectually curious. I just came from a meeting at PLATO. PLATO is an acronym meaning Perpetual Learning and Teaching Organization. It's at UCLA Extension for old folks who want to continue learning. There are fourteen people in each discussion group for fourteen weeks. Once a week, one of us makes a report on a subject. For example, my subject these next fourteen weeks is Arthur Miller. We each take one of his plays and report on it, and then there's discussion. The subjects range from psychology to history to poetry—the whole panoply. It's wonderful. Someone said to me, "Why do you take it?" and I said, "It gets me out of my pajamas."

Another thing that gets me out of bed is my wife kicks me out. When I married her, I was fifty and she was twenty-five. It's the best thing that ever happened to me. She's my third wife, by the way, and I say she's one of the best.

BOB SCHILLER was born on November 8, 1918, in San Francisco, California.

HAL DAVID

"Raindrops Keep Falling on My Head," "What the World Needs Now Is Love," "Alfie," "Do You Know the Way to San Jose?" These are just a few of the standards written by Academy Award-winning lyricist Hal David. In writing his lyrics (with composer Burt Bacharach), Hal David searches for believability, simplicity, and emotional impact.

I CAN'T SAY I'M AS ACTIVE as I was in my heyday—but I'm pretty close to it. I've given up tennis because all the guys I used to play with aren't playing anymore. But aside from that, I'm on the board of ASCAP. And I'm chairman of the Foreign Committee, so I travel all over the world for them. I'm on ASCAP'S Legislative Committee, too, so I go to Washington to deal with questions of copyright.

I'm also chairman of the Songwriters Hall of Fame. So between ASCAP and the Hall of Fame,

I have almost more board meetings than I really want. But it keeps me very involved and a close part of the business I love. And that keeps me young. I know what's going on, it isn't passing me by. And consequently, I get calls from record companies to write things. I contributed to an album of eleven Christmas songs that'll be coming out in September.

Stress was very much a part of my life in music. I have two sons who are grown men now. And if you're raising children, you know that creates stress, too. But the older I get—certainly for the last twenty years or so—my reaction to stress has changed. Now I let stress roll right off my back. That is pretty damn important.

When you're young, you can't avoid stress. If you're a songwriter, you get things turned down. It's inevitable. Burt Bacharach and I did a movie which turned out to be a lousy picture, but we had our songs in it. Then we were called in to do another film, and when they finished that picture and did the editing, our songs fell out of the movie. That's upsetting and annoying.

But at this point in my life, unless it involves my children or my wife, the frustration and annoyance doesn't last long.

I'm very fortunate that I've had a good career, so people display a certain amount of respect for me, whether they mean it or not. And it's always flattering. And I get enough calls to write, from record companies and for films. So I feel I'm still in the music business.

My attitude toward tension changed through the years. When I came out of the service and came back to New York after World War II and started writing songs, I was knocking on doors but couldn't get in to see people. And then when I got in, I was getting rejection after rejection.

And then I started writing some successful

"Nothing keeps you feeling as young as being involved in your own career, in your own field, in your own life."

stuff. But still there was stress and doubt. I would ask myself, "Am I really any good?" I don't ask that anymore. But when I started to achieve success, I kept looking over my shoulder and thinking, "They're going to catch up with me and realize I'm not so hot."

But I can't avoid stress entirely. Burt and I had a show on Broadway last year called *The Look of Love.* It was a sort of concert version of our songs. We had a big producer, a great director, a talented choreographer. I thought we really had a shot.

I have an apartment in New York, and the morning after the show opened, I went to my door at four in the morning to get the *New York Times,* and I looked at the review. It was awful! The show ran for three months and the reviews made me sick!

The first really bad review we got was when we were a long way into our career. We did the score for a Columbia movie—it was a musical version of that classic film *Lost Horizon.* The story of Shangri-La. We wrote what we thought was a very good score. It was recorded. We thought we would produce some hit songs. But it was a terrible movie. And the reviewers not only killed the film, they killed the score.

Burt and I had a history of good reviews. So when we had the terrible responses that greeted *Lost Horizon,* it was a blow. Burt stopped writing for about a year. It threw me, too, but I came back quickly, so I may be more resilient. I was working again in another couple of months—I didn't live with the disappointment.

I hope I never retire. I'm still writing. If I weren't writing, sooner or later they'd stop calling me. Not that they call me every day, but they call me enough. As far as writing goes, there are definite advantages to being eighty-four. I really know how to do it now. In constructing a lyric, in writing a song, in recording it, I feel confident. I don't panic.

When young people show me their work, I try to be helpful and encouraging. I tell them: The only way to learn how to write is to write. And find out the people whose work you love, and examine their songs, and learn how they do it.

And write and write and write.

At the beginning, it's easier for people to say no than to say yes. And people turn you down without a second thought, because they don't know who the hell you are, so how can you be any good? So you've got to believe in yourself, because if you don't, it just won't work. If you don't believe in yourself and keep working, the rejections will destroy you.

To my contemporaries I say: Keep working. The main thing, assuming you love what you do, is don't retire if you can help it. Nothing keeps you feeling as young as being involved in your own career, in your own field, in your own life. And mentor people in the things you're good at.

Volunteer. I've been on too many boards, but they're fun. I go to the meetings and meet the kids and I go the workshops. And it just revitalizes me.

HAL DAVID was born on May 23, 1921, in New York City.

SENATOR ROBERT C. BYRD

Robert Byrd is truly an elder statesman. Some call him a "walking encyclopedia" on both the American and the Roman Senates. He had cast a total of 17,591 votes as of April 2006, far and away the most of any U.S. Senator. Robert Byrd is one of the country's most respected legislators and never shrinks from urging the people that now is the time to return to the values that made the country great.

I MAY NO LONGER BE ABLE to run a hundred-yard dash, but my mind is as sharp as the day I took office, and my passion to serve my state and my country has never been stronger. Gray hair—or white hair, in my case—and wrinkles are signs of maturity and that life experiences and hardships are important sources of wisdom.

Some people fear and dread growing old. I don't. I think there are some good examples to follow, if only we take the time to learn.

Individuals of exceptional accomplishment have been known at every age and in every quadrant of the globe. Neither geography nor chronology of life is a barrier to continued achievement. Confucius was still teaching at his desk at age seventy-three in 479 B.C. Michelangelo was still painting, sculpting, and writing poetry when he died at the age of eighty-nine on February 18, 1564. Rosa Parks served as a role model in social activism until she passed away at the age of ninety-two. Indeed, it seems that very little can hold some people back.

It may seem cliché, but with age comes experience. That has been the case for hundreds of years. From the Book of Job in Chapter 12 we read, "With the ancient is wisdom; and in length of days understanding." I frequently find that I have an advantage in my dealings in the Senate because there are not many matters that come before me that I have not previously dealt with and learned from in one form or another.

For me, age is just a number. The passion that I have for the Constitution, the fervor that I feel for the liberties of the American people, and the courage that I draw from the heroism of our founding fathers—that is where I draw my inspiration. That is where I find my own fountain of youth. The greatest thing a person can do for this country is to continue to serve, to engage in public service. What was the challenge that President Kennedy offered? "Ask not what America will do for you, but what together we can do for the freedom of man." It is that ideal that drives me in public service and in defense of our Constitution, the premiere spark of genius in the framers' mind.

I embrace life through the lessons of my faith. I am a Christian. I don't go around making a big deal over that fact. But my faith teaches me a great many things, including the way to live life in service of one's neighbor. "In as much as ye have done it unto one of the least of these my brethren, ye have done it unto me." In large part, my Senate career follows that Biblical direction. I have sought to lift this country, to help people overcome adversity, and build a better future for themselves and their families.

Recently, I had the chance to give the commencement address at Marshall University in Huntington, West Virginia. It was inspiring to talk to those newly minted graduates, and to see the pride in the faces of their families. I told them, like I tell most young people, the days in their life's journey won't always be blue skies and sunshine. Storms and rough weather will surely come. But, remember this—problems are for solving. Almighty God, in His infinite wisdom, gave man a brain for the purpose of using it to better his lot. Never, never give up. Never become the scourge. As George Bernard Shaw once observed, "I don't believe in circumstances. The people who get on in this world are the people who get up and look for the circumstances they want."

I have spent my life overcoming obstacles and jumping hurdles. I didn't have enough education, so I got more. I wanted to help West Virginia, so I went into politics. I wanted a law degree in order to be a better Senator, so I went to school at night. I wanted to understand the Constitution to which I have sworn an oath many times, so I studied it—read the Federalist Papers, read Roman history, learned about the roots of the Constitutional language, and the lives of the framers. None of it was easy. I had to work for all of it. Our young people can, too. Great satisfaction comes in being the master of oneself, being able to discipline oneself to beat all the odds and achieve a goal.

That's the real fun in life: Achieving something when everyone says you can't. Pulling it off against all odds. One's feeling of pride is what makes life the exciting adventure that it is.

"To be ignorant of what happened before you were born," admonished Cicero, "is to remain always a child." If Cicero were to look at history lessons for America's schoolchildren today, he might conclude that they will never grow up.

Washington, Adams, Jefferson, and Madison lived in a revolutionary time, a revolution fed by their own eloquence and erudition. These men read widely and deeply. Their interests and their libraries spanned the ages and included works on philosophy, history, economics, agriculture, and the arts—every facet of the human condition. Their knowledge of history, of the mistakes and triumphs of past civilizations and forms of government, permitted them to formulate a simple, flexible political doctrine that worked with our human flaws, and allowed individual talent to thrive, regardless of the circumstances of one's birth. They believed that the ultimate security for this new government lay in an informed populace, one that could recognize would-be tyrants and prevent their return to power.

We, too, live in a revolutionary time—a time of great technological change and globalization. We face new and uncertain threats. In our fear, we have sought protection from a more powerful and intrusive central government. But if we are to remain a role model of government, by the people and for the people, we must not simply wear red, white, and blue and proclaim ourselves patriots. We must cherish the heritage of governance bequeathed to us by our founders. And even more importantly, we must understand its underpinnings and historical roots, lest in our ignorance we allow the return of tyrants.

We cannot let others think for us, no matter their office or their media ubiquity. We must as a people have the wisdom to think, and think well, for ourselves. We have not lived under a tyrant, so we have only history to teach us what one looks like.

Perhaps at no time in our history has the study of history been more important. History is not the recitation of dead facts—it is relevant for the present and for the future. Our schools should give history its proper place, and encourage a love of it.

"Gray hair and wrinkles are signs of maturity, and life experiences and hardships are sources of wisdom."

For more than half a century, I have repeatedly taken a sacred oath to protect this Republic and our Constitution against all enemies, foreign and domestic. Today I see programs and policies that threaten the foundations of the Constitution and of this country. I am not willing to sit idly by and allow that to happen. I will continue to stand in defense of the Constitution and the people's liberties. The American people need to wake up to what is happening to their country.

A poem by Louisa May Alcott reads:

A little kingdom I possess,
Where thoughts and feelings dwell;
And very hard I find the task
Of governing it well.

Like Alcott, most of us find self-control difficult. We do get mad. At work, while driving, even at home, people get on our nerves and make us very angry. We are tempted, as the saying goes, not just to get mad, but to "get even."

The Bible advises against such a solution. It holds us to a higher, nobler standard. In the Sermon on the Mount, Jesus advised us to turn the other cheek when someone strikes us. Well, that is still too noble for many people. But the place for all of us to begin is with self-control.

In Washington, in Congress, and really throughout the country, we must cultivate the ability to listen to one another. We've got to always keep in mind that the other side can be right and that legislation can often be removed by constructive amendment. No political party has a corner on the market of wisdom, and no proposal or policy is beyond the possibility of improvement.

I always have hope. There's a story from the Constitutional Convention that might best answer this question. Benjamin Franklin was the oldest man at the Constitutional Convention in Philadelphia. He was eighty-one years old. At the end of those meetings, after the documents had been signed by the representatives of the people, Dr. Franklin was asked about the president's chair at that convention. It featured a sun. Was it a rising or a setting sun? Ben Franklin believed that it was a rising sun, the rising sun of America.

I believe in the Senate. I believe in the people of this great nation.

And I still believe that we see a rising sun, not a setting one. Some days may have clouds obscuring the view, but those clouds are not enough to hold back the sun's rays.

ROBERT BYRD was born on November 20, 1917, in North Wilkesboro, North Carolina. He moved to West Virginia with his adopted family when he was one year old. Senator Byrd is the longest serving Senator in the history of the United States.

*"In growing old,
we grow more foolish and
more wise."*
—La Rochefoucauld

.

EPILOGUE

The informal essays in this book are based on conversations held during the winter of 2005/2006. While this work was in preparation and production, some of its contributors left us:

Art Buchwald
Ahmet Ertegun
Ray Evans
Cy Feuer
Kitty Carlisle Hart
Frankie Laine
Jack Valenti

Half a century ago, in 1950, Cy Feuer produced the landmark musical *Guys and Dolls*. One critic wrote: "The big trouble with *Guys and Dolls* is that a performance of it lasts only one evening. I didn't want to leave the theatre. I wanted to hang around on the chance that they might raise the curtain again." When he died in May 2006, Cy Feuer hadn't left the theatre. He was meeting with Kurt Vonnegut about producing a musical version of one of his novels.

Kitty Carlisle Hart was dashing about the country, giving her sparkling concerts.

Art Buchwald was writing witty pieces for the *Washington Post*.

Jack Valenti was editing the proofs of a new book on the joys of speechifying.

Ray Evans was singing along at presentations of his work.
Frankie Laine was impatiently waiting for his voice to return after surgery.

Ahmet Ertegun was a vibrant part of his company's musical renaissance.

Like *Guys and Dolls*, Cy Feuer and his 79 collaborators in this book have been getting ecstatic reviews and audiences have been blistering their palms for years. Their lives have been a triumph, spirited, noisy, tough on the surface and shamelessly sentimental underneath.

God bless our 80 wonderful guys and dolls. The years are never long enough between the overture and the final curtain.